Nothing but the Dirt

Nothing but the Dirt

Stories from an American Farm Town

Kate Benz

University Press of Kansas

Published by the University Press of Kansas (Lawrence, Kansas 66045), which
was organized by the Kansas Board of Regents and is operated and funded by
Emporia State University, Fort Hays State University, Kansas State University,
Pittsburg State University, the University of Kansas, and Wichita State University.

Library of Congress Cataloging-in-Publication Data

Names: Benz, Kate Guerriero, author.
Title: Nothing but the dirt : stories from an American farm town / Kate Benz.
Other titles: Stories from an American farm town
Description: Lawrence, Kansas : University Press of Kansas, 2022.
Identifiers: LCCN 2021057682
ISBN 9780700633456 (paperback)
ISBN 9780700633463 (ebook)
Subjects: LCSH: Courtland (Kan.)—Social life and customs—21st century. |
Country life—Kansas—Courtland—History—21st century. | Courtland
(Kan.)—Social conditions. | Courtland (Kan.)—Economic conditions.
Classification: LCC F689.C78 B46 2022 | DDC 978.1/24—dc23/
eng/20220308
LC record available at https://lccn.loc.gov/2021057682.
British Library Cataloguing-in-Publication Data is available.

Printed in the United States of America

10 9 8 7 6 5 4 3 2 1

The paper used in this publication is acid free and meets the minimum
requirements of the American National Standard for Permanence of Paper for
Printed Library Materials Z39.48-1992.

"Let the fields be jubilant, and everything in them."
Psalm 96:11

To the three men I admire most:
the Father, Son, and the Holy Ghost.

To Justin, my favorite son. You are destined for great things.

And to Bryan, the love of my life. I'd rather be on a dusty trail
with you, than sitting in a castle with anyone else.

Contents

Preface

You get a lot of strange looks when you excitedly tell people, "I'm going to Kansas!"

This is usually because most people are living vicariously through Instagram posts of friends and strangers jet-setting to various posh destinations: Paris, L.A., London, Tokyo, New York, the Virgin Islands, Thailand. "But *Kansas*?" people always ask. "Really? You're excited to visit a town of 285 people located in the middle of a cornfield that's ninety minutes away from the nearest shopping mall because why? Are you sure you're feeling okay?"

In the summer of 2013, my little red Fiat was packed with me, my son, Justin, and all his worldly possessions bound for the University of Colorado, Boulder, to begin his freshman year. Just over fourteen hundred miles and twenty-one hours west of our home in Pittsburgh, Pennsylvania. The idea was simple: to Boulder, we'd take the interstate. But to make the solo journey back home, there would be no interstates, no hotel reservations, no GPS. Only a road atlas and a general sense of direction: home is east.

My dream had always been to take a cross-country road trip, an idea I had fallen in love with after reading *Blue Highways* by William Least Heat-Moon, cover to cover, once again, and ten times after that. I wanted to *see* forgotten corners of America. And I had wanted to see it alone.

This was my chance. And so, after a teary good-bye in the parking lot of his dormitory (Justin was just fine. Me? I was a mess), I started on my adventure. I really hadn't done any planning before the trip. No research. Just one Google search: "best road trip route across Kansas" or something like it. Repeatedly, Highway 36 got the accolades.

Out of Boulder I went, picking up 36 as it skirted past Denver, through multiple lanes of blaring horns and choking exhaust fumes, past ugly, industrial grit, and a lot of power lines until many lanes became just one, and the land opened and the sky widened and everything, including my mind, began to quiet. The windows were down. The radio was loud. And I was in my glory.

One lane east. One lane west. This was Highway 36, once hailed as "The Fastest Route from Indianapolis to Denver!" as claimed by a faded sign on the side of the road. One of many I would stop and photograph as I crossed the state line into Kansas, getting out of the car to look at whatever caught my eye: rows of sunflowers dancing in the breeze, roadside curiosities, cheery signs that welcomed you to St. Francis, Bird City, McDonald, Atwood. I stopped to look at rolling fields and grazing cows and walked through country cemeteries filled with fading tombstones and chirping crickets, the only sound to be heard. I toured buildings that were once part of the Pony Express. My diet consisted almost entirely of homemade pie à la mode that came from mom-and-pop restaurants like Paul's Café, where a cup of coffee was fifty cents and prices doubled for finger snappers. I watched the sun make its slow descent over the horizon, watched it break the dawn, and stayed at a keychain motel in Norton with 1950s vibes.

For miles at a time, I passed no one and saw nothing but land and sky, small towns, and big farms. I was falling in love with rural Kansas the way that you fall in love with someone you'll later call your soul mate. It was beautiful and peaceful. A powerful simplicity. I felt joy/peace/overwhelming calm, like floating in warm bathwater. I felt something else, too. See, I had always known of God, but I had never really *known* God. But on that day, I felt Him. He was everywhere. With me. Surrounding me. Just . . . there. And I know how weird that sounds. *You felt God's presence while Fleetwood Mac was blasting on Sirius Radio and pie crumbs were stuck to your lips?* Why, yes, I most certainly did.

On my second day in Kansas, I continued down Highway 36, stopping in Prairie View, Phillipsburg, Athol. It had taken me six hours to drive less than two hundred miles. I took pictures of old buildings and more faded signs and stood in the geographical center of the forty-eight contiguous United States in Smith Center. I turned up the radio even louder, stuck my arm out the window, caught a breeze, and took a loop through Mankato. Twenty miles or so later, I saw the sign for Courtland. It was midday on a Saturday afternoon. I was tired. Feeling . . . lazy. Courtland didn't sit right on 36 like so many of the others. It was buried at the end of a long stretch of road. It would take effort to go there. *Eh,* I thought to myself. *Pass.*

I drove about fifty feet down the road when I got the message, loud and clear: TURN AROUND. Just two words. TURN. AROUND. Clear as a bell. Not a suggestion. **TURN AROUND.**

I glanced in the rearview mirror, saw no one, and jerked the steering wheel to the left, making a U-turn in the middle of the highway. At the crossroads I had just breezed through sat the Depot Market, a very cute, Norman Rockwell-ish building sitting by itself, all bright and blue and cheery with a big sign out front that was propped up in a wagon with steel wheels: "ANTIQUES." Thinking there were some inside, I pulled into the gravel lot, parked under a shade tree, and went inside.

"The antiques are in Courtland," said the young girl behind the counter, which was surrounded by wooden crates overflowing with freshly picked zucchini, peppers, potatoes, corn, peaches, and apples. I told her I was on a road trip. Asked her about Courtland. "Is it worth going to?"

It was, she told me. She said she had grown up there, had graduated, and decided there had to be more to life than wide-open spaces and fresh country air. She wanted excitement. She wanted L.A. And so, she went. And L.A. was . . .

"Not Courtland," she laughed.

She told me that she missed her hometown. That she missed the people and the community. "Everyone waves to you here," she said. She talked about realizing that maybe there *wasn't* more to life than wide-open spaces and fresh country air. I felt myself envying her wisdom. It sounded like divine insight usually reserved for people five times our age. She had me hooked.

There's a one-mile stretch of road that takes you from Highway 36 into Courtland. And as I drove it, I could feel something embedding its hooks in me. I hadn't even seen the town yet, but I was smitten. Which made zero sense. Courtland was seemingly nothing more than one main drag and four blocks worth of buildings—some vacant, some occupied—and most of them were closed for the day. No opulent town squares. No cobblestone quaintness. No cute boutiques or yummy bakeries. No impressive monuments. There were three or four pickups parked on the street. It was blazing hot. And yet, I felt deliriously happy.

The only joint in town that was open was AnTeaQues. Half café, half antique shop. I parked the Fiat on a very empty Main Street, walked in, sat down, and immediately struck up a conversation with an older fella named Charlie. "You're a writer? We have a newspaper here," he said. "You're kidding, right?" I asked. "Nope," he replied, leaning back in his chair. "My wife works there. I help her fold papers every week." When I finally left about an hour or so later, I had another feeling: delirious sadness. For the next thousand miles and fifteen hours, I had just one thought: *How can I get back to Courtland?*

When I got home, I Googled the *Courtland Journal* and fired off a letter to editor/publisher Bob Mainquist. I described how I had fallen in love with his town, kind of laughingly asked if they were hiring, and gave him my number. Unbeknownst to me, he ran my letter on the front page of the paper. I found this out when I got a voicemail from some guy named Luke Mahin, who oversaw the Republic County Economic Development office and said he could give me as much detailed information as I wanted about Courtland, housing, and state incentive programs in place for people looking to move there.

Subsequent road trips to visit Justin always included a pit stop in Courtland. I'd say hello to Luke and Mr. Mainquist and his wife, Colleen, and buy a treasure at AnTeaQues. But it wasn't until 2017 that I experienced one of those "duh" moments. I was a writer . . . why was I not writing a story about this town? In September of that same year, I talked to Luke and Mr. Mainquist about my idea, who both gave me a starting point: "Go to Pinky's for morning coffee with the farmers!"

A few weeks later, I made the sixteen-hour drive, settled into an Airbnb that just happened to be owned by Luke's brother, Caleb, and woke up at 4 a.m. the next morning. Armed with a Moleskine and a few pens, I flopped myself into a chair at Pinky's Bar & Grill at 5:30 a.m. to introduce myself to the morning coffee drinkers; fourth- and fifth-generation farmers who I had never met before, had no idea who I was, kinda understood what I was doing in town after I explained myself, and patiently let me ask one question and then ten more, morning after morning, for an entire week. I had envisioned writing a short story that I'd pitch to a magazine. By the time I packed up and headed home, I had a Word document bursting with twenty thousand words. A quarter of the way to a book. So much for the short story.

I returned seasonally throughout 2017 and into 2019, staying for a week or so at a time, to get the story of how this rural, remote farming community of fewer than three hundred people managed to stay on the map. Every time I swung through, a new business was opening, a building was being repurposed; the younger generations were returning home, determined to redefine the rural, agricultural-based economy. Everyone together, surviving the market, the weather. Because always: the market, the weather.

My objective was to tell the story through the people who lived there. That's why you'll never really "see" me in it. But believe me, I'm there. On that hot August day in 2013, I left my heart in the middle of a Courtland cornfield. This book exists because it began with one conversation that led to another and then twenty more. I had no ties to Courtland other than a weird love affair with it, and every single person I talked with welcomed me, my pen, and my ten thousand questions with gracious hospitality I will never forget. Only a few names have been changed, and those upon request, presumably to protect the guilty.

To this day, when I talk to people about Courtland, Kansas, I like to say that I have found my geographical soul mate. Those people like to give me strange looks and inform me that I probably need meds. But I promise you, I'm of sound mind. They just don't know what they're missing.

Acknowledgments

A project like this one didn't happen because I just woke up one day, had an idea, and hopped in the car. It happened because along the way, well before the idea for this book ever dawned on me, the good Lord began to string together individual events to create a path that would eventually lead me right into Courtland, Kansas. My endless gratitude to the following for luring me there:

First and foremost, to God, of course, whose presence was palpable, a most enjoyable road trip companion, whose directive to TURN AROUND ensured I wouldn't miss out on meeting my geographical soul mate.

To William Least Heat-Moon, author of *Blue Highways*. I have no idea how old I was when I picked up his page-turner, maybe fifteen or so, but it seared into my heart a burning desire to take a solo road trip along the forgotten lanes of America. I could not wait to get behind the wheel and go. Almost twenty years after reading it, I was finally able to.

To the Benz family and their generosity to ensure Justin could attend the University of Colorado, Boulder. It was on my return trip home to Pittsburgh when I stumbled upon Courtland. And to Tim, for graciously keeping an eye on my beloved dog Birdie while I traveled, catering to her every whim, sending plenty of photos and videos my way, and dutifully handling the separation anxiety she and I both experienced whenever apart; stuff that became legendary in some parts.

In Courtland, much thanks to the mystery gal at the Depot Market who piqued my curiosity, the late Charlie Delay for talking to a stranger, Mr. Bob Mainquist of the *Courtland Journal* for reading and printing my letter to the editor (him), and Luke Mahin with the Republic County Economic Development office, who saw that letter on the front page of the paper and took the initiative to reach out, introduce himself, and tell me more about this fascinating town.

I wouldn't have a story to tell if it weren't for the people who generously shared theirs with me. My heartfelt thanks and genuine admiration first and foremost to the farmers and morning coffee drinkers: Steve, Larry, Joerg, Kenny, Mikesell, Carlson, Jake, Slug, Dan, Don, and Jim, for letting me invade their quiet mornings day after day after day and pester them with my very presence. And to Betty for her gracious hospitality and always opening the door despite the "Closed" sign.

Also, Mrs. C, Pastor Sandra Jellison-Knock, Shanna Lindberg, Shannon Langston and Linda Swanson, Mayor Tim Garman, Steve Benne, Gaynell Delay, all the liars on the Liar's Bench, Norm Hoard, Scott and Brenda Hoard, Al Urich, Cindy Hedstrom, Jana Carlson, Jenny Russell, Christy and Troy Newman, Sherie Mahin, Dan and Kathy Kuhn, Quinten and Melissa Bergstrom, Mark Garman, John Garman, Tanner Johnson, Pete Gile, Dan and Mary Reynolds, Brian Griffiths, Jeff Sothers, Beverly Sothers, Brock and Angie Hanel, Craig and Lisa Tebow, Peggy Nelson, Lynette Engelbert, Lacey Kaufmann, Joan Brown, Jennifer Mahin, and everyone else who took the time to stop and talk to me, answer my phone call or text, show me something, or point me toward another person I could chase after with my pen.

Many thanks to Caleb and Gayle Mahin for the crash pad, conversation, and cinnamon rolls, and Don Lieb and Peggy Nelson for generously offering me another crash pad whenever I dropped into town to work on this project. And to the regulars at The Barn, who also tolerated my presence and never failed to liven up the dinner hour.

There's no way I will pass up an opportunity to give a special shout-out to the following: to Mrs. C for the emergency food delivery service when my flight was canceled and also for the amazing applesauce recipe and baking advice. To Mr. Bob Mainquist for serving as an excellent sounding board and friend, and for his tremendous help with this project. To Luke Mahin for the advice, direction, insight, and "sagery." To Jim Hudson for letting me hop in his golf cart for a tour of town. To Steve Brown for tolerating an endless string of "just one more question" questions and for always giving me back my pen, despite a strong desire to throw it out the window. To Norm Hoard for being a fine dinner date and driving me into the beautiful countryside to see where his family farm once stood. To Dan Peterson for the tour of the irrigation pipes, and the opportunity to give the old steel wheel tractor a spin. To Mayor Tim Garman for always making me smile, letting me tap into his WiFi, and for showing me the true meaning of having "cold feet." To Dan Reynolds for letting me tag along in Truck 2 for an entire day, and to his wife, Mary, for the delicious lunch afterward. And to Kenny Joerg for the wheels, visit to the sale barn, laughs, and most definitely, for being a gracious and fun chauffeur to and from and to and from the airport again, thanks to one too many canceled flights.

To the Courtland Community Arts Center for supporting this project in so many ways without an ounce of hesitation. And to Josey Hammer for the wonderful photographs and innate ability to capture the soul of your subjects. Your eagerness to jump into the back of a hearse to get the perfect shot puts you in the Hall of Fame.

To my manuscript readers, both official and informal, who provided invaluable insights, corrections, challenges, and in one way or another saved me from myself: my parents, Jim and Veronica, my brother, Christopher, University Press of Kansas peer reviewers Marci Penner, Max McCoy, and the one who chose to remain anonymous. Also, Nick Levendofsky, Wade Reh, Bob Mainquist, and Warren Farha. Blame me for any errors or misinterpretation of facts found within these pages.

A sincere thank-you to my editors, Kim Hogeland, Bethany Rose Mowry, and Joyce Harrison, my copyeditor, Janet Yoe, as well as Andrea Laws and the entire crew at the University Press of Kansas, perhaps the best cheerleading team there is. Also, to Senator John Heinz History Center president Andrew Masich for all the advice and enthusiasm from the get-go, and photographer John Altdorfer for listening to me get all dreamy about Courtland, Kansas, more often than I'm sure he would have liked.

To my parents, Jim and Veronica, for all of the support and prayers along the way and to my favorite son, Justin, a most brilliant writer if I do say so myself.

And to my hubs and best friend, Bryan, for never once thinking that my starry-eyed adoration of a rural, Kansas cornfield was weird . . . at least, to my knowledge. Regardless, I love and adore you.

EARLY FALL

Commodity Prices (per bushel)

	September 1920	September 1973	September 1984	September 2017
Corn	$1.33	$2.50	$2.89	$3.27
Wheat	$2.45	$5.25	$3.49	$4.65
Soybean	$2.68	$6.18	$5.99	$9.35

The Coffee

The farmers need coffee. All you can drink for a buck at Pinky's Bar & Grill. Right there on the corner of Main and Freedom in Courtland, Kansas. Population 285.

Steve and Larry, Mikesell, Slug, Hootie, Don, Carlson, Kenny, and the other Kenny, who says it's confusing to have two Kennys, so just call him by his last name, Joerg. Pronounced *George.* "It's Prussian," he says. Sometimes, ten to fifteen of them will show up at Pinky's well before the sun has a chance to crack through the horizon. Before Betty has technically opened for business. This is why she keeps the interior lights dimmed for the first two hours that they're there.

"Oh," they say, sipping their coffee in partial shadows. "Is that why you don't turn the lights on until seven?"

"Yeah," she says. "So I don't have to look at ya!"

Sometimes they get in later. Mostly earlier. The other day they started showing up before Betty even had a chance to park her Cadillac. "That's what I call my golf cart," she says.

The E-Z-GO is one of many golf carts that zoom up and down the streets. They're just easier than getting in the car when your commute to town is only four blocks. Everyone gets them from Dennis at C&W Farm Supply, right across the street from Pinky's. He buys them, fixes them up. Maintains them. He's the one who got Betty's golf cart winterized with a zippered, plastic covering to keep the chill out when the sky grows cold and the wind howls.

Betty's E-Z-GO is electric. It starts with the turn of a key that's hanging from a shiny, scarlet lanyard embroidered with "*Huskers* N *Huskers* N *Huskers* N . . ."

Betty couldn't care less about sports. She's a Husker because she was born up there in Nebraska. When the farmers start to annoy her, she'll put on her Huskers T-shirt and annoy them right back. But they're probably already

annoyed with the Huskers license plate in the front door of the bar and the Huskers sticker on the front of the E-Z-GO. Because when you're this close to the border, you pass the years being annoyed as hell by the Nebraska Cornhuskers.

The E-Z-GO transports Betty from her house across the tracks, down to the bar, and back home again, six days a week. Pinky's is closed on Sunday, but Betty is still there cleaning. And although it's closed on Sunday, and she's running the vacuum, there will still be a knock on the door, first thing in the morning.

"I let them in so they can have their coffee," she says. "Why not? They wouldn't go away anyway." So, Betty will open the door. As she has done every day for the past five years. And during those past five years, she's only taken off three days.

"Actually, it was *four* days. There was the time I went to Colorado for my aunt's 100th birthday. So, I've had four days off in five years."

She's tried hiring someone to take her place in the morning, and a few gals have worked out for a little while, but it's hard to find anyone reliable these days. No one wants to work . . . even when they *are* at work.

Betty is seventy-three. When Pinky's went up for sale five years ago, she had an idea and called her brother Wayne. "I told him we should buy the place. Because I'm crazy," she likes to say.

When the farmers are having a good week, Pinky's is having a good week. The guys come in for coffee, come back for lunch. Come back again to have a beer when the sun is hanging low and they've powered down the New Holland T5.

But if the farmers get into trouble because of the market, the weather—always, the market, the weather—then Pinky's gets in trouble.

"If they go, then I go next," says Betty.

Courtland is a rural farm town of 285 people. It sits just about smack dab in the center of Republic County in North Central Kansas, thirty miles south of the Nebraska border, and right along Highway 36; two lanes that were once hailed as the "SHORTEST ROUTE!" from Indianapolis to Denver until they poured the concrete for I-70, leaving Highway 36 to itself.

When you see someone else traveling along 36 as it gets closer to Courtland, they wave. And when someone needs to get somewhere faster than you're driving, they flick on their turn signal, merge into the opposite lane, and merge back in front of you at a remarkably safe distance; a process that does not include blaring horns or the middle finger.

There are no billboards planted alongside the road advertising for defense lawyers or anything that glows open for twenty-four hours. There are no strip malls in Courtland. No Walgreens, Starbucks, or Burger King. No Super Walmart. No Dollar General. All the businesses here are family-owned, and many are owned by women.

With a population of under three hundred people, you wouldn't expect much. But it's hard to find a building on Main Street that's standing empty. There's Pinky's, the post office, and stores that sell plumbing supplies, farm implements, and antiques. There's a local, family-owned bank. A commodity broker. A community swimming pool, community garden, elementary school, two gas/service stations, an arts center, weekly newspaper, city hall, library, volunteer fire department, and a mayor. Young people who grew up in Courtland are moving back to raise their kids here. A lot of them grew up on a farm. But instead of farming, they are opening a brewery, gym, boutique, and hair salon, and figuring out how to inject new life into the local economy. They love rural life but want a new way to define it.

Most of the buildings tucked into Main Street were put up by the hands of the Norwegians and Swedes who settled here in the 1800s. "New" residential construction on streets like Liberty, Freedom, and Republic means it was built around 1974. No clusters of cookie-cutter townhouses or sprawling apartment complexes with on-site fitness facilities and puppy parks. There are no traffic lights in town. No neon. The only thing that flashes are the railroad crossing gates when trains from the KYLE or BNSF are passing through. But the sky is wide and blue, the land vast and green, and the air is sweet. Other than the grain elevator on the south side of town, there's nothing here that can keep you from seeing the sun rise or set. It is peaceful. Quiet. The sounds that you hear come from the rhythmic hum of farm machinery or the hand of God.

Courtland sits on the sidelines of Tornado Alley, but when the sky turns black and the clouds begin to roll, lightning will flash in jagged, horizontal streaks—*crackle! pop! hiss!*—that electrify the atmosphere, leaving you completely awestruck, absolutely terrified, or most likely, a little of both.

It is twenty miles west of Belleville (population 1,835) and eighteen miles east of Mankato (population 808) with an economy that, for more than a century, has existed thanks to what God and the farmer have put into the ground. Farmers here will plant, grow, and harvest crops that feed more than 166 people in the world every single day, almost seven times the number of people they fed in 1960.

This is the Wheat State. The Breadbasket of the World. The seventh highest agricultural producer in the country, growing $16 billion worth of food every year. There are fourth-generation farmers here who have been working the same land that their great-grandfathers did with horsepower that came from actual horses, not a John Deere. When a farmer says he's retiring, most people, including the farmer, laugh. "There's no such thing as a retired farmer," they say. "Just ask his banker."

When Betty turned sixty-five, she tried retiring but couldn't handle it. "There was nothing to do," she says. "I don't knit, I don't play cards, and I got bored."

She had raised three kids of her own—Ricky, Tammy, and Shawn—who gave her six grandkids and two great-grandkids. She had also been a foster mom for seventeen years, then cared for her mother when she got sick. So, when she talked to Wayne, they decided that he'd buy the bar and Betty would run it.

Over the years, Pinky's has been a pool hall and a drugstore, but when it opened in 1903, it was the Cozy Hotel, offering rooms for fifty cents and baths for half of that.

Betty's dream is to turn the upstairs back into a hotel. "It'd be so awesome," she says. But the roof went a few years ago, and it's in pretty bad shape up there. She thought maybe the historical society could help her out, but nothing yet, and she doesn't have the $300,000 to turn those fourteen empty rooms and two bathrooms—His & Hers—into a hotel again.

"Every one of those windows was a room," she says, pointing to the boarded-up windows on the second floor.

So, oh well. The dream will have to wait for now. It's okay. She still enjoys coming here seven days a week. It keeps her happy. Keeps the coffee drinkers happy, that's for sure. Because while the dream can wait, the coffee drinkers can't.

"I get here at five o'clock in the morning to get the cinnamon rolls and coffee done," she says.

By the time 7 a.m. rolls around, the place will be going full tilt for the all-you-can-drink coffee for a buck.

Yeah, the farmers smirk, *for the ones who pay.*

While they drink their coffee, they'll take their usual seats at their usual tables and maybe grab a cinnamon roll. "Betty's hockey pucks," they joke. They might place an order for eggs over easy, biscuits with gravy, or buttered toast and bacon that Betty will make on the open griddle. Sometimes they call in their order so that it's ready when they arrive, which is why the phone at Pinky's Bar & Grill is ringing at 5:16 a.m., 6:25 a.m., and 7:13 a.m.

They'll all sit there. Pay a buck. Or not. Drink a cup of coffee. Or two. And talk about stuff. Stuff like rain and sex and the market and sex and politics and sex and farming and sex and cattle and sex and use words that'll make you blush. "Bring earplugs, boots, and a sifter," she says.

Or they'll talk about the Kansas City Royals. Right now, they all hate the Royals because they just keep losing.

"Well, not hate," Joerg clarifies. "We're just very disappointed."

"Yeah, disappointed," they all agree. "That's more politically correct."

"The starting pitching just went to hell," whistles Jim. "Like that game last night? Three home runs by the Rangers."

That's when they'll yell at the TV, say they *hate* the Royals. Come into Pinky's the next morning and shake their heads and sigh before they move on to talking about rain and sex and the market and sex and politics and sex and farming and sex and cattle and sex and use words that will make you blush.

Things toned down a little bit after Joerg's wife, Pat, died unexpectedly a few weeks ago. Got kinda mild, actually. Then it picked up again. Got back to normal.

"I'm warning you," Betty says. "Bring earplugs."

The stuff that the guys like to talk about used to embarrass her so badly, her face would turn red. "Now I just turn on the TV and tune them out," she says.

They'll go through about three or four pots of coffee until they have to plow something, plant something, harvest something, haul something, feed something, or fix something. The previous owner used to put them to work peeling a five-gallon bucket of potatoes while they sat there and enjoyed the all-you-can-drink coffee for a buck.

"I should do that," Betty says.

People tell Betty she needs to get away more. She won't, though. Why would she? She's happy here. "Besides, it's a weird world out there," she says. "There's no respect. No morals. And frankly, the world is more than welcome to stay *out there*. Gives us more space," she says.

There's nothing she has to worry about in Courtland. Her family might not be here, but her friends are. And yeah, some of them love to make her face turn red, love to torture her about her hockey pucks, love to knock on the door even when they see a "Closed" sign, but if push came to shove, every single one of those morning coffee guys—Steve and Larry, Mikesell, Slug, Hootie, Jake, Jim, Don, Kenny, Carlson, Joerg, and all the rest of them— would go to bat for her.

"What more could I ask for?" she smiles.

The Morning Coffee: Friday

It's somebody's birthday.

That somebody isn't saying much about it, though. But everyone is going to know it's somebody's birthday because the List is on the counter.

The person celebrating their birthday will be picking up the coffee tab this morning for everyone who signs the List, instead of the other way around, and no one has any idea why.

Pinky's is where most of the farmers start their day. Where they needle and poke and harass and laugh and talk and worry about each other. *Why weren't you at coffee this morning?* Where they gossip, pray for rain to fall, curse it when it won't stop, and can carry on entire conversations that begin and end in two sentences.

"Dove season starts today."

"Yep. Good to eat when they're wrapped in bacon."

When the farmers start coming into Pinky's a few minutes before 6 a.m., they'll add their names to the List, a notepad of lined paper that sits in front of the Bunn coffee machine. *Probably not going to get any celebrities today though,* they'll snicker. *But you never know.* Obama was in here once and signed the List. Trump too. Oh, and that guy who passed away last year. He came back from the dead and signed the List.

When there's no birthday and no List to sign, everyone uses the honor system and throws a buck into a dirty white plastic cup to cover the all-you-can-drink coffee. Almost everybody.

"We do have some cheapskates," they say. "But we know who they are."

At 5:40 a.m., the front door swings open. Steve Brown. Tall. Swagger. Faded Wranglers. Boots. White cowboy hat beat to hell. And a T-shirt. Winter, spring, summer, fall; always, a T-shirt.

His dad, Larry, arrives next. Wireframe glasses. Faded ballcap. "NRA 140 Years of Freedom." Silver wristwatch. Supersized travel mug that was most likely gleaming white in another lifetime. Totally straight-faced. A look that implies this isn't his first time at the rodeo, so don't even try. By far, the hardest one in the room to read. Until he says things like, "Did Jim leave for Kansas City already? I wanted to tell him to have a safe trip."

Then Slug. As wide as he is tall. Faded overalls. Floppy canvas hat. Always smiling.

Followed by Mikesell, Hootie, Kenny, and Joerg. If you're looking to let your hair down, call Joerg. Impeccable sense of humor, semiretired, totally into his golf game.

"Or just the nineteenth hole," says Steve.

They all come in while the oven is warming the cinnamon rolls and Betty is busy answering the phone.

"Where's your wife?" Steve asks Joerg.

"I don't know," Joerg drawls, sipping his coffee. This is not in reference to Joerg's late wife, Pat. It's in reference to Carlson, who has been Joerg's best friend for like, forty years.

The phone rings again. Breakfast orders. Betty arranges everything into neat, equally spaced quarter sections on the griddle. Bacon up top, sausage down here, eggs over there. When their food is done, she'll place it onto a white plate and add four pieces of buttered toast separated by two plastic containers of Welch's Jelly: Concord Grape or Mixed Fruit. "Family Farmer Owned."

Betty cracks open two more eggs as the front door swings open again. It's Jim. Retired from the KYLE Railroad, a short line that runs through town and on into Colorado. He makes it halfway to the table before everyone starts unloading on his University of Kansas T-shirt.

"Stupid Jayhawks!"

"Get a new shirt, Jim!"

"Oh, shut up," Jim says. He scribbles his name onto the List, pulling an empty chair from an empty table, and joins the group. He rubs his eyes, props his head on his hand, and takes advantage of Slug, who is currently mid-pour.

"Put a tad in there, Slugger," he says, holding out his mug. "Well, to the governor," he adds before taking a sip.

The one thing that Betty doesn't do is pour the coffee. "They're big boys, they can take care of themselves," she says.

"You took care of that cute little thing from Oklahoma," Joerg points out. "You poured *him* coffee *twice*."

Betty has no idea what to say about this, so she just rolls her eyes. The cute little thing from Oklahoma isn't here today. So, if the guys want to fill their mugs, they can just help themselves or take advantage of whoever happens to be closest to the Bunn, which is plastered with warnings.

"WARNING: Remove Funnel Slowly"

"WARNING: To reduce the risk of electric shock, do not remove or open cover"

"WARNING: HOT LIQUID"

Two pots are sitting on the Bunn's warmers. One of which is already half empty. And next to the Bunn are four tall, plastic pitchers filled with water, as well as a sugar jar and a small container of creamer.

Cream and sugar? They laugh. *Yeah, okay.*

Hanging on the wall are banners announcing the upcoming schedules for the Royals and NASCAR, and an advertisement for Anheuser-Busch. "WE BUY MORE FROM AMERICAN FARMERS THAN ANY OTHER BREWER."

"None of us drink Budweiser," says Steve. "Except for Slug."

"Well, Busch Light," he smiles.

Everyone's still irritated with the damn Royals, though, because they just keep losing. But last night's JV football game?

"We kicked ass."

"High school team's lookin' pretty good this year, too. Lots of speed."

Pike Valley High School serves seventy-one students in Courtland and nearby Scandia attending grades 9 to 12. The Panthers play eight-man; barely enough to scrimmage. "But the smaller schools, hell, they only play six," says Joerg. And while Jim tops everyone's mug off with a fresh pot, most of the talk continues with the damn Royals and the speed of the Panthers and what the weather radar is showing, until around 7 a.m. when Betty turns the lights up.

"I'm out," Larry says, grabbing his travel mug.

Mark Garman's in, though. He's followed by one of the youngest farmers in town, who is very sweet and can be kinda shy and has thus become the preferred bullseye for a good ol' fashioned browbeating, teasing, and torture from the farmers. Lovingly doled out, of course.

"Anyone need a refill?" he offers, grabbing the pot.

"Goddamn! Every time!" Joerg says as his mug overflows and splashes onto the table.

Mark is thirty-four. The young farmer is thirty-eight. They are the youngest in the room by at least a decade. Maybe two or three, depending on who's in the room. Both are Fort Hays State University grads. The young farmer got his BS in wildlife biology. He farms full-time. Cattle, soybeans, and corn. Third generation.

"My grandparents and parents farmed here. Because of them, Courtland was the only place I could try farming," he says. "But I also wanted my kids to have the same childhood experiences that I had."

Mark studied political science and justice. He does farm a little bit; 172 acres with his older brother. But doing it for ten, twelve, eighteen hours, seven days a week, 365 days a year?

"Farming is a lifestyle, not just an occupation. I lived that lifestyle for the first twenty years of my life and wasn't sure I wanted to continue with it. And not all farmers have enough land to just keep their kids on and farm with them. You can only squeeze so much money out of an acre," he says. "Both of my brothers that now farm went out and had other jobs that they used to save money and purchase some land and start farming with Dad's help in lending machinery to begin with." Farming might be what Mark ends up doing, but he's always been a little fuzzy on the whole what-am-I-going-to-do-with-my-life thing. "Short answer," he says. "I'm single and thirty-four. I still have no clue what I want to do with my life. I absolutely love living in the country, but I don't believe traditional farming is what I want to do."

What Mark does like to do is work on a wind farm about thirty-four miles south of Courtland, performing routine services, hydraulic and electrical troubleshooting, and main component exchanges on sixty-seven massive, three-bladed white turbines with tips that slice through the prairie winds at 120 mph. Each turbine is spread out evenly to the east and west of Highway 81, converting the wind that whips across the open plains into electricity that supplies power to grids in Kansas and parts of Missouri. A lift takes him to the top of each turbine, 262 feet above the ground. "I'm lucky. Most newer turbines have climb assists, a rope that pulls you up a little as you climb the ladder," he says. "Older sites just have plain old ladders."

He's not usually here for the morning coffee, but he just wanted to get some breakfast. While he waits, the door swings open. More guys. More coffee. More conversations.

"Took off to Tipton in that John Deere."

"Yeah?"

"Yeah. 'Bout Randall, the AC quit. 'Bout Jewell, alternator quit. By the time I got to Tipton, I was worn out."

"Yeah. Sounds 'bout right."

By 8 a.m., the Bunn has brewed its third pot, the huge stack of white mugs from the Swedish-American State Bank, located down the street, has been reduced to one, and Joerg has taken over pouring duties.

"I see your ladder is still up out there."

"Yeah, don't ask me about that. I'm already out 750 bucks."

"Aw, hell."

The flatscreen is muted but turned to the Weather Channel. Because always, the weather. When the farmers check their phones, they're either looking at the radar or the market, not their email accounts or Twitter feeds.

"Well, corn's down two, beans are down ten, wheat's down four," says Joerg.

Right now, everyone's hoping for some rain. Been rough out here the past few months. The soybeans are turning silver and yellow. Just dying in the ground.

"Too bad we can't get just a little bit of somethin' from that hurricane. Hell, two inches would solve everything."

"Another hurricane is coming in right behind it."

"Oh. Really?"

"Yep. Real humdinger."

Two inches of rain would be great. It's been dry as a bone. Market's bad, too. "What the hell is the Board of Trade doing up there anyway?" Steve asks. "When did they stop giving a damn about the farmer? Everyone's losing, what, sixty-five cents a bushel on corn right now? And wheat, hell, that's at three bucks a bushel. *Three* bucks. It costs four bucks just to put each of those bushels into the ground."

This is nothing new. It is pretty much the same hand the American farmer has been dealt for the past hundred years. Franklin Delano Roosevelt saw it. When he ran for president, his target audience was the guy with the dirt under his nails, calling for "faith in the forgotten man at the bottom of the economic pyramid," a campaign strategy that sounded familiar during the push to "Make America Great Again."

"You know," Steve adds. "When the farmers need to produce, they produce."

Which is kind of like a catch-22. Because when a farmer in Kansas is told to produce, every other farmer in the country is told to produce, and when everyone is doing what they're told to do and producing, there ends up being too much of a good thing. When that happens, commodities either sit in bins and do nothing, or suppliers go into a selling frenzy, which drives prices of commodities down even further. The government and the people are usually happy because food is cheap. The farmer isn't happy, though, because he's losing sixty-five cents a bushel on corn and a buck on each bushel of wheat.

When he produces too little, prices go up. But that isn't exactly a golden ticket, either. If prices are up and supply is down, it's usually because some farmers somewhere are about to have a coronary thanks to bad weather, barely any crop to sell, and therefore hardly any income for a year's worth of backbreaking work. What he can unload is sold at a premium, but premium prices irritate consumers who then blame "those rich farmers" for how expensive a loaf of bread is at Kroger's.

"There are forty-two loaves of bread in one bushel of wheat. If we've got higher-priced food, it's not the farmer's fault. It's the middleman," says Kenny.

"The farmer gets blamed for a lot of crap," says Steve.

When food is cheap, people are buying stuff. And when people are buying stuff, the economy is strong. Out *there*. Back here, when food is cheap and people are buying stuff, well, then your farm is barely breaking even and you might have to borrow money just to pay your income tax. And if just one guy decides to sell his wheat cheap just to break even, everyone has to sell their wheat cheap because it's better to sell your wheat cheap than to not sell your wheat at all.

"The government loves cheap food because people love cheap food. It keeps stability in the food chain," says Joerg.

To get a bushel of wheat out of the ground and into the forty-two loaves of bread sitting on the shelf at a grocery store is a process that involves multiple steps. And most of us eating that bread are in large part completely oblivious as to how the wheat even gets into our slice of Sara Lee.

The first step begins with the wheat field. After the farmer has tilled the soil, put fertilizer in the ground, bought the seed, planted it, raked it, covered it with soil, watered it, weeded it, protected it with insecticide, cultivated it, and harvested it, he sells his wheat to the local grain elevator for whatever the current market value is. Good market value is $9/bushel, which is where prices were in 2008. Bad market value is where it's been for the past few years: around $3/bushel. This is what's currently responsible for the migraines since that's pretty much what dad got for a bushel of wheat in 1973, and not too much more than what great-grandpa got in 1920, when $2.45/bushel was considered a good, square deal thanks to World War I, the Wheat Price Guarantee Act, and high demand from our Allies.

The local grain elevator then sells the farmer's wheat to the regional grain elevator, who either loads it into a train or truck to be taken to a port and shipped overseas to places like China or sells the wheat to a miller. If it goes to the miller, the miller then pulverizes the wheat into wheat flour, which is sold to a food processor, like Sara Lee. Sara Lee then bakes the forty-two loaves of bread and sells them to a distributor who gets them delivered to Kroger's, where you can buy your loaf of Golden Wheat for $2.99.

So, forty-two loaves of bread at $2.99 each equals $125.58. Of which the farmer made $3.00, or whatever price the market is going for at the time.

"Each time that wheat changes hands after we sell it to the elevator, someone adds money to it. But if we're only getting $3/bushel, you can't make a profit," says Kenny.

When that happens, there's a problem. Which may morph into what experts predict will become a national crisis with farm debt soaring to a historic high of over $400 billion.

There's a reason for this. In 1980, the American farmer received thirty-one cents for every dollar spent on food. Today, that number is down to only fifteen cents. Everything else goes toward the cost of operating the farm: production, processing, marketing, transportation, distribution, and wages . . . for everyone but the farmer. So, to pay their share of expenses to keep feeding the world, most farmers have to get more loans, or tap into their savings or crop insurance—if they have any—just to keep their heads above water.

Privately held crop insurance works just like your car insurance does, charging annual premiums (which, on a thousand-acre farm is around $6,000) and paying out a guarantee (usually between 65 and 75 percent) when something has devastated your crop. But there's a cutoff date for getting your seeds planted. So, if you're having a late planting season thanks to Mother Nature's mood swings and miss it, you're flying by the seat of your pants and praying that a summer hailstorm doesn't wipe out your entire crop and leave you with a whole lot of nothing. Which happens more than anyone cares to remember.

There are also government subsidies that often get labeled as "farmers' welfare" and always make headlines: "Damages the economy!" "Prone to scandal!" "Undermines US trade relations!" "The agriculture industry would thrive without subsidies!"

Subsidies are payments that are in place to supplement the income a farmer should be getting but is not, like when the market is paying you $3/bushel for something that costs $4/bushel to grow. They were another idea that originated from FDR, have been around for almost a century, and without them, the average farmer would never survive the market or the weather. Which tells you a lot about how lucrative farming is for the average farmer.

"At least Trump is doing something to even the playing field with the tariffs," says Joerg. That playing field included what had ballooned into a record-shattering $375 billion annual trade deficit with China by 2017, representing a gap in the number of Chinese imports into America versus American exports into China; a volley the president returned by imposing a 25 percent tariff on more than $200 billion of Chinese imports.

In the wake of the tariff war, President Trump directed Secretary of Agriculture Sonny Perdue to come up with a short-term plan to protect agricultural producers while he duked it out with China for what he called "free, fair and reciprocal trade deals to open more free markets, in the long run, to help American farmers compete globally."

So, new programs were created. "To make sure our farmers did not bear the brunt of unfair retaliatory tariffs," Perdue said. This is when the USDA got to work to try to cut the American farmer some slack, similar to what FDR came up with during the Great Depression and the Dirty Thirties as part of the New Deal; a way to give the American farmer a break and the American economy a boost.

The first program that Trump proposed was the Food Purchase and Distribution Program, which promised to buy up to $1.2 billion in commodities that were at high risk for being targeted for retaliatory tariffs from the Chinese; food that would have otherwise gone to waste but instead would be redistributed to nutrition assistance programs like Emergency Food Assistance and child nutrition.

The second thing he did was put $200 million into the pocket of the Foreign Agricultural Service's Agricultural Trade Promotion Program so they could figure out which countries could fill the gaping hole that China left behind when it slapped a 25 percent retaliatory tariff on our soybeans and exports to our biggest customer came to a screeching halt.

The third was the creation of the USDA's Market Facilitation Program, which functioned like the deficiency payments that President Reagan offered to farmers as part of the 1985 Farm Bill. Under the MFP, President Trump gave the USDA the green light to dole out up to $9.6 billion in 2018 and $14.5 billion in 2019 in direct payments to farmers who were getting burned by retaliatory tariffs to make up for the drop in prices.

"This assistance will help with short-term cash flow issues," said Perdue. "Our farmers work hard, are the most productive in the world, and we aim to match their enthusiasm and patriotism as we support them."

The MFP covers nonspecialty crops like corn, cotton, dairy, soybeans, wheat, sunflower seeds, and sorghum, specialty crops such as sweet cherries, almonds, walnuts, and cranberries, and also dairy and hogs.

To sign up, a farmer can download a pretty straightforward, two-page application that includes questions about the state and county they farm in, what commodity they're planting, and their total planted acres.

Here's how the MFP program worked in 2018 with beans, wheat, and corn. Soybeans were trading at about $9/bushel. So, to cushion the blow from the tariff, the subsidy payout that the government gave to the farmer was $1.65/bushel. The number of bushels per acre could vary, largely due to weather conditions, but in 2018, the average American farmer was able to get around forty-six bushels of soybeans per acre of land. This meant that if a farmer had five hundred acres of soybeans, Uncle Sam gave him a check for $37,950, which supplemented the $207,000 a farmer would get for his beans at market.

Wheat was interesting. A wheat farmer received a subsidy of fourteen cents per bushel in addition to the $4.77/bushel he would make at market. The American farmer can get around thirty-seven bushels of wheat per acre of land. If he had five hundred acres of wheat, his paycheck would have been $2,590 from the US government, added to the $88,245 he would get paid at the grain elevator.

But nothing even came close to beating corn. Enjoy your subsidy of one cent per bushel, farmer! Most growers in Kansas can get an average of 129 bushels of corn per acre of land. The average market rate for corn these days has been around $3.49/bushel. So, if he farms five hundred acres of corn, he could expect to get around $225,105 at market, plus an additional check for $645 in subsidy payouts.

The difference in the MFP prices, whether for corn, beans, wheat, or whatever, reflected the impact that the trade war had on prices for each particular crop.

The program changed in 2019. For nonspecialty crops like beans, wheat, and corn, it offered a payment rate of between $15 and $150 per acre that got multiplied by your farm's total plantings. The payment rate was determined by the state and county you lived in, and how hard that area was hit by the retaliatory tariffs. Republic County fell on the lower end at $60 per acre.

And while they can appreciate the effort, no farmer hears about a government subsidy, powers down the combine, and starts planning for early retirement. A subsidy is kinda like a Band-Aid on a bullet hole. There's nothing financially sound about getting an additional $645 bucks for five hundred acres of corn that nets $225,000 at market. But at least subsidies are *something,* the farmers will say as they sip their coffee. And something is better than *nothing.*

"Yeah, it helps. You won't hear a farmer bitching about the subsidy payment," says the young farmer. "I think of it as a hand-up, not a handout."

Before the subsidies inspired by the trade war, Forbes had put the spotlight on ten mega-farms in America that, between 2008 and 2017, each received an average of $18 million through sixty of the USDA's federal farm programs that included price loss coverage, agricultural risk, conservation, and crop disaster. If math isn't your thing, that amounted to $1.8 million a year; $150,000 a month; $34,615 a week. And if you're a curious taxpayer and want to know whether anyone in your neighborhood is part of the Millionaire's Club, OpenTheBooks.com—"Every Dime. Online. In Real-Time"—has made it easy to find out. Just type your zip code into their interactive mapping platform to see who's getting $1 million or more in taxpayer-funded farm subsidies.

But what they don't tell you is how much money that same farmer *lost* during the year. Between the exorbitant cost of operating his farm and the low commodity prices he can sell his products for at market, he probably lost a lot of cash. The cost of operating a farm today can be ten times higher than it was in 1973 just based on the price of land and farm equipment alone, yet when you look at the market prices of wheat, corn, soybeans, and dairy in a then versus now scenario, the needle for profits has barely moved. If at all. Meaning that a farmer today could be making just about the same amount of money per bushel of crop that dad made when President Richard Nixon was in the Oval Office.

There are family farms in Courtland that have received subsidies over the years for their soybeans, wheat, corn, sorghum, livestock, and sheep; some more significantly than others. But for the most part, it's not like the average farmer in Courtland or anywhere else in America is rolling in the dough because of the subsidies he's receiving. It's kind of the opposite.

"Farmers' welfare" makes for a good headline, but when those words are lumped together, it kinda gives the impression that farmers are snoozing in the combine, waiting on free money from the government. In reality, they're working up to eighteen hours a day or more, virtually year-round, trying to grow something that they've rarely been fairly compensated for over the past hundred years.

"I think most farmers would agree that if we could get a decent price, we would not want subsidies," says Joerg. "What we want is a fair price and we don't get that. Without subsidies, it would be pretty tough because of weather situations. And any insurance we get is something we pay for."

There is a conservation program—like FDR's Agricultural Adjustment Act of 1933— that pays a farmer to take his land out of production for a set amount of time to curb an overabundance of supply. The theory is that when you lower supply, you increase demand, which in turn boosts commodity prices when they are extremely low and barely cover your costs. But not everyone is a fan of any of it.

"Too many rules and regulations," says Steve. "Not worth a damn."

But even when the soybeans are turning yellow and silver because they need two more inches of rain and the tough year is starting to look quite bad thanks to the boys in Chicago, and you had to tap into the last of your savings just to keep your head above water, and you're already late planting or harvesting thanks to Mother Nature's mood swings, everyone forgets their problems when they hear you've got a worse one.

When Hootie had a massive heart attack a few years ago in the middle of the harvest season, everyone added another hour or two to their eighteen-hour days and brought their combines and grain carts and semi-trucks to his fields to finish cutting his wheat while he went under the knife.

And when Joerg's wife, Pat, died unexpectedly a few weeks ago, 350 people came to the funeral in a town with a population of 285.

Because that's what neighbors are for. It's just what you *do*.

"We have our own little world out here," Joerg says. The world out there, well, that's out of their control. "If it was, there wouldn't be killings and shootings or anything like that. We just have more respect for each other. We're the deplorables, you know."

A lot of liberals, some conservatives, and most news anchors still want to know why most people in rural areas, flyover states, rust belts, and bible belts voted for Donald Trump. *How could you?*

It was more about voting against Hillary than it was voting for Trump, some say. I really do believe in his economics, say others. At morning coffee, they'll tell you that during the election, there were twenty-two hundred votes cast in Republic County and nineteen hundred went to Trump. And the farmers that pulled the red lever will tell you that the trade war with China and tariff on our soybeans are having little effect on what was already a bad market and the farmers that pulled blue will tell you it's killing them. But even the ones with the biggest "MAKE AMERICA GREAT AGAIN" bumper stickers can only tolerate so much of the antics.

"We hate his antics," Joerg adds. Oh yeah, everyone nods. Everyone could do without the antics.

But they put up with the antics because Donald Trump was someone who stood up in front of Middle America and said, "I hear you." The popular narrative is about "acceptance" and "respecting differences" and "tolerance." Until it's time to accept and tolerate someone conservative, pro-God, pro-life, pro-anything that isn't a popular ideology trending on Facebook. It's cool to rip on Christians, fun to slam anti-abortionists. But raise one eyebrow about *my* choices? *My* religion or lack thereof? *My* lifestyle?

Bigot. Racist. Sexist. *You intolerant, stupid redneck. You dumb country bumpkin.*

"Deplorables," Joerg smiles, shaking his head.

By the time 10 a.m. rolls around, the tables are empty again. So are the coffee pots. The phone stopped ringing. The someone who had the birthday paid the coffee tab for everyone who signed the List. And Betty is beyond disappointed.

After everything she warned about, the earplugs and a pair of boots and a sifter needed to survive the morning coffee, everyone *behaved.*

No talk about sex, sex, sex, or words that would make you blush. Nothing that would embarrass you so bad you'd turn red. *Nothing.* Even Mikesell just sat there like a Boy Scout.

"You *always* need to wear boots if you're talking to Mikesell," she says. "I'm disappointed in all of them."

The Farmers:
Steve Brown

It could be 30 degrees outside, and Steve Brown is going to be wearing a T-shirt.

Not like Kenny and Mikesell and Hootie and Joerg, who are all bundled up. Warm and cozy.

"Pansies!" he says.

"Who ya calling a pansy?" they'll shoot back. "Damn heater's on in your truck!"

The truck is a Dodge 2500 permanently caked with mud. It's a toss-up between Hair Nation or Christian music playing on satellite radio and a rifle is usually riding shotgun on the passenger seat. *You got in the truck with Brownie?* they all howl. *He drives like shit! Goes a hundred miles an hour. He doesn't even pause at the stop sign down on 36.*

Steve Brown has been farming in Courtland for fifty years. "Ever since the day I was born," he says. His parents, Larry and Joan, also farmed. Joan's father farmed. Larry's father and his father's father farmed, too. The old wood-framed house that Larry was born and raised in is still standing on their property a few miles north of town, in the shadow of two MFS corn bins with the G-115 galvanization.

"Dad can't stand to see the house torn down," Steve says, opening a circular trap the size of a fist. Kernels of dried yellow corn plunk into a plastic, five-gallon bucket that he'll empty into a metal trough for cows that are waiting expectantly. He gets why his dad doesn't want to tear the old house down. He just hates to see it looking like this, home to a couple of raccoons and a fourteen-year-old cat that Steve feeds daily with a scoop of dry food.

Steve's voice is strong, like he knows exactly what he's talking about, but just slightly high like he's perpetually amused by whatever is happening

around him. Most of his sentences are punctuated with laughter. Or, sayings
like "Oh, Mylanta," and words like "Fuck." Kinda radiates rugged, Marlboro
Man vibes with the swagger and the slow eyes and the mustache and the
midwestern twang. If the white cowboy hat that's been beaten to hell isn't on
his head, it's a faded ballcap. The boots. The Wranglers. The T-shirt. Winter,
spring, summer, fall; always a T-shirt.

Steve is married. Has two grown kids. Neither of them farm.

"I told them to go out in the world and try that first and see if they like
it," he says. And he did try the whole daughter-working-for-me thing once.
"She got fired. I just like shit done right."

Steve loves living in Courtland. Wouldn't trade it for the big city. Hell no.
He can do whatever he wants here. Can be left alone. Gets to see the seasons
changing.

It's just different out here. If the end of the world happened, if people were
smart, the first thing they'd do was find their way out to Courtland, Kansas,
because these guys will still be alive, he'll say. They're the ones who know
how to live off the land. And besides, it's just so much more relaxed and
friendly here than it is out there. People do things like go out of their way to
wave to you as you drive by. Even if they have no idea who you are. If you're
driving through town, they're waving. They give a damn about you and your
family, too. And when you're pissed off and barking at everyone, they get it.

Not to say it's all Mayberry out here. They'll tell you it has its Peyton
Place-ish moments. And there is the occasional crime that pops up on the
county police blotter, usually sandwiched between reports of a wandering
cow out on Highway 36. The crime that happens here is occasional and petty.
Drugs, usually. Pills mostly. Sometimes, the people who want them are the
ones who break into houses to either find pills or find stuff to steal and sell
to get pills.

Breaking into a house like Steve's probably wouldn't be the brightest of
ideas.

A lady from the media once got a hold of him when he was in Kansas City
buying a gun to add to his collection. She had a cameraman, a microphone,
and a question for him.

Steve had an answer. *You try to take my guns,* he said, *the streets will run red.*

"I had a full beard when I said it, too. I looked crazy."

Steve will tell you he feels naked without his pliers and his guns. He has
the pliers because every farmer needs a set of pliers. And the guns? Well, that's
just how you're raised out here, knowing how to shoot pheasant, dove, and
game, or anything that's coming after your cattle. It's how you protect what
you're trying to raise. How you live off the land. Which is very dry lately.
No measurable rain for six weeks. But there's a surplus of last year's wheat still

sitting in the grain elevators that's driven prices down to $3/bushel, which is about fifty-five cents more than it was in 1920.

Apart from the occasional spike in commodities prices that can occur due to things like world wars or catastrophic natural disasters, profits in the farming economy haven't worked out in favor of most farmers over the past hundred-plus years. When it does, it's usually because something terrible has happened to the other guy growing the same crop as you. Like in 2012, when the US experienced its worst drought in fifty-six years, which obliterated everyone's beans. It caused such a shortage and frenzied buying that soybean prices spiked to $18/bushel, an all-time high. So, to keep their head above water, most of the farmers had to come up with a new plan.

"We try to grow ourselves out of poverty," he says. The idea is that the less you're getting per bushel, the more the incentive to farm more land and grow more food to try and bridge the gap. "Never works," he says. Mostly because everyone else has the same idea. "Doesn't do you any good to get nervous about it because you can't change it. Just gotta get over it. Patience is a virtue. God teaches that a lot."

It also doesn't do you any good to fight with your neighbor when you're in a mood. Yeah, you might get barked at or be the one doing the biting, but the next day, you're buddies again. You have to get along with each other out here because one day you might need help, and the guy you were fighting with yesterday is the same guy who's pulling your tractor out of a ditch when the wheels slip and it flips over with you in it.

He'll tell you he used to be hot-headed, worrying about everything, stressing out over the weather, the damn Board of Trade. "They manipulate the market to line their own pockets. They don't give a damn about the farmer." *Rain makes grain,* traders like to say. "Which okay, yeah, rain makes grain, but the boys in Chicago are also pushing pieces of paper, trading on speculation," he says. And what's too much and what's too little is anyone's guess for the boys in Courtland. "It's up to Mother Nature and God. We grow to the best of our ability."

Before, when Steve would think about all these things, he'd get pissed off. Really pissed off.

Now, well, he still worries and stresses and gets pissed off, but he just tries to handle it differently. Stopped drinking about five months ago. He did take one small sip out of a mason jar recently, just because. Someone hands you a mason jar, you take a sip. Or, he'll fire up the Ranchero 500, the one with the 600-turbo engine that he got from Missouri. Sometimes, he'll take his wife for a ride. Most of the time, she passes.

How everyone else handles their stress is between them and God. Some of the farmers have had to dry out a couple of times. Tried not to worry and stress about how they're going to pay the bills when the bills keep going up and the income keeps going down, get seed planted when the ground is too dry, harvest their crop when the ground is too wet. Sometimes they stay away from the bottle. Sometimes they don't. When things have gotten really bad, when the yields aren't enough to pay the loans and the bank comes calling, and suddenly, the land that was in your family for three or four or five generations is about to have a foreclosure sign stuck into it, and the worry and the stress get too overwhelming and you just can't see beyond it, an alarming number of farmers in recent years have been finding relief in the barrel of a .22.

"Doesn't happen often around here," he says. "But it does happen."

There is a lot of blood, sweat, and tears that go into farming. Not like Steve wants some pat on the back or anything. No farmer in Courtland does. They just wish a lot of people out there realized what they do back here to ensure those grocery store shelves are stocked with what we want when we want it.

That twenty-four-hour convenience is the result of ten, twelve, and eighteen hours or more of work a day, seven days a week. Blazing sun, pouring rain, biting cold. Because when that pivot's stuck and it's 110 degrees outside? You're the one trying to pull it out so your crops can get watered. And when your cow is calving in a −15 degree snowstorm, you strip down to your T-shirt and help her. "It'd be nice if people could live it for just one year, to appreciate the work that goes into farming," he says. "You can read all you want in books, but until you experience it, you just don't know. Nothing is textbook out here."

Farming isn't some cute hobby that involves planting seeds and puffing on a corncob pipe while you wait for your money to sprout out of the ground. Being a farmer is like getting advanced degrees in business, economics, finance, accounting, mathematics, biology, ecology, chemistry, meteorology, animal husbandry, and veterinary medicine, intertwined with a little bit of clairvoyance and a lot of knowledge that's been handed down generation after generation, although chances are good you'll never be compensated accordingly. Not in your lifetime. Not monetarily or otherwise. Because fertilizer has gotten expensive. Seed has gotten expensive. And that tractor has gotten *really* expensive.

But the profits? Not so much. In 2017, the cost of equipment, seed, fertilizer, chemicals, labor, and land—basically, everything you need to farm—set the farmer back around $640 per acre of corn planted. But his profits from that acre? Also $640. Same for soybeans: an investment of $483 per acre. Profits of $483 per acre.

Congratulations on a year's worth of backbreaking work: you barely broke even. Which has been the same story year after year after year, for decades.

There's been plenty of talk about the injustice over someone at McDonald's not being paid a fair wage of $15/hour to flip hamburgers, yet wages for America's directly hired farmworkers haven't even risen 1 percent since 1989. In 2017, the average hourly pay was $13.32. And when they go to sell what they've grown from the ground, our farmers are often being paid either the same, just slightly more, or, sometimes, a lot less, per bushel compared to what dad got in 1973 and great-grandpa got in 1920.

Take the going price for wheat, which is $3.65/bushel. Plug it into an inflation calculator. That $3.65/bushel in today's market is equal to $0.30/bushel in 1920, which is less than the $2.45/bushel a farmer in 1920 was *actually* making.

In 1985, a farmer could get $3.49/bushel of wheat. Now plug that into an inflation calculator. The $3.49/bushel he got in '85 is equal to $8.60 today, nowhere near the $3.65/bushel he's getting today.

There is also very little downtime, very few vacations, and no such thing as calling off work because "Ow, my back hurts." You are planting, harvesting, hauling, mowing, weeding, plowing, and tending—to cattle, crops, or machinery—all the time.

And in addition to being at the mercy of the weather and the boys in Chicago, you're also at the mercy of Meatless Monday, gluten allergies, and low-carb diets that have inspired millions of people to fear the wheat you're growing and the cattle you're raising. Whatever you've put into the ground is also very appetizing to deer, raccoons, grasshoppers, and all those winged things that look like pretty Monarch butterflies but are actually moths—hungry ones. Never mind the coyotes that are looking to make a meal out of your newborn calves.

"Everything is eating what we're trying to raise," he says. All that work, those ten-, twelve-, and eighteen-hour days to grow something that can disappear in the blink of an eye and very little of it is within your control.

"One month ago," he says, pointing out the window of the Dodge, "that field of beans had the potential of fifty bushel. Now, I'd be shocked if it were twenty bushel because of the drought." Which is a problem. Because at fifty bushel/acre, and \$9/bushel, well, do the math, he says.

"If I'm getting \$9/bushel, fifty bushel would have been \$450. I get only twenty bushel, we're talking only \$180. Then subtract all your expenses, and that's what you're left with. That's what you live on."

What you live on at twenty bushel is not much.

If you have a great year, a twelve-hundred-acre farm might net you \$100,000 or more. When there's rain at just the right time and in just the right amount. When the boys in Chicago seem like they're giving a damn, and beans are going for \$12/bushel, corn's going for \$7 to \$8/bushel, and wheat's going for \$9/bushel.

So yeah, netting a hundred grand a year after you've paid all your expenses, paid your loans, paid the mortgage, paid the property taxes, put in your ten-, twelve-, and eighteen-hour days, 365 days a year, means you're having a good year.

But during the lean times? When soy's at \$9/bushel, corn's at \$3.50/bushel, and wheat's at \$3/bushel? The way it's been for the past few years? "Hell," he says. "You might not pay any income tax." And just because you're not paying income tax doesn't mean you aren't still figuring out how you're going to cover your expenses, pay your loans, your mortgage, and don't forget about that property tax, which on an average fifteen-hundred-acre farm could set you back anywhere from a couple thousand to tens of thousands, depending on an impossibly complex equation set forth by the Director of the Division of Property Valuation of the State of Kansas that evaluates a litany of factors including your potential for crop productivity based on the composition of your soil.

"No other income but off the dirt," he says. "Nothin' is given to us out here."

It's why a lot of farmers have wives who decide on a career that doesn't involve combines. It's a steady income. Insurance benefits. Something to help cushion the blow of a very bad year on the farm; something to help keep the farm in operation instead of in foreclosure.

Since Steve was seven or eight, he's been putting in ten-to-twelve-to-eighteen-hour days in good years, lean years, tough as hell years. But take him off the farm, off those twelve hundred acres of row crop to harvest, away from his two to three hundred head of cattle, including the hundred head of red heifers that he wakes up every morning at 5:15 a.m. to feed, and then what?

"What would I do?" he asks. "I have no idea."

When Steve can get away, he goes on mission trips with his church, Concordia Wesleyan. "Celebrate Recovery. Healing from life's hurts, habits, and hang-ups. Thursdays @7PM." He helps other guys get that, too; the one they call when they feel themselves slipping. Concordia Wesleyan also builds churches in places like Mozambique and Ecuador. There's talk they'll go to Australia, which Steve hopes is true, because he'd really like to go there. And when he's in Mozambique or Ecuador, he gets a real appreciation for how we live like kings over here. Even in the lean years like this one, when things are going backward, and farmers have had to sell their biggest asset, land that's been in the family for generations because that's the only option he has left if he wants to survive.

Ideally, Steve would like to retire in twenty years when he's seventy, although he knows there's a damn good chance he'll be working until the day he dies. Because even if he's in a financially secure enough position to retire, once he does, he'll wonder the same thing that every other retired farmer thinks. *What do I do now?*

Hopefully, part of what you do is enjoy a big check from the person renting your land and farming it themselves; usually a split of 60 percent to the person renting it, 40 percent to you. Pay the income tax and property tax and the rest is yours to enjoy. It's a big deal, choosing who is going to take over something you spent your life babying. It's nice when it's your kids, but that doesn't happen too often anymore. These days, kids go to college, get a job in some big city, enjoy paid vacations, matching 401(k) plans, and air-conditioned offices, just like their parents encouraged them to do. And even when they do return to a farm town like Courtland, they know enough to look at the profit margins, the skyrocketing expenses, those ten, twelve, or eighteen hours a day in the sun/snow/rain, and say, "Yeah, no thanks." So, land like Steve Brown's ends up being sold to a corporate farm that owns tens of thousands of acres and hires hands instead of blood to work them. Today, 98 percent of all farms in the United States are family-owned, but those same families represent less than 2 percent of our total population.

Call the American family farmer a dying breed and yeah, Steve Brown will agree with you. Almost entirely.

"Strong minority," he says. "We're the strong minority."

The Pastor

Pastor Sandra Jellison-Knock is about twelve hours away from preaching two sermons in under two hours. She delivers messages to two churches and sometimes two nursing homes, without notes, always from memory, never in front of a pulpit, always with a microphone in her hand. And she never gives the same sermon twice, even on the same day.

"I believe in a community of worship. So, I try to tailor my messages to fit the community and the people in it, speaking to what they're going through."

Pastor Sandra knows she's not going to sleep tonight. She's just accepted that fact because sleeping on Saturday night doesn't happen.

"Never been able to," she says.

Most of the people in her congregations have no clue. They don't know that she doesn't eat until after church is over. They can't tell that she doesn't like talking in front of people. "Sometimes I have flop sweats! I'll be up there thinking, 'Oh, this ship is sinking,' and afterward I'll say to someone, 'Was it obvious that was a flop?' and they'll have no idea what I'm talking about."

Pastor Sandra has short brown hair, glasses, and is wearing a black T-shirt emblazoned with the letters UMC across the front in green rhinestones. She has small, silver hoop earrings on and gray New Balance sneakers. She just got back from a Blessing of the Bikes over in Scandia. "Motorcycles," she says. "You know, just to pray for everyone's safety as they ride."

Pastor Sandra has been the lay pastor at Courtland United Methodist and Scandia United Methodist for two years, going on three. "In Courtland, there are about a hundred members on the record, baptized kinda thing. We usually get about thirty to thirty-five attending each Sunday." Since it's a farming community, the community prefers early church. This year, service in Courtland is at 9:15, Scandia is at 10:45, and each year, they switch. "Easter is what's usually tough because, obviously, everyone wants the pastor there for sunrise service. So, we just do it together and have one service."

She is aware of the general perception that people who live in the bible belt are going to church five days a week and walking around with John 3:16 signs in their hands.

"It's not that," she says. "To be fair, because I live in a clergy bubble, I spend a lot more time around church people. But I would say for a lot of other people here, church is still really central to their day in, day out life. There are also folks who have a strong belief, but church has become less central to their week, just like anywhere else in the nation or around the world. Is it just because people are so much busier? Or, maybe they're discouraged, I don't know. Church attendance has certainly dropped off, as it has everywhere in the world. The other thing I see is people that are really searching, and there's something about being in a small community that is more family-oriented that is part of what they are looking for. So, even if they left home for a while and moved back, they know there's something about that small-town feeling of 'we're all in this together' and have some tie to some church through their family or a memory. It's a part of that community feel."

Pastor Sandra grew up in Hays, Kansas, population twenty thousand, two and a half hours southwest of Courtland. She graduated from Fort Hays State University, then seminary school, and got her first church when she was twenty-three years old. "Part of the Pink Collar Ghetto," she says dryly. "As women entered into leadership positions back then, which was around 1985, there was this general feeling that pastoral positions would be viewed as less prestigious and offer lower pay as women stepped into those roles. I'll be honest, preaching is a lot like teaching or farming; you do it because you love it, and you're called to do it. You don't really do it for the money."

Her husband, Randy, is an ordained elder, and they live in a parsonage house around the block from Courtland UMC, a tidy ranch next to one of the houses where Dan Kuhn's Mexican workers live during the summer.

"Oh, I am always so excited to see them!" she laughs. They bring her watermelons. She gives them donuts.

Hi!

Hola!

"There's definitely a language barrier so it's probably why we've gotten into the whole 'giving food' thing. And that's friendly!"

She also loves to jog. "Don't laugh. My goal was to do a 5K in twenty-five minutes. I used to jog down to where the Carlsons live. But I kept injuring my hip. I think I'm getting old. Now, I walk two miles and stay mainly in town. I love when Sherie Mahin has the kids outside and I can high-five them as I walk by."

Being in Courtland is a new chapter for Pastor Sandra and Randy. In 2013 their son, Keenan, was killed in a head-on collision, right after he graduated from high school, three days after prom.

"I am not a sad woman. But it was the day of the Boston Marathon bombing, and there was just this overall feeling of sadness that I was experiencing all day long. I had ordered a pizza for dinner, and Keenan was late getting home, and I remember thinking, 'That's strange.'"

A few minutes later, two state troopers were standing on her front porch.

"We were living in Washington, which is another small town about an hour east on 36. I'd say there are only about one thousand people or so who live there. And six hundred showed up for his funeral. They needed two services to handle the crowd."

State troopers lined the streets. So did the local police. So did a group of bikers called the Patriot Guard, because of rumors that members of the Westboro Baptist Church in Topeka had planned to picket the funeral with their "God Hates Fags" signs.

"Most obituaries in Kansas don't mention a man's boyfriend or include photos of a gay couple at prom kissing, so it stands out."

Keenan was gay.

He never tried to hide it from anyone. He wanted to take his boyfriend to prom, so he met with the principal and had a stack of paper and notes this thick. The principal was so kind and said, 'I've been waiting for this day for four years. Keenan, there's nothing that says you can't bring him to prom. But just understand that there is the chance that afterward, there will be a rule created to ensure it doesn't happen again.'

A few days before the prom, Keenan introduced his boyfriend to the parents of his graduating class of thirty-two students. "That was my concern. I wasn't worried about the kids. I was worried that a parent would yell something during the promenade. But it was fine," she says.

Keenan was also black.

"Keenan would have been our nephew. His mom was adopted by Randy's parents. We didn't have kids. We had tried, but it just never happened, which we were okay with. When she was pregnant, she asked us if we would want to adopt her baby. And Randy and I both looked at each other at the same time and said, 'Yeah, we do.' When he was an hour old, she gave us custody."

Keenan loved Kristin Chenoweth and *Wicked*. He had plans to attend the Fashion Institute of Design in L.A. "His dream was to make it to the finals on *Project Runway* and to show in Bryant Park. He was so delicious. Do you want to see pictures of him?"

While he was growing up in rural Kansas, he did get picked on at school. "Little stuff," she says. "But yeah, it did happen from time to time." He also felt that the United Methodist Church as a whole rejected him, but never the little churches he attended on Sunday. "For the most part, there were no issues. He loved Jesus Christ and felt that Jesus Christ loved him. People have this perception that if you vote a certain way, you therefore must be intolerant. But people in small towns feel a sense of ownership, like, 'This kid is part of my family.'"

When the United Methodist Church voted to prohibit homosexual lay-persons or allow gay marriages, only one family told Pastor Sandra that they would have left the congregation had the vote swung the other way.

"Just one family said that to me. So many families said, 'This really hurts. I have a niece, brother, or child who is gay.' And that's what a lot of people outside of a small town forget about the people living in a small town. In big cities, most people either have someone in the family who is gay or knows someone who is gay. Well, it's the same here."

As a pastor, what's most important to her is that people learn how to understand grace in a larger way. Grace for others. But grace for themselves, too. "Which is so hard, right?" And she sees a lot of grace in Courtland. "It's just the support that you see, even in difficult times. You might see somebody who's at a hard point in their life who has had a tragedy or a life crisis reach out to someone else who is going through the same thing. And that person might be someone they don't know that well or even someone they don't necessarily get along with. Because a small town is like a family; there are times you are going to rub each other the wrong way. But you still show up with a casserole when you hear that someone close to them has died."

She pauses for a minute before continuing.

"To be honest, I don't know if people living in small towns have time to be sittin' around hatin'. There's a sense of community here and the ability to have empathy, too. I love it here. And I mean, look at me. I have this hyphenated last name. We had a black, gay kid. Our politics don't mesh as much with theirs. I thought the Ziggy Marley concert we went to down in Salina was the best concert ever. People probably think we're a little weird. And yet, I never felt shut out. What I feel like is that people want to know that you want to work *together*. Especially around here. And I feel like that, more than anything, is what makes them think of you as 'one of us.'"

The New Business:
Soul Sister Ceramics

The shop is cute. Really cute. Like, super cute. Bright white walls, wood flooring, cheery blue door. Throw pillows and handmade purses and totes, kitchenware, glassware, candy in jars with bright turquoise lids, handcrafted jewelry, colorful stationery, cards, and day planners, macramé, and thick, cotton throws with tassels that are displayed on painted step ladders. A lot of what you're seeing on the shelves has been made in Kansas: Leaf Logic Tea, Rough & Rye roller ball fragrances and lotions, Kansas Earth & Sky Candles, Fresh Seven Coffee Beans.

"I didn't really have any buying experience," says Shanna Lindberg. "I just bought what I liked. And I was able to make so many connections on social media just searching for #madeinKansas."

Shanna is tall with glossy, reddish-orange hair and clear eyes. Faded distressed jeans, linen top, a pair of sandals with a four-inch stacked heel. She can dish it out and take whatever you throw at her.

"It takes a lot to offend me. You'd have to insult my kids or my shoes to do that," she laughs.

The whole idea started because Shanna and Michelle Lindberg were bored, really. No relation. Best friends who happened to marry cousins.

"We were just hanging out one day at Michelle's house and our kids were playing. And we said to each other, 'You know, we need a hobby. What can we do?' And there was this mug that we had both always loved that was ceramic, and so, that was it."

They got the kiln off Craigslist. The wheel, too. Started making ceramic earrings and necklaces. "Things that were small and hard to mess up," Shanna says. They put a bunch of their stuff up for sale on Etsy. People started buying. They figured they might as well rent out their kiln and wheel so other people could enjoy it, setting up shop in the Courtland Arts Center on Main Street. People kept using it.

"It actually got to be a pain, carting all that pottery around," Shanna says. "So, we started looking for a place to open a business. We looked in Scandia and found a building right along 36. And we thought it'd be perfect. Everyone would see us as they drove by. It had a ton of windows. But he wanted $20,000, which was way more than we were willing to spend. We talked about it, and ultimately, we really wanted to find something in Courtland. And we always thought the old gas station in town was adorable."

The old gas station in town *was* adorable. Brick, little faux chimney on the side, Spanish tile roof, made to look like a cottage tucked into the corner of Liberty and Main. The analog gas pumps were still standing here, too, and there was a service bay attached to the side. It had been vacant for years. Used for storing the town Christmas lights and not much else. It was dingy and dusty and probably the last place anyone would have expected to see gourmet loose leaf tea and handmade beaded earrings up for sale.

They talked to the Mayor and city council about buying it. Settled on a price. Then, Shanna and Michelle went to the Swedish-American, got a loan that their husbands cosigned, and started thinking about a name.

"We always said we were Soul Sisters. So, that's what we went with."

When someone in Courtland has a renovation project, it's usually Bryan VanMeter that they've got on speed dial. Three months after he swung his hammer, Soul Sister Ceramics had a ribbon cutting and grand opening that got sixteen hundred views on Facebook Live in a town with a population of 285.

Congratulations!

What an awesome place!

Such a cute shop!

Everyone went crazy over the industrial lighting fixtures, galvanized tin trim, and shiplap walls; the new windows and all the bright, natural light that pours in, creating zero need for any filters on their Instagram posts, which tend to get a lot of likes.

Love it all! I'm stopping in tomorrow.

The cottage, which was once the office for the service station, is where the boutique is. They turned the old service bay into a bright, airy workshop where unpainted ceramics line the shelves: pitchers, mugs, serving platters, creamers, and smaller pieces for kids to paint, like mermaids and butterflies, frogs, ice cream cones, tractors, and fire engines.

When you pull up a red, metal stool to sit at the table and paint, you're sitting around what was once the old service station's car lift. "We just topped it off with some wood and filled in the pit that was underneath," she says.

It's 10:15 a.m. on a Saturday. Fifteen minutes after opening and there are already four kids and three adults with paintbrushes in their hands, including the family from Concordia, who drove thirty minutes to get here. Shanna is pouring paint and helping pick colors and assuring everyone that yes, that rusty/brown/red color that you're painting on that ceramic Christmas tree will cure green when it's fired in the kiln.

"No one ever believes me, but I promise, it's really green," she says.

When they're done painting, Shanna will take the pieces home and fire them in the kiln. She used to keep a list of people's names and phone numbers, calling each one when their pottery was ready. "That was taking up so much time. Now I just tell them it'll be ready for pickup in a week. I also used to deliver each piece or ship it out. But I realized that if I'm doing that, then it's a missed opportunity for them to come back and shop. Plus, I love to see the reaction of people when they see how their pottery turned out."

Soul Sister is open five days a week, Tuesday through Saturday, from 10 a.m. to 5 p.m. "My son can walk here after school." When Shanna's not at the shop, she's running her kids to baseball and gymnastics, with practices and games and tournaments that are usually thirty-, forty-five-, and sixty-minute hauls each way; getting the crockpot filled in the morning so that dinner is ready in the evening; taking a meal out to her husband, Nathan, while he's out in the fields tending to their farm. She also coaches gymnastics twice a week in Concordia. Thirty miles south.

"We all saw our mothers work and do ten things at once, so we're used to it," she says.

Michelle has her nursing degree. Shanna got her degree in journalism from Kansas State. "I never really thought I'd move back. It's not like I hated it here, but I thought, 'There's so much to see out there in the world,' and then I went out *there* and, I don't know . . . it just wasn't me. But when I came back, it was like, 'Okay, how is a journalism degree going to do me any good out here?' And I think a lot of people, especially the younger generation, feel that way, but you just have to get creative and make it work."

Soul Sister hosts painting parties for Ladies Night, birthdays, and holidays, and if you're over twenty-one and feel like making it a BYOB, go for it.

The largest party they've hosted so far was for twenty-five people. "4-H Club," she explains. "They were squeezed in here like sausages. And I've had other people call who had bigger groups but there's no way we could fit them. And some people just get bored and want to come in and do something creative, so we get walk-ins all the time. There are some days we are crazy busy and other days when no one comes in to paint at all. But that's where the boutique serves as a good balance. If the boutique is not busy, then the ceramics side usually is, and vice versa."

Their Facebook and Instagram posts regularly lure people in from Concordia, Beloit, Clyde, and Clifton, people who drive fifteen, twenty-five, and forty miles to get here. When Soul Sister celebrated its first anniversary, forty people showed up throughout the day to paint and shop.

"I would never have the loyalty in a bigger city that I have here," Shanna says. "For the younger generation that's moving here to raise a family, we know that growth is necessary if we want to stay here. And I think the overall perception is that if you're a small store, your prices are going to be higher. But I don't mark my prices up very high because I want to keep everything as affordable as possible."

She and Michelle both grew up around here. Michelle is married to a seed salesman. Shanna's parents farmed and she married a farmer.

"It's funny. Right after we got married and I saw a few bills for the farm, I freaked out. But then Nathan was like, 'No, that's totally normal,' and I was okay with it. I grew up on the farm, but parents always shield that stuff from the kids. So, even for me, it was a shock at first."

Shanna and Michelle were never really worried about whether Soul Sister could survive in a town of only 285 people or whether they'd feel the domino effect when the farmers were trying to skid through another bad year. They came up with an idea, had a dream, and went for it.

"People here are so supportive and generous. They're going to support the local businesses rather than ordering on Amazon," says Shanna. "Over Christmas, I had about ten people come in and say, 'I want to buy local.'"

The Farmers:
Hootie Rayburn

From your window seat at an altitude of thirty thousand feet, Republic County looks like an obsessively meticulous checkerboard of brown and green squares and rectangles, each representing a section (640 acres) or half a section (320 acres), that are all tucked inside of one big square (the county). In it, there are 575 farms totaling 361,076 acres. Mostly soybeans (119,000 acres), corn (106,000 acres), and wheat (56,000 acres) plus thirty-nine thousand cattle and calves grazing in 92,000 acres of open pasture.

The main roads in Republic County include Highway 81, running north to south, Highway 36, running east to west, and Route 148, running east to west to kinda south. Each is two lanes. And in between all of them are a series of dirt and gravel roads running north to south and east to west; the gray, dotted lines you'd see on a Rand McNally road map.

Oak Road is one of them, over which Hootie Rayburn is navigating his half-ton GMC 1500 Sierra about an hour after he left Betty, Steve and Larry, and the rest of the boys at Pinky's. Like Steve, Hootie is a fourth-generation farmer. He started in 1975 when his dad let the Rayburn boys rent eighty acres.

Okay, look; you can use my equipment. But you boys have to pay the expenses. Whatever money is left over is yours.

Since graduating from high school, Hootie's been farming. Full-time, part-time, but always farming. These days, it's full-time. He owns about 1,500 acres. Rents 350 more. "And, oh, about eighty head of cattle right now; forty cow/calf pairs," he says. He also works part-time as a law enforcement officer for the county. He's certified, which means he's on call 24/7, so he's learned how to function properly on about two hours of sleep. Hootie is very tall with grayish hair, a pair of wire-framed glasses perched on his nose, a grin almost always on his face. Jeans. Plaid button-down shirt, tucked in. Boots.

"My farm is small," he says, a swirling cloud of dirt kicking up behind him, from which varying sizes of gravel rain down and ricochet off the truck and into the fields as he drives toward the 50.7 Lateral, a man-made water source that will irrigate his fields when Mother Nature refuses to. A gold badge and a walkie-talkie are sitting on the center console and Garth Brooks is singing about having friends in low places on satellite radio.

"They aren't that well maintained," he says of the county roads, his shocks absorbing the blow from a small crater.

Some ways out into the northern section of the countryside that surrounds Courtland, Oak Road intersects the 50.7 lateral, an eight-and-a-half-foot-deep, twenty-five-foot-wide channel carrying water from Lovewell Lake.

"Love Well Lake?" Hootie laughs. "You mean Lov'll, girl. Lov'll is about, oh, seventeen miles that way as the crow flies," he says, pointing his hand out the window.

Mother Nature has always taken a schizophrenic approach to watering the Midwest. Some years wet. Some years dry. Some years flood. A lot of years drought. In the aftermath of the Dirty Thirties, the nearby Republican River flooded and killed a hundred people, leaving only two options for the farmers here: irrigate or migrate. That's when a weary handful of them finally conceived a way to circumvent Mother Nature's mood swings.

Build a dam and some canals and laterals. Get that sweet, Republican River water under control and into our fields.

Good idea, politicians replied.

Six years and one presidential veto later, FDR finally signed legislation in 1943 that would guarantee Colorado, Nebraska, and Kansas each a certain acre-foot of the Republican River flow, which is exactly what it sounds like: the volume of water it takes to cover an acre of ground to a depth of one foot. Kansas was guaranteed 190,300 of them.

In 1955, construction started on Lovewell Dam. Fifteen years later, a hundred miles of main canals and 150 more miles of laterals and pipelines transformed dry land into irrigated land that would help keep alive everything the sun would otherwise burn to a crisp during a dry spell. Today, Kansas Bostwick Irrigation District No. 2 is responsible for delivering that water to forty-three thousand acres in Jewell and Republic Counties; to farmers like Steve and Larry Brown, Slug, Kenny, and Hootie, who can each use up to fifteen inches of water per acre during the irrigation season to help grow whatever they've put under the soil.

Not like that water's just free for the taking. Back in the day, if geography and gravity were on your side, making it possible to have a lateral dug on your property, the United States government didn't go through the hassle of constructing one out of the goodness of its heart. Instead, Uncle Sam asked that you sign on the dotted line of a loan. No one had any clue how valuable irrigated land would become, though, and there were a few farmers in the area who weren't about to hedge their bets and *pay* for the *privilege* of having water delivered from an irrigation system instead of directly from God.

It's a long-term contract, the government said. *Vote yes. Sign here.*

Any farmer who signed was agreeing to repay the government for constructing the irrigation system. Which farmers are still paying for today at a rate of $4.38 an acre until 2040 when their loan to the United States government will be officially paid off. That $4.38 an acre is on top of an operations and maintenance tax of $44 an acre, which you're on the hook for whether the water levels in Lovewell are such that you can use your full allotted load of water (fifteen inches an acre), less than half a load (six inches), or absolutely nothing, which can happen in a dry year.

"A dry year is anything below ten inches of rain during the growing season," Hootie says. "Our average is about twenty inches."

If you get *too* much rain and your field turns into a mud bog, and there's no need for irrigation water at all, it's not like you can carry that water over and double down the following year, just in case there's a drought. It is what it is and when the year ends, whether you use your water or not, game over.

Once in a while, some exceptions are made. Like back in 2005 and 2006, when it was discovered that Nebraska was using way more water than they were supposed to be using, leaving Kansas farmers who were totally dependent on Lovewell and its upstream reservoir with hardly a drop. As a consolation prize, Nebraska was ordered to pay Kansas back with water to make up for what they had overconsumed in addition to a chunk of change worth $5.5 million. Kansas Bostwick Irrigation District No. 2 also dropped their assessment taxes to $10 an acre.

But just because you've got Lov'll Lake and a canal system of mains and laterals to irrigate your land doesn't guarantee you're *actually* going to get water.

"In farming," Hootie says, "we hope we have irrigation water, but Mother Nature plays about 80 percent of a role in that."

And even if she lives up to expectations and puts water in the lake, it's not like you can just crack open a cold one and wait for the mains and laterals to do the work for you. Someone has to go out and turn on the pump so that the pivot—those giant, metal caterpillars on wheels stretching for half a mile across a field—can spray your crops with nine hundred gallons of water per minute.

"This is a gated pipe," he explains, pointing to a series of connected metal pipes that are sitting in the dirt. The pipes run parallel to endless rows of

soybeans that will be used to feed livestock in the US or China, but not necessarily to make the soymilk you're drinking, since most of the beans grown
in Courtland aren't food grade.

The pipes are laid down manually, every year, a few days before irrigation
season begins on June 1. And every day during irrigation season, Hootie will
spend three hours opening a gate every thirty-six inches or so in the pipe to
make sure his 140 acres of beans get watered. When he does, the water bubbles out into thirty-six-inch rows that he cut through the field with a hiller.
"You have to cut the furrow down through so the water spreads. Otherwise,
it'll just pool near the gated pipe and everything more than a few feet out will
dry up and turn brownish-yellow and become worthless."

When irrigation season ends on September 15, each of the pipes that were
manually laid down will be manually removed and stored until the following
year when the process begins all over again.

Hootie likes to refer to irrigation season as "leisure time."

"When we get a chance to goof off, we do," he says.

Because farming usually means eighteen-hour days. There are no such
things as sick days, vacation days, or mental health days during planting and
harvesting seasons. When you have a chance to get that crop, you get it.
That's your livelihood out there. Which sometimes doesn't amount to very
much.

"We have good years and years where you just pay bills," he says. "Farming
can get intense."

Farming can also get very expensive very quickly, especially if you want
the modern stuff that's got an enclosed cab to protect you from the ele-
ments and is all computerized, digitized, air-conditioned, and outfitted with
GPS systems that allow you to throw your John Deere 7920 into autopilot
and watch it beep, bleep, bloop its way through tilling, harvesting, planting,
mowing, seeding, and spraying, to accomplish in one hour what used to take
dad all day long to do. It's the equivalent of buying a new, highly efficient car
versus one from 1935 that chokes out exhaust fumes, burns through fuel, and
has nonexistent safety or convenience features.

But let's say your family doesn't own farmland, and dad doesn't own any
equipment you can borrow. You're just an average Joe, and you just want an
average Joe farm.

"Okay, so first you need a planter," Hootie begins. "An older one will run
you $50,000 while a newer one is about $300,000. Then you need a combine.
Again, if you're okay with an older one, say, a '91, that's about $75,000 and
a new one? I'd say around $300,000 . . . and that doesn't include the heads.
Because you're going to need a corn head, bean head, and a wheat head to get
what you've planted into the ground out of it, and that'll be at least another

$250,000 to $300,000 for the heads. You'll also need one or two tractors, preferably between 150 and 300 horsepower, which will set you back $150,000 to $300,000, plus the swather and baler for hay, a sprayer, grain cart . . . "

When you're done buying your machinery, you'll need some seed to plant. About $50 to $60 for a bag of milo, a grain used primarily for cattle and hog feed, which will cover ten acres, and $60 to $70 a bag for soybeans, which covers an acre's worth. You'll cough up between $250 and $400 for each bag of corn that will cover a little over two acres per bag, paying a premium for the years of research and science that have gone into developing an ear of corn that is basically resistant to everything.

And don't think you can save a buck by saving last year's seed to plant this year. Most seeds have a patent on them, and the seed company can slap you with a lawsuit if you aren't buying brand new seed every single year. Some guys risk it. Others don't dare. But you better be sure your neighbor isn't the kind of guy to snitch when he sees you buying a measly five bags of beans to plant across your four hundred acres.

You'll spend about $25 an acre in weed killer so all your patented seeds can grow without being choked out. Plus, another $85 to $95 an acre for liquid or dry fertilizer. And don't forget to set aside $18,000 to $20,000 a year for the diesel it takes to run all your average Joe machinery.

Cattle are a good idea because it's another source of income, a way to diversify. And just like commodities, prices of beef can fluctuate depending on the market. A good, young cow can run you anywhere from $2,000 to $3,000 depending on the breed, if they're bred to a high-quality bull, and how fast they gain weight. Even an older cow can go between $1,500 and $1,700 a head. But you can't just throw them into the pasture and let them do their thing. Figure on spending at least $100,000 on feeding them, watering them, caring for them, housing them, and transporting them.

Now you're ready to buy some land. Around here, dry land, meaning no canals or laterals with total reliance on rainfall, goes for $3,000 to $4,000 an acre. If you want irrigated land, it runs anywhere from $6,000 to $8,000 an acre.

You want to be an average Joe farmer in America? Then expect to be in over $3 million to get your six-to-eight-hundred-acre, average Joe farm up and running. And for most people, that means one thing: loans. Lots of them. But good luck getting one because most banks will laugh you out the door unless grandpa just willed you a couple of thousand acres of land that you can use as collateral or you have a sugar daddy who's willing to cosign the financial risks of your new career.

Because a $3 million farm loan is a risky one; one that also needs to be paid back. Regardless of whether the market is paying $3 a bushel for wheat instead of $6 or $9 a bushel. Regardless of whether there's a drought and the water levels in the canals and laterals are way down and your crops are dying. Regardless of whether it wouldn't stop raining and you miss the deadline for planting your wheat and therefore can't claim on your crop insurance when a hailstorm shows up in the middle of June and takes five minutes to obliterate what took you almost an entire year to grow.

When loans aren't paid back, you have an economic crisis on your hands. And that usually turns into a game of dominoes that starts with the farmer and negatively impacts the entire town before spreading like a disease into the rest of the world.

When a farm gets foreclosed, jobs are lost. When jobs are lost, there is no money to eat at the local restaurant. When there's no money to eat at the local restaurant, the local restaurant is forced to close. Which means more jobs are lost. And when more jobs are lost, people who can't pay their bills are forced to move. This is when classrooms start to shrink, and schools begin to consolidate and eventually close. So, even more jobs are lost, forcing even more people to move. And with hardly anyone left in town, who's paying the taxes for the municipal government to remain in existence?

When you have no school and no municipal government, and people are forced to move because there are no jobs left in town, entire towns start disappearing from the map. This is usually when people who aren't farmers finally start to pay attention and decide they're going to help the American Farmer by buying a ticket to a Farm Aid concert.

"I don't know of any farmer out here who's ever gotten a check from Farm Aid," Hootie says.

A large part of the problem is that what the market always wants is a hearty crop they can get on the cheap. Because what most people want is a hearty loaf of bread *they* can get on the cheap. The market really doesn't care how much time, energy, and money you've put into your farm, whether beans are turning yellow and silver because it hasn't rained in three months. It doesn't care that you're being paid the same amount of money per bushel of wheat, and sometimes even less, than what dad got in 1973 or a measly fifty cents more than what great-grandpa got in 1920. That's your problem.

"That's why many farmers have some sort of second income, whether it's a second job or income from their wife's job," Hootie says, speeding past Slug in a cloud of dust. He flips the bird. Slug smiles back, returns the gesture, and they both laugh hysterically.

When Hootie has a lean year and things are so bad that all he can do is pay the bills, at least he has the income coming in from his job as a part-time law enforcement officer. Before he had his heart attack in 2013, he also used to earn some money flying a Cessna 172—a high wing—for the Drug Task Force.

"It's worth it because you enjoy living out here. We have ups and downs, just like everybody else. Good years, bad years. Sure, if I screw up out here, I screw up and pay for my own problems. But it's the lifestyle, what *you* want to do with your life," he says. "We ain't got any better life out here. Everyone's willing to help out if you get in trouble. When I had my heart attack, I was lying on the operating table and everyone out here was finishing cutting my wheat."

Some static comes out of the walkie-talkie. He turns the volume up. Listens. "Nothing important," he says.

He rests his arm on the window. Maneuvers the GMC further down Oak Road, around another corner and another crater, kicking up another cloud that trails behind the truck like a dusty parachute.

"When you farm, you're working for yourself. You put in the hours and take the risk. But doesn't everyone?" he asks. "I mean, what's the guarantee that tomorrow you won't go into work and get laid off?"

The Farmer's Wife:
Mrs. C

There's a peach pie baking in Jan Carlson's oven. Carlson's wife. Mrs. Carlson. Mrs. C, actually. That's what her students always called her.

"I'm not sure it's gonna do what I want it to," she says as the timer goes off. *Ping! Ping! Ping!* Like a neighbor with one finger on the doorbell who won't go away.

She gets up from the kitchen table, which is neatly covered in a red checkered cloth, and extracts the pie from the oven. It's very gooey and bubbly and doing all the things a delicious smelling pie should be doing. "The best thing for a crust is plain old lard," she explains, giving it a once-over before placing it back into the oven. "Butter's too light. Crisco is okay. But nothing compares to lard."

It is the middle of the afternoon. A hot summer day that was 79 degrees before dawn and 98 by noon according to the digital temperature sign outside the Swedish-American State Bank, which everyone ignores because they get it. It's hot. Carlson popped in a little while ago, a few hours after he had his coffee at Pinky's, but now he's in the barn or in the fields or out somewhere with Joerg.

"Oh, I know . . . his wife," she says, rolling her eyes.

There's a lot of patience that goes into making a good pie. Almost as much patience as goes into being married to a farmer.

"It's a little like being married to a gambler," she says. "The only difference is you don't have the lights and the glitz."

When Jan Goodwin met Robert Carlson in 1964, she was a sophomore in high school selling snow cones on the midway at the North Central Kansas Free Fair. He was a senior showing dairy cattle. On their first date, they hopped into a car. Dragged Main. Had a Coke at the Kravmore in Belleville. Talked. Danced. And the rest is history.

"I chased him till he caught me," she laughs.

They got engaged. Headed two and a half hours south to start their freshman year at Fort Hays State University. Jan was going to get a degree in elementary education. Carlson was studying agricultural economics. He had grown up on his family's Grade A dairy farm a few miles west of town in Formoso, milking forty-five to fifty head of Holsteins every day at 5 a.m. and 5 p.m., but he was tired of it. Carlson wanted to try something different from farming.

Then Vietnam happened. And the draft. So, Carlson went to take his physical. He flunked. An old high school football injury—his shoulder—sidelined him. Again.

Soon after, he was walking through the student union at Fort Hays and ran into a representative from the Peace Corps. They talked. She handed him some information. Gave Carlson an idea. His plan B. He didn't mention anything about his plan B to Jan. And they had never even talked about the Peace Corps. But he thought it'd be good for them to get out of Kansas. Out of *Courtland*. Away from the Grade A dairy farm. See the world. Do something. Help somebody. Have an exciting adventure. Everything about it sounded *enchanting*.

So, the first thing he did was sign them up. The second thing he did was tell Jan. "How do you feel about going into the Peace Corps?" he asked.

"Uh, okay . . . " she replied. "Where are we going?"

"Don't have a clue!"

They had their pick of three destinations. Iran was their last. Which is exactly where the Peace Corps sent them. In May of 1971, they walked out of Fort Hays with their degrees. Got married in June. And although everyone in Courtland thought they were crazy, on August 1, a Boeing 747 dropped them off halfway around the world in Tehran, Iran. They were given some training —language training, tradition training, environmental training—and then sent to the village of Borujerd on the northwestern side of the country, right next door to Iraq.

"We had not a clue what we were getting into," Carlson says. "Iran was one of the toughest places to go, especially for a woman. Jan became known as 'Pack Your Bags Jan' for a long time. But she did stay, and I'm proud of her for that."

"I was just baggage," says Mrs. C. "Along for the ride. They wanted Robert and his life skills. The shah was trying to drag Iran into the twenty-first century, kicking and screaming, by modernizing things." Things like farming.

At the time, harvesting in Iran was still done by hand. Milking cows was still done by hand. Plows were pulled by a donkey.

So, Carlson's job was to teach them about modern innovations in the farming industry. How machinery could speed up all that planting, tilling, harvesting, and milking. He taught them about ditch irrigation. Built them a dairy barn. Showed them how to use the electric milking machines instead of their hands.

He ordered the machinery, too; a planter that came from Israel and a John Deere combine. The field hands would catch the wheat in burlap sacks, which were immediately taken to the bazaar and sold.

And although they were half a world away, Borujerd, Iran, turned out to be not so different from Courtland, Kansas. It was a farm community. It was small. Everyone knew everyone else and their business. But it was nice. People were nice. They made friends. Like Don, who had grown up in Southern California. Don had also decided to join the Peace Corps, landed in Borujerd, and ended up following the Carlsons back to Courtland, where he still sees Carlson almost every morning at Pinky's.

The Carlsons spent two years in Iran. In 1973, another Boeing 747 brought them back to Kansas, although on the return trip they were a party of three. They had adopted a little Iranian girl. Robin. She was a year old. And although a jet brought them back to Kansas, it was family ties that brought them back to Courtland.

"He planted me in a cornfield," she says.

Jan got a job in nearby Jewell teaching kindergarten. Carlson worked at the grain elevator in Courtland, running the fertilizer department and working part-time with his dad, John, on the family farm, which had switched from dairy to beef. "Dad didn't want to do it by himself when I went to college. Those cows had to get milked at 5 a.m. and 5 p.m. every single day, on the dot."

Not too long after they settled in, a neighbor stopped by. *I want to ask you something. How does it feel? Having a foreign kid as a child?*

"I never felt more hurt or surprised by that question," says Mrs. C. "Because I had never given it another thought. Robin was mine. But it turns out, he was asking me that question because he and his wife were considering adopting a foreign child, too. And they ended up doing just that; a little boy from Costa Rica. So here we were, in this little country town, with kids from Iran and Costa Rica living a mile from each other."

Things were going well for the Carlsons.

Then, April 5, 1977, happened. When two juveniles escaped from the Atchison Youth Center. Showed up 172 miles west at the Carlson farm wearing Maltese crosses and looking out of place. *We're looking for a place to hunt rabbits*, they said.

A few hours later, John Carlson was found with a .22 caliber bullet in his head. He had been working on his disc harrow, cleaning the stalks and mud out, getting ready to go back into his fields and get back to planting when the two boys returned.

Why'd you do it? the prosecutor asked.

Sonofabitch wouldn't talk to us.

"He was hard of hearing from riding an open tractor all those years," Jan says. "He didn't talk to them because he had his hearing aid out and couldn't hear them."

"Dad was in the wrong place at the right time," Carlson says.

Afterward, his mother moved to Courtland, and Carlson quit his job at the elevator so he and Jan could take over his father's four hundred acres. If he's being honest, he'll say he really didn't want to. "I had to," he says. "If I didn't, we would have had to sell the family farm."

When he took it over, the entire community made it their business to help him. The farmers showed Carlson how to match up cow/calf pairs. Showed him how to operate the equipment. Showed him whatever he needed to be shown to keep the farm up and running while Mrs. C continued teaching. "I had to keep teaching if we wanted to keep the family farm."

One day, she came home from school and saw a bill for fertilizer in the mail. She opened it. Then, almost fainted.

"Don't worry," Carlson assured her. "It's okay."

"Are you kidding me?" Mrs. C cried. It was more than she made in an entire year. Way more than the Carlsons had in the bank.

"Credit," Carlson explained. "You farm, you buy on credit. If you want to be a farmer, all you have to do is ask, 'Where do I sign?'"

Mrs. C had been raised by a father who never even used the word "credit" in his vocabulary. You wanted something, you paid cash for it.

What have I gotten myself into?

She has asked herself that question a couple of times over the past fifty years. She asked it when the only time the kids would see their dad was when she made him a meal ("The real deal," she says. "I wasn't making him a sandwich. It was an actual, full meal") and they hopped into the car and drove out into the fields to give it to him. When he was out there planting, harvesting, weeding, mowing, hauling, from dawn to dusk, coming home exhausted and stressed out, getting a few hours of sleep and then doing it all over again the next morning, and the one after that, and thousands after that.

She asked it when she was teaching full-time, running a household, raising Robin, Jon, and Amber, tending to the garden, canning, checking the irrigation, doing whatever needed to be done, and feeling like a single parent while she was doing it. When she got lonely. Stressed out. When she was tired of being planted in a cornfield. Tired of driving forces they didn't have any control over, like the market, the weather.

Still to this day, the market, the weather.

This is the first time in forever that the Carlson farm hasn't had any wheat.

Not to say it wasn't planted. It was. As it has been for the past forty years. But the market was so low at under $3/bushel that Carlson decided it was just better to plow it all up and plant something else. All that investment in seed and fertilizer, all that work planting and harvesting and hauling. And then, nothing.

"Over the last few years, everybody in the world raised wheat real good, so nobody wanted it," he says. "It's almost like you have to capitalize on someone else's problems. If a foreign country has a drought and don't raise any wheat, then our wheat is more valuable because it'll get shipped over to them."

The ups and downs, the uncertainty . . . it's frustrating. Really frustrating. "But the men . . . the men have the land in their blood," she says. They get angry, stressed out, make money, lose money, curse Mother Nature and her mood swings, thank God for his faithfulness, pray for rain, beg for it to stop, do it all over again.

"Farmers are a breed that is never happy no matter what happens," says Mrs. C. "But they love it here. Just can't give it up. And being a farmer's wife is not for the faint of heart. You gotta be tough. There's a problem? Put your big girl pants on. Figure out an answer. Make a decision. Move on. You gotta be confident in yourself. Adaptable."

When their kids left the farm for corporate jobs in North Carolina, Texas, and Colorado, and her thirty-five-year teaching career came to an end, Mrs. C had to reinvent herself.

Which she did. She got active at her church, Courtland United Methodist. Meets up with the other ladies on most Wednesday mornings at AnTeaQues for coffee or tea. "You want the real story?" she laughs. "Come talk to us. Not the Pinky's crew."

She can't make it every week. Doesn't always have time to sit and visit and relax or even to read the weekly *Courtland Journal*. Because there are things to do. Like caring for her ninety-year-old mother, babysitting kids from the neighborhood whose parents used to be Mrs. C's students, driving Carlson to all those doctor's appointments. Because the sun plus forty years of working in it usually equals skin cancer, and when you've been riding in an open cab tractor since you were eight years old, your hearing is probably shot, too.

Ping! Ping! Ping!

Mrs. C gets up from the table and the red checked cloth. On the wall are decorative signs: "My Favorite People Call Me Nana," "Love You to the

Moon and Back," "I Love You a Bushel and a Peck and a Hug Around the Neck."

She opens the oven door, sees that the peach pie has finally done what she wanted it to, and sets it out to cool. The kitchen she's standing in was once one of four rooms that comprised the house that Carlson's grandparents built in 1901. His dad was born and raised here. Took his last breath here. The house has been added on to, upgraded, and renovated over the years. But it's been in the family for three generations. Where Jan and Carlson raised Robin, Jon, and Amber. Where they invite all the guys to come to hang out in the Shed, Carlson's massive man cave, with the row of recliners, big-screen television, and a spread of chips and dip, sliced veggies, cookies, and home-made vegetable soup that Mrs. C puts out for them to eat.

Pack Your Bags Jan has stuck through a lot. They've both stuck together through a lot.

"We had a few good years," he says. "Land values went up in '74 and '75, prices of grain went up and there were a lot of people who said, 'Wow, this is great!' and got overextended. Then they got their hands slapped."

The eighties were rough. Got up one morning and you were worth half of what you were worth yesterday. Everyone was maxed out, the market was bad, the land was devalued, and no one could pay the 18 percent interest on their $500,000, $700,000, and $1 million loans, losing farms that had been in the family for three, four, and five generations.

Carlson wasn't sure they'd survive it. "Well," he said to his banker at the Swedish-American. "We have another year like this . . . we might have to line 'er up."

But the Swedish-American stood behind him. As did Mrs. C. It was just another storm to weather. She's still standing behind him now. It's bad again. The market. The weather. The loans. The stress.

They hope the kids don't sell the farm when that decision must be made, even though Carlson doesn't really want them to come back and try to farm. "It's a tough life. Tough because of the financial burden, the uncertainty. So many ups and downs and they all have such good jobs out there," he says.

And for all the talk that rolls through a town of only 285 people, no one ever makes it known whether they've made a killing or lost their shoes. So, when the weather turns what should have been a good year into a very bad one, when you're out there plowing up your wheat because the market thinks $3/bushel sounds about right when it cost you $4/bushel to put it into the ground, when there's too much corn in Iowa and prices in Courtland tank, you can sometimes wonder if you're the only woman in town who's ending each day with a pounding migraine because your husband is about to lose his mind.

But when something terrible happens—injury, illness, tornados, a .22 caliber bullet—your crisis inspires a community outpouring. People show up. Do whatever needs to be done. Then, they ask if they can do a little more.

So yeah, farming is often a tough life. "But it's also a wonderful life," says Mrs. C. "A good life. As much as part of me would like to say I'd do things differently, I wouldn't. We never wanted for anything." "But," she laughs, "I like to say that while I'd never dream of divorcing him, I've definitely thought about killing him."

The Young Couple

You locked your second-floor windows, that's what you did. At least where Jennifer McCarty grew up. Not like she was raised in some shady section of Lancaster, Pennsylvania. Not like she walked around looking over her shoulder all the time.

Locking your windows was just *what you did*.

And when she found her way to the University of Nebraska, Kearney, and switched her degree from dentistry to teaching, she locked the windows in her apartment. Locked her car, too.

Then she came to Courtland.

"The only risk you take if you leave your car unlocked in Courtland is someone opening the door to leave you cucumbers," says her boyfriend, Luke Mahin.

Luke grew up in Courtland. Born and raised. Graduate of Fort Hays State University, class of 2010. Just inherited his grandma's golf cart. Has a slow, easy way about him. Always on the verge of smiling. He's a partner and account executive at JenRus Freelance, director of the Republic County Economic Development office, sits on the board of the Courtland Community Arts Council, and is 110 percent in on their mission to grow and diversify the local economy. When Shanna and Michelle got the idea to buy the old gas station and turn it into Soul Sister Ceramics, they went to Luke for advice. And if you even hint around about wanting to move here, he'll let you know that Republic County is one of seventy-seven in the state designated as a Rural Opportunity Zone and will gladly email you the link to apply to the program.

The ROZ is the carrot that former governor Sam Brownback and the Kansas legislature started dangling in 2011 in an attempt to boost rural populations by enticing you and your family to U-Haul it out here and reinvigorate small towns with your presence and hard-earned money. Mainly by offering new residents financial incentives like state income tax waivers for up to five years and student loan repayments up to $15,000 over five years.

Young people are moving back to Courtland. Maybe not necessarily to climb into the combine and start farming, but they are opening new businesses on Main Street. When the 2010 Census came out, a lot of people were pleasantly surprised. *The two areas of growth were the number of residents ages twenty to twenty-four and thirty to thirty-four? Really?*

"They're looking to come back here for the quality of life," he says.

Luke also serves on the North Central Kansas Food Council to encourage the marriage of what the farmer is pulling out of the ground to what's being put on your plate, which is encouraging because most of what's on the menu in Republic County has been deep-fried. He manages the Courtland Arts Center and Courtland Fun Day, is a member of the Courtland Pride Club and keeps a photo of the Courtland water tower as his Facebook cover.

"Because you're obsessed with Courtland," says Jennifer.

"I am not!"

Luke's mom runs a day care in town and his dad is the maintenance foreman at the irrigation office. He has a twin brother, two other brothers, one sister, and for the longest time, didn't know what a house key was because the Mahins never locked the front door.

When Jennifer bought the house on Centennial that she shares with Luke, the owners had to look for the key because *they* had lived there for three years and never locked the front door, either.

Jennifer bought the split-level a few years ago. When she and Luke decided to move in together, there were two houses on the market in Courtland. They knew this because of word of mouth, not because of a listing posted on Realtor.com. And when they got wind that this one was about to go up for sale, Jennifer took one look and fell in love with the big living room, the fireplace, the big windows, and the huge, fenced-in yard for her dog, Gus.

Gus is a standard poodle. He has white fur, loves Jennifer and Luke, and hates everyone else. "He's very judgmental," she says. Gus loves to wear handkerchiefs that are handmade by her mom, who lives in Lancaster, Pennsylvania, but is about to move to Scandia, seven miles east of Courtland.

"She loves making those handkerchiefs," she says. "It gives her something to do."

"It's ridiculous," he says. Luke likes Gus. Even though he almost killed him. "Not on purpose," he points out.

"You didn't listen when I told you not to let him out," she says. "I *said*, 'Be careful! He's gonna escape!'"

Which is exactly what Gus did. So, Luke got into his car and went looking for him, whistling and calling his name. *Gusssss!* He was parked in the middle of the street, waiting for Gus to respond, when . . .

"You backed the car up and ran over him!" Jennifer says.

"I did not," Luke replies. "He ran into the back of the car! Although I did think, 'Oh man, she is going to kill me. Gus is dead.'" Gus wasn't dead. But he was staggering around in a daze. Had a big gash in his snout. Was all bloody. So, Luke picked him up and carried him to the front door. "Open the door!" he yelled.

"You killed Gus!" she cried.

The whole thing left Gus with a shaved snout, stitches, some antibiotics, and a brand-new handkerchief from Jennifer's mom. Luke was presumed guilty on all counts until a neighbor said he saw Gus run head first into the back of Luke's parked car.

"It was validation," Luke says. "I finally had a viable witness."

Jennifer has never found any cucumbers in her car, but the neighbors have given her plenty of food plenty of times: things like rhubarb crisp, apple crisp, banana bread, cookies, jelly, ham salad, meatloaf, and spaghetti.

When people ask Jennifer how in the world she got to Courtland, Kansas, from Lancaster, Pennsylvania, Luke always pipes up first. "She's breaking Amish!"

"Shut up! I am not!"

Jennifer and Luke met three years ago when they were set up on a date by Luke's brother, Caleb, and his wife, Gayle. Gayle and Jennifer worked at the same school just across the border in Nebraska. Caleb asked if she was single. Showed her a photo of Luke. "Is that the only brother you have to offer me?" she asked.

He had other brothers. But Luke seemed like the best match. And eventually, either Jennifer or Luke friended the other one on Facebook.

"No, *you* friended me first."

"I did not!"

"Yes, you did!"

Well, whatever. Despite how great Caleb and Gayle were telling her that Luke was, Jennifer had gone on like, ten bad dates in a row, leaving her not very optimistic that anything remotely promising would happen with this one.

Eventually, she decided to give Luke a shot. And at first, it was kind of awkward. They started out on the phone and usually talked over each other. *Go 'head. Sorry, go 'head. Sorry.* But eventually, they started hanging out. Then they started hanging out a lot.

In the beginning, she'd come down to Courtland to spend time with

Luke on the weekends. Which was fun. Always something to do. "Courtland wasn't so bad," she'd tell people.

She almost believed it. Until she left her apartment complex and its pool and walking trails and the Target and Starbucks and McDonald's and shopping malls that were five minutes away. She got a teaching job over in Belleville. Unpacked her bags and . . . was bored.

"The first summer here was rough," she admits.

She found herself making dumb excuses to justify driving an hour and twenty minutes south to Salina so she could get a Coke and French fries and shop for cute stuff. Jennifer always looks cute. Blond hair up in a bun. Cute. Sandals and a sundress. Cute. Glasses on. Cute. She missed Target. Old Navy. Kohl's. Hobby Lobby and McDonald's especially. Because yeah, Amazon and Instagram boutiques might be your best friend out here, but it's not the same as *going* into the store. Looking around. Browsing. Seeing all that cute stuff in person.

"Enjoying civilization," she adds.

But eventually, she got used to not having all that stuff around. And she and Luke go all over the place; up to Nebraska, over to Colorado, down to Kansas City. Beer festivals and ski trips and concerts and hiking trips. In addition to her teaching job, she also got a job waitressing at AnTeaQues and bartending at the country club in Belleville, where Carlson and Joerg like to show up every Wednesday for Hamburger Night and beer after playing eighteen holes.

Luke and Jennifer are PowerUps, a mixed bag of young professionals between the ages of twenty-one and thirty-nine who have decided they will live in rural corners of Kansas because they want to, not because they're stuck there. It's not a club that you join and sell flavored popcorn to fundraise. It's organic; more like a movement. It believes in a set of core principles and values. Things like making it a point to buy from locally owned businesses like Soul Sister, taking on active leadership roles, engaging with others instead of just tweeting enraged tweets about whatever bothers you, and developing an inclusive network of peers so that the PowerUps have a say on rural issues that affect all of Kansas.

This is why Luke and Jennifer are living here, working here, putting money earned in Courtland back into Courtland. It's one of the reasons they're excited about the brewery that Luke and his dad plan to open in the old Senior Center on Main Street.

Luke and his dad have been brewing beer for years. It started as a hobby, but people liked what they were brewing. A lot. So, Luke and his dad started thinking. Decided to just go for it. They're calling their brewery Irrigation Ales.

"Our specialties are saison, wheat, oatmeal stout, lagers . . . "

"No, your lagers are NOT good!" Jennifer says.

"Yes, they are!"

"No, they're not!"

Turns out, they are. At least, the Kansas City Bier Meisters Homebrew Competition thought so when they slapped a blue ribbon on Irrigation Ales' Mexican lager. That was even more exciting than finding out their stout won "best of show" at a brew fest way over in Norton, Kansas, 110 miles west.

A lot of people in town are excited about the brewery. Like the members of the Courtland Fermentation Club. But Betty's kinda worried it'll be a blow to her bottom line. Nothing personal; but another beer joint in a town of 285 means that if you're spending money on a Mexican lager at the brewery, you're probably not going to be spending money on a Budweiser at Pinky's.

"But it's okay," she says. "We all do what we can."

So far, the Mahins have used their own money to bring Irrigation Ales to life but will eventually get to the point where they take out a loan; either from other family members or something more formal like a revolving loan fund from the county. RLFs are low-interest loans—the maximum rate is 3.5 percent below prime with a minimum rate of 4 percent—that tend to favor riskier start-ups that usually get a flat "no" from a bank. It's a good deal. Even the Swedish-American right across the street taps out at a rate between 5 and 7 percent. As far as a revolving loan goes, there is no catch, other than a requirement that your business, whether new or existing, remains in Republic County. The first year of payments are interest only, and once money is paid back into the fund, it's reloaned out to another new business in the county; hence the whole "revolving" thing.

And using local malted grains like barley in their saisons, wheats, stouts, and lagers would be great, but for the fact that local malted grains are really, *really* expensive to buy because there is very little available. "Plus, there are no malting facilities around anyway. So, because the barley is so scarce, Irrigation Ales would be looking at paying around $1.50 per pound versus what we can get online for like, forty to eighty cents per pound," Luke says. "But more and more Kansas brewers are looking at making one-offs using local grains, which is what we'll do, too."

The brewery will add even more life to Main Street, which is good because while Jennifer has gotten used to living here, she still misses civilization. Although, she notices things when she returns to it. Like, how she'll wave to people and no one waves back. "Everyone in Courtland waves to you," she says.

Like, how there's as much poverty in an area like Courtland, which is primarily white, as there is in areas that are primarily black or Latino. The difference in addressing it here versus out there is what Luke calls "undercover social services." If you're a good person and you need something, someone will give you a helping hand: a place to sleep, something to eat. Whatever you need.

"If you're willing to work," he says, "it's hard to find yourself struggling."

Because that's what neighbors do out here. They leave cucumbers in your unlocked car and cut your wheat when you're on the operating table. Even if you aren't the most pleasant person to be around.

And if you're "different," well, yeah, your neighbors here are probably going to have an opinion about your lifestyle. Just like they do no matter where you're living: big city, bustling suburb, Kansas cornfield. Because it doesn't matter if you are heterosexual, metrosexual, homosexual, born in America, crossed the border illegally to get here, say "Merry Christmas," "Happy Festivus," or "Feliz Navidad," are black, white, or brown, a workaholic, on welfare, a sugar daddy, a cradle robber, a cougar, a working mom, a stay at home mom, ten kids, no kids, married for fifty years, living in sin, or about to walk down the aisle for the third time; somebody somewhere is going to have *something* to say about how you are living your life, regardless of whether you're in a big metropolitan city or a midwestern farm town.

And while collectively, Courtland might put a high value on the traditional nuclear family model and conservative values, every single house does not have a white picket fence running around it. Which is why no one can remember anyone being run out of town, chased with pitchforks, or burned at the stake for having a "lifestyle" that doesn't mirror one of those aw-shucks stories you hear on *A Prairie Home Companion*. There have been and still are blended families, homosexuals, teen moms, and single moms and dads, even in a town occupied by 285 people and surrounded by cornfields.

"My partner is moving here in a few weeks," said one gay resident. "He's going to live with me. You know, I only ever had one person in town say something ignorant to me. And I looked at him and said, 'Do you see how big I am? Do you understand that I could come over there and take you outside and bounce your head off one of those poles?' He's been fine ever since. I've never tried to hide who I am from people here or felt that I needed to. To be honest, I've had more problems with that living in big cities like New York and Denver than I've ever had here. And I think that says a lot about a town like this."

"Everyone knows that everyone can play a role. You can't just kick people out. People know you have to be tolerant of everybody," Luke says. "If you're not an asshole, people are going to get along with you . . . but I don't know what the point of no return is."

"If you're rude or argumentative," Jennifer offers.

"And we get stereotyped, too," he adds. "People think we drive covered wagons to school, or we're all . . . " he pauses, picking at an imaginary banjo. People think that a lot, actually. When you begin to describe Courtland to anyone who has never been there or even mention the word "Kansas," you tend to get a lot of sweeping assumptions, also known as stereotypes, about "those people out there."

"Those people out there are racist."

"Those people out there are homophobic."

"Those people out there are right-wing, Bible-thumping Jesus freaks."

"Those people out there are rednecks."

Courtland might not have an annual gay pride parade, or even a Starbucks or Target or McDonald's or any other twenty-four-hour oasis of convenience the world considers essential for survival, but they have something else that feels like genuine inclusiveness, not just lip service or a trending hashtag.

"People want to make you like part of their family," Jennifer says.

"But you have to make an effort, too," Luke adds. Like, wave to people who wave to you. Talk to your neighbors. Say hello when you see someone walking down Main Street. Get involved in the community by supporting the Courtland Arts Center and taking a tango lesson with the Republican Valley Dancers or buying a ticket for "Cocktails & Appetizers: An Asian Affair" or shopping the Courtland Christmas Vendor Show. You can volunteer for a Courtland Fun Day committee, join the Courtland Pride Club, the Courtland Fermentation Club, Bridge Babes, the Do Nothings, or the Courtland Crusaders, who make sure all the planters in town are blooming with something beautiful.

"We all know that we're one thing away from having another difficulty," Luke says. "Everybody row or the boat sinks."

"It's relaxing, safe, and they are so nice here. Whereas, people won't just do anything and everything for you somewhere else," Jennifer adds. "But I'm still locking my windows. That's just what you *do*."

The Lunch Spot

Most everyone who comes into AnTeaQues for lunch between 11 a.m. and 1 p.m. Tuesday through Friday has a spot. Their usual spot at their usual table. Norm has his spot. Mr. Mainquist has his spot. The table back there in the corner is where Beryl and Rita like to sit. Sometimes Gaynell will join them.

AnTeaQues is the place to enjoy a cup of tea, get some lunch, shop for antiques. Other than Pinky's, it's the only restaurant in town. There is no menu here. But there are two daily specials.

"Whaddya got today?"

"We've got ham with peas and potatoes au gratin or a hamburger and chips," Shannon says. "Yellow cake with chocolate frosting for dessert. What would you like to drink?"

Shannon Langston and Linda Swanson opened AnTeaQues about nine years ago. They're both registered nurses. Have been friends for, like, oh gosh, thirty-five years. Raised their kids together. Took them on camping trips and went on ski vacations together. And because they were doing everything together, they figured they might as well open a business together, too. Linda's shy. She'd rather you talk to Shannon about it.

Shannon moved around a lot when she was growing up. All around South Dakota, Nebraska, Kansas. Her dad built bridges, a process that took about two years. Build bridge. Move. Repeat. In 1974, her family landed in Courtland and Shannon never left.

Well, she did live in Scandia for a while, but she doesn't consider living in Scandia *leaving Courtland* since it's only seven miles east.

When Shannon was fourteen, she bought her first antique: an old icebox. It was a mess. So, she refurbished it. By the time she was done, she was hooked.

"My mom always said I should have been born in the 1800s," she says.

When people aren't coming in to drink tea or eat the homecooked daily specials that Shannon and Linda start making at 4:30 a.m. Tuesday through

Friday, they're on the other side of the store looking to score something: a Glenwood gas stove, wicker picnic baskets, a Sylvania Projection Lamp, metal coffee pots, tongue and groove cabinets, dressers, and desks, hand-painted china, hatboxes, a Zenith tube radio, a black rotary phone . . . castaways from days that are long gone with prices that make you feel like you're getting away with something.

"I hate ripping off the public," Shannon says. It's the one thing she cannot do. "That's why I won't make my million."

The building AnTeaQues is in was used as a mercantile for years. It used to be walled off into two sections; goods on one side, and a lot of card playing and duckpin bowling on the other. It's one big open space now. The kitchen, where Shannon and Linda whip up the two daily specials, was once the cold room; eighteen-inch-thick walls to keep butchered beef good and fresh. If you look up, you can see some of the original iron meat hooks still screwed into the tin ceiling.

Before Shannon and Linda opened AnTeaQues, they spent four months scraping all the glue off the floor. "Glue leftover from the ugly linoleum that everyone put down back then," she says. Four months of scraping, scraping, more scraping. Linda was determined to get every last bit of it, but Shannon finally convinced her that the imperfection in the floor kinda added something to the place.

Shannon and Linda also salvaged the original flooring from the old roller-skating rink that was down the street. Back in the day, everyone would go to the roller rink on Saturday nights. Until they didn't anymore. It went out of business in the sixties. For years, the Farmway Co-op used the building for storage. When they finally tore it down, the flooring was piled up and left in an old shed. "By the time we came along, that shed was so twisted that we had to get in *like this* to carry the wood out," Shannon explains, contorting her body.

Which they did. Went into that twisted shed *like this* for an entire day, removing each ten-to-twelve-foot-long plank of wood one by one by one. It took them a week to scrub them all down. Then another to wash and air them all out. When they were dry, they took a few hammers and nailed them to the wall in the back room.

When they decided to move the massive refrigerated coolers to make room for more vendor booths, Shannon walked across the street and into Pinky's.

"I'll buy you a beer if you guys help me move some coolers," she told the guys.

So, the guys came over. Took one look at the coolers. Laughed.

Only one beer to move these?

Around 3 p.m., long after the lunch crowd is gone, Shannon sits down at

one of the tables and begins wrapping silverware in white paper napkins, arranging them into a neat row. Knife, fork, spoon. Like swaddled babies. The silverware used to belong to the local chapter of the Masons, over in Scandia and was about to get thrown away until her son-in-law grabbed them.

"Coffee and friends make the perfect blend" reads the sign on the wall, right above a red coffee maker and some Nestlé Coffee-Mate. They used to have a Keurig, but it just sat there for two years.

"No one could figure out how to use it," she says, picking up a napkin. "We like things simple here. I still use a flip phone. Because those smartphones, how often do you have to charge them? Like, a few times a day? I charge my flip phone once a week or sometimes only every ten days."

She also doesn't allow her waitresses to bring their phones to work. "It's only two hours," she tells them. "You'll live."

Which none of them really like, especially the younger ones who will *die* if they can't check their phone every two minutes. And while Betty can't find an adult to help her out at Pinky's, Shannon can't find any teenagers who want to work at AnTeaQues on the weekends during school or while they're on summer break.

"Kids are so busy these days. They've got so many things they're doing after school, or they just don't want to work. I can't get any help, actually," she says. "And you can make good money here. You can make thirty to forty bucks in tips every day."

When she's done wrapping the silverware, she might go across the street to check on their other building, the one that holds all the architectural salvage, all the doors and windows, and things that people bring in after they tear down an old barn or prairie house.

Shannon's always had a lot of things to check on. She checked on patients when she worked as a nurse over at the hospital in Belleville for thirty-five years. Then she checked on her dad when he got sick.

He's got two weeks, the doctors said.

Says who? Shannon wondered.

She drove her dad back to his house. Checked on him often. Cared for him. Enjoyed his company for two weeks, then two more, then two more after that. He lived for another eleven months.

Shannon is always busy. Whipping up the two daily specials with Linda in the kitchen. Selling antiques that are priced to make you feel like you're getting away with something. Putting in a day's work and then driving around to check on the patients she still cares for as a home care nurse. Between all of it, she will clock eighty hours a week. Sometimes more. Which is fine. She's always worked two or three jobs. Really, it's no big deal.

"I might not make my millions," she says, "But I'm happy."

The Mayor

Right now, the Mayor of Courtland is waiting for some green beans.

A drink would be nice, too. Anything wet, actually. Because it's hot outside; 98 degrees of blazing hot Kansas sun in another cloudless sky and not a drop of rain in sight.

Not a drop of anything in sight for the Mayor. Not Coke or iced tea or even water. He is occupying one of many occupied seats at AnTeaQues during the lunch rush, ordering one of two things that are on today's menu: chicken tetrazzini or sloppy joes.

He's gotten his chicken tetrazzini, but not his green beans. Or his drink.

What Mayor Tim Garman has gotten for the past thirty years is an election he never loses. "Sometimes I don't even sign up," he says. During those elections, someone just writes his name on the ballot. And when he's up for reelection, he already knows what his campaign slogan will be.

"Vote for Someone Else," he says.

If he wants to end his political career, it'll probably come in one of two ways. "If I died or moved away," he says.

The Mayor was born and raised in Courtland. "Gem of Republic County, Good Schools, and Enterprising People!" "A CITY FROM WHICH NONE DEPART BUT WITH REGRET AND TO RETURN WITH PLEASURE!"

The political thing started when he decided to join the city council back in '81, one of five members that met with the city clerk once a month to go over city business. And he was perfectly happy being on the council until the previous mayor, Sparky, quit. So, Tim decided to run.

"I won. Because I was unopposed," he says.

The Mayor is also the guy who brought the Courtland city cable TV system into existence a year later. CCTV Channel 6 that he ran right out of his house. He brought the internet in 2001, installing an antenna on top of the grain elevator that spits out a signal for everyone to use. And if you're his neighbor, chances are good he'll just give you the password to his Wi-Fi.

"Are you still using my internet?" he'll ask. "I thought I could feel a little extra weight."

The Mayor owns a red Mustang convertible, a small Jeep SUV, and an E-Z-GO golf cart, which he also got from Dennis at C&W Farm Supply. The E-Z-GO is his vehicle of choice when it comes to his morning commute of four blocks to city hall, which is a few doors down from AnTeaQues, and he likes to get to his office around eightish. Inside are leather-bound copies of the *Kansas Statutes*—annotated, official—a silver belt buckle commemorating the Courtland Centennial, a handful of awards, an aerial photo of Courtland, and a sign: "I'm somewhat of a bullshitter myself but occasionally I enjoy listening to an expert. PLEASE CARRY ON!"

When he sold the family business, Garman & Son, which his grandfather opened in 1925 as L.E. Garman Implement Co., he thought he was retired.

He thought wrong. Because in addition to his mayoral duties, he also has a part-time gig working for Tibbets-Fischer, a funeral home over in Belleville. When they need someone to transport a cadaver, they call the Mayor, who arrives in a gray, late model Chevy minivan with the back seats removed, to transport the bodies from Tibbets-Fischer to the mortuary. Or, from wherever they died to Tibbets-Fischer. "Wherever they need to go," he says. He didn't get this job because he's the Mayor. He got this job because he made it his job. "I thought it'd be nice to help out."

When he's not hauling dead bodies around, you can find him volunteering at the city fire department or hanging out in his music room playing bass guitar, drums, piano. Jamming.

"Very poorly," he says. "Self-taught. I have joined the long-term care jammers at the rest home. Can't hardly go wrong there."

His newest hobby is ham radio: signal WoFOX. "Wolf, zero, fox." It was his dad's. Six or seven bands. On a good day, his signal will reach someone as far away as Australia. They'll talk about politics, news, arthritic knees. On a bad day, he can't even connect with someone in Wichita.

Mostly, though, he's tending to his mayoral duties. Which in large part entails keeping people and businesses from leaving town.

"It's what I work on the most and worry about," he says, pausing. Okay, "worry" is not the right word. "It's what I'm *concerned* about." "Concerned" is a good word. Courtland's existence is dependent on the farmer's existence. He gets the whole domino thing.

After lunch, he'll head back home in his golf cart, finish the edging he had started earlier this morning. He hadn't planned on edging his yard today, but then the neighbor starting edging and well, you know how that goes. And if someone, dead or alive, needs him later, whether he's in the middle of edging his yard, or trying to get the "wolf, zero, fox" signal past Wichita, he'll be there.

"My day never ends," he says. "There are no set hours. If somebody calls me, I'm working."

The check comes. Which is more than the Mayor can say for the chocolate cake he wanted for dessert.

"Sorry," Shannon says, pointing to the toddler sitting next to him. "He got the last piece."

The Newspaper

"We may get up to four pages, and that won't hurt my feelings."

The *Courtland Journal* is usually up to six pages, but this is a holiday weekend. Labor Day. And while much of the country is taking a break from laboring, Bob Mainquist is getting his weekly newspaper ready for the printing press. He'll make the thirty-five-minute drive across the border into Nebraska because the Superior Printing Press still prints a thirty-two-inch-wide paper. No one prints a thirty-two-inch paper anymore. If a newspaper is even still being printed, it's barely twenty-two inches wide. "But that's not really a paper," he says. "That's more like one of those dang scandal sheets."

When you've only got four pages to print, well, what can you do? It's usually slow in the summer, and even slower on Labor Day weekend. He'd prefer six pages, though. Six would be good.

"This is Gaynell," Gaynell Delay says into the receiver. "Do you have news?"

Verlene Veteto doesn't have any news to report. Nothing to fill Gaynell's Hometown Happenings column; comings and goings she gets from people writing in, from calling them on the phone, from leaving messages.

"This is Gaynell. . . . If you have news, call me."

It's slow out there. Not much of anything to report. At least Rita Allen had something.

"Chris Garst of Topeka spent Saturday to Monday with Rita Allen. Alene Lundberg was a Friday night supper guest of Rita Allen. Staci Allen of Lee's Summit, Missouri spent Saturday and Sunday with Rita Allen."

On the corner of Gaynell's desk, sandwiched between the Dell hard drive and a tube of original Chapstick, are a few loose pieces of lined notepad paper. Ninety-five-year-old Norma Aspegren's flowery cursive delivers the latest news from Scandia (population 372), 7.5 miles east.

"Darnell and Jana Carlson of Courtland who accompanied Norma

Aspegren and Jane Ann Calgren and Brandt Calgren attended the 100th birthday open house for Virginia Fuller held at the United Methodist Church at McCool Junction Nebraska, Sunday afternoon, a former resident of Scandia. Virginia looked so good. She sure didn't look like a 100 years old . . . "

Nothing from Betty Bouray, either. Not this week. Betty lives fourteen miles north in Republic (population 116). Although next week she'll have plenty to report for her column, Republic News.

"Story Hour at the Rae Hobson Memorial Library was held with three children and one adult. Story hour is held every Tuesday following school. . . . Don't forget to mark your calendar for the Pawnee Meet and Greet 2 pm at the Pawnee Indian Museum. . . . Troy and Christy Newman hosted their 14th annual family cookout at their home on Sunday, September 10th. For years after their wedding celebration in September of 2004, Troy grilled meat brought by friends and families throughout the evening . . . ".

Gaynell is in her seventies and has been working at the *Journal* for thirty years. "Once you get the printer's ink in your blood, you can't get it out," she says.

She used to run the linotype and has a few burns to show for it. Now she comes in every Monday to gather the news—*call me*—and again on Wednesday to drop off 504 subscriptions next door at the Courtland Post Office, which gets delivered to mailboxes in Courtland, throughout Republic County, and as far away as Pennsylvania, California, Colorado, Louisiana, and Texas. Yearly subscriptions are $28.21 in-state, $33.00 out-of-state, and single copies are a buck.

Since no one seems to have much news to share this week, Gaynell's column won't be as long as it usually is. Neither will Betty's or Norma's. Nothing from the Kansas Farm Bureau or the Huck Boyd National Institute for Rural Development at Kansas State University, no unapproved minutes from the Republic county commissioners, or any word from the River Valley extension agent, either.

And even with the church notes from Ada Lutheran, Courtland United Methodist, Amana Lutheran, Covenant Church, Our Savior's Evangelical Lutheran, and Living Waters, a list of the daily specials from AnTeaQues, the professional directory, and the ads, like the 8x10 from C&W Farm Supply ("TURBO-MAX Harvest Starts Here. This True Vertical Tillage machine is available in 7 models"), the *Journal* is stuck at four pages. And while it's not hurting Bob's feelings, it's also not putting him over the moon either. Because normally, even when it's 10 below outside, there'd be enough news to fill six pages.

"Thanks so much to all guys who dug out my car, my driveway, and front walk. What a blessing! Yes, you really can get stuck in your own driveway, especially if you're a stubborn retired teacher who thought she could bulldoze through all that snow. It was a teachable moment and I did learn the lesson! Many, many thanks. Janet Nelson."

But there's nothing this week. Not even a birthday party notice, like the one for Ralph Dunstan. "Celebrating 95 Years. 2–4 p.m. Open House. Formoso Fire Hall. No gifts please."

"But it's better to have four pages of relevant material than six pages of filler," offers Steve Benne.

Steve's in charge of a lot of the ad layout and most of the sports writing. "I don't claim to be a good writer," he laughs. "I just try hard."

The Panthers rolled to a 58–8 victory on Friday playing eight-man against the Lakeside Knights over there in Downs, thirty-nine miles west, then twenty-two miles south of Courtland. "The Panthers are lookin' good this year; have a lot of speed. Two of the fastest in the state," the farmers will say as they sip their morning coffee at Pinky's. "Lookin' real good. But they lost a lot of beef on the line."

Steve's also writing about the Pike Valley Lady Panthers volleyball team, which stands at 2–2. Had to fight a little harder during their game with Rock Hills. Won the first set 26–24. Lost the second 23–25. Rallied for the third set win with 25–18. "Solid group of girls with great potential . . . great start to the season," he types.

Bob gets in around 7:30 a.m. every Monday, about an hour before Gaynell and Steve, just as he's done for the past twenty-seven years. "I was never really a newspaperman. I taught at Pike Valley High School to support my bad habit: farming," he says. But Bob's late wife, Colleen, had started working at the *Journal* and when the previous owners finally wanted to sell, the Mainquists felt the paper was too important to the community not to buy it.

"I think I was supposed to be the janitor or something but that didn't work out too well," he says.

Bob took one agriculture journalism class when he was in school and he didn't like English so much. And he doesn't use a program like Adobe PageDesign to prepare the paper for printing. Instead, he lays out each page on a light table and assembles the paper by hand every week. Articles are typed up and printed from the computer, trimmed using a pair of scissors or the Dahle Cut Cat, and run through a waxer. Then, everything is pieced together onto the page like an aesthetically pleasing puzzle.

Hanging on the wall above the lightbox is a pegboard pinned with packets of MPS Newspaper Border Tape and Chartpak Graphic Tape. Bob doesn't like to use them, though. They're getting hard to come by. It would take at least 120 inches to tape off a page like the Fantasy Football Contest—forty-one

spots for forty bucks a pop—that will run for the next ten weeks. So, instead, he created the borders by hand with a black marker.

People come to the *Journal* to drop off a notice to be printed or pay for their subscription or just sit and gab for a bit. There are shelves lined with colorful cookie jars that Colleen collected, and the air conditioning takes the edge off in the summertime. People pop in to buy greeting cards, too, because the nearest store to buy them is eighteen miles west in Mankato or twenty miles east in Belleville. There are birthday cards, congratulation cards, get well cards . . . three display racks full of cards to choose from. "The dollar ones, well, they haven't done so good," Bob says. Not the "Hula Loves You" or the "Ze birthday cake, she is good, no?" cards. "But the two-dollar ones, well, they go pretty well. The one of the boy peeing on the tree is still our best-seller." Which he'd like to order more of. But apparently, it's been discontinued.

"Probably not politically correct anymore," he says.

By noon, just in time to grab lunch at AnTeaQues, the four pages are starting to look good since Steve suggested moving a few things around to keep all the high school sports photos together in one place. "Makes it easier for parents and grandparents to cut out," he points out.

"Good idea," Bob agrees. Which meant that Bob had to move the obituaries to page two, which he doesn't really like to do. He prefers the obits to be on the back page. No matter, his front page is still strong with the

announcement that Central Valley Ag and Farmway Co-op have officially
united. "Historic milestone. Combined, the unified cooperative will have
more than $400 million in members' equity . . . "

News that loops twenty-four hours a day, seven days a week is left to CNN
or MSNBC or FOX or the AP. The *Courtland Journal* isn't trying to compete.
Because what CNN or MSNBC or FOX or the AP can't bring you is the
news that's happening here. The news you can't get anywhere else. News
about Virginia Fuller's hundredth birthday celebration, Troy and Christy
Newman's fourteenth annual family cookout, the co-op merger, and when
"Pike Valley Downs Lakeside in Third."

Sometimes, you'll see a note from the editor tucked in between the regular
columns. Something interesting. Food for thought. Like what Bob read in a
bulletin from Amana Lutheran:

"Welcome! We extend a special welcome to those who are single, married,
divorced, gay, filthy rich, dirt poor, yo no Ingles . . . you're welcome here if
you are 'just browsing,' just woke up, or just out of jail . . . we welcome those
who are inked, pierced, or both. We welcome tourists, seekers, and doubters,
bleeding hearts . . . and you!"

"Community papers like ours, well, we may have a little bit of a chance
to hold on better than a bigger paper," he says. "But there are no guarantees.
I've run it longer than anyone else did. Does that make me a newspaperman?
No. It just makes me the idiot that's got one."

The Liar's Bench

It's 4:55 p.m. Even hotter than yesterday. Still no clouds. No rain either. The digital temperature sign outside of the Swedish-American State Bank wants to be sure everyone's aware that it's 101 degrees, just in case they didn't notice. And seven guys are sitting on six benches that line the sidewalks outside of Pinky's. Catching up on the latest.

"Friend told me you had a problem with your cows getting out."

"Yeah, well that does happen. . . . Life goes on."

The only one that's here from the morning coffee crew is Mikesell. The six benches that they are all sitting on have collectively been dubbed the "Liar's Bench." Everyone in town knows what the Liar's Bench is. When you ask, they snicker, roll their eyes, shake their heads.

"That's because you don't want to believe everything you hear here," says AJ.

Although most of the guys hanging out on the Liar's Bench are not part of the morning coffee crew, they all know about it: the sifter, the boots, the earplugs, all the things that make Betty's face turn red.

"I'd rather be in bed than listening to all that BS," says Cousin Steve. Although he does get up at 3:30 or 4:00 every morning because he can't sleep.

"It's his conscious," says AJ. AJ is retired. He farmed for forty years. Crops and cattle. Mostly crops. He misses it. Still wears the "Anderson Fertilizer Service" hat. Before he farmed, he worked at the state penitentiary.

"I spent a little time there," he likes to say.

Then he came back to Courtland.

Why, AJ?

Good question, he smiles.

Which was harder, AJ? Working at the state pen or on the farm?

"Farm," he smiles. "Back then, Courtland was really something. They'd have a drawing every Wednesday and Saturday night . . . yeah, that was it, right? Wednesday and Saturday nights. For a turkey or something."

Courtland had a blacksmith.

A roller rink.

A movie house . . .

"Or was it an opera house?"

"Well, movie/opera house."

And three filling stations.

"Or four?"

"Was it four?"

"Yeah, four filling stations."

"It was unique," AJ says. "A really unique place."

AJ nicknamed everyone in this town. Like Cousin Steve. AJ nicknamed him.

He nicknamed Larry Brown "LB." *Here comes LB!*

And Uncle Sam, too. Also known as Howie Mandel. Who they also call Mr. Big. Don't ask him how he got the name Mr. Big.

"That's what his wife nicknamed him," Mikesell laughs, taking a drag from a Marlboro Light.

"No, she didn't," says Cousin Steve, rolling his eyes.

There's also Lug, so named after he forgot to tighten the nuts on his tire one day, which caused it to fall off and roll down the hill.

"That was a bad day," AJ laughs.

Most of the guys sitting on the Liar's Bench are retired farmers. Well, three or four are retired. Mikesell is still farming. "But I am *tired*," he laughs, taking another drag.

Four of the benches are dedicated in memory of someone. There was JD Stutt from Decatur, Texas . . . you know, that trucker. He was a local favorite.

And Brandon Melby. He was only a teenager. Died unexpectedly. That was a shame.

Paul W. Segerhammar was a classmate of Cousin Steve. They spread his ashes in the grass next to Pinky's.

And Delbert E. Roper. Delbert was a farmer.

There's one more memorial, a sticker adhered to the corner of the front window of the bar. "In memory of Cayden Dunston. September 17, 2009–October 15, 2011." Oh man, that was sad. Cayden was standing behind the wheel of one of those big tractors and no one realized it. Just . . . sad.

"That's why no one likes John Deere, right?"

"Nah . . . buddy a' mine says when you buy a John Deere you usually have to buy two because one is usually broken down."

A few feet away from the Liar's Bench is Main Street, which has just been paved with a heaping of asphalt right down the center.

"That's the county," Cousin Steve says. "The city's responsible for the area from the sidewalk to the edge of the blacktop."

"Small town politics, that's what that is," Lug says.

So, for now, just the center of the street has been paved. Black and gummy under the 101 degrees that are beating down from the sun.

The guys on the Liar's Bench got here around 2:30 or 3:00 in the afternoon, just like they always do. Get out of the sun. Into the shade. Light a Marlboro Light or Eagle 20's. Drink Mountain Dew. Pepsi. Wave to people driving by. High-five the kids in day care as they walk by. Sit in silence. Talk about the weather, the corn, the damn Royals.

"Starting pitching just went to hell. *To* hell."

And other . . . stuff. "Like sex," Betty says, taking a break from the bar to come outside for a smoke. "Or the brass pole."

Someone thought it'd be cool to put a brass pole in the back of the bar. For, well, *you know.*

"Entertainment," Mikesell says.

Everyone laughs. Yeah, *entertainment.*

"See," Betty says. "I told you you'd need earplugs."

The awnings above the benches absorb maybe 1 or 2 degrees of blistering, dry heat. The sky is wide and open and a very pale blue. There is an occasional, whisper-soft breeze that is far too warm to be anything remotely cool.

"If only we could get a few inches of rain, even just two inches," Mikesell says. "Sure would help things."

The farmers come to the Liar's Bench because they might get to enjoy a ten-hour day instead of an eighteen-hour one during irrigation season. Damn near a *vacation.*

Sometimes they just meet up, play cards, whatever. But mostly, they come to the Liar's Bench. Sit. Keep tabs on each other. Talk about . . . oh, *stuff.*

"Waitin' on a train?" someone laughs, walking past.

"Yeah," Mikesell replies from behind his polarized sunglasses, raising another Marlboro to his lips. "Somethin' like that."

The Gas Station

"Hoard Oil . . . this is Norm."

When the phones first started ringing at Norman's Standard in 1954, the Chevys were the easiest cars to work on. You could get your hands into the guts of a Chevy engine. Wrench on it. Change the oil. Change the spark plugs.

Which Norm did. A lot. You had to change the spark plugs every fifteen to twenty thousand miles if you wanted your car to run top-notch. If you got lazy and didn't change them, your car would *putt-putt* down the road. And when you finally limped your way into the service station—*ding! ding!*— Norm would get you set up with four, six, eight, or sixteen new spark plugs to get you on your way again.

Norman Hoard had about 150 bucks to his name when he first started. He was nineteen. Gas was twenty-six cents a gallon at the Standard Oil gas station on Highway 36. And he and his high school sweetheart, Doris, had just said, "I do."

Norm and Doris met in junior high. She could play the piano and the trombone and was good at softball and tennis. She was a cheerleader, too. One day, Norm sat next to her at the movie theater over in Formoso and held her hand.

It was love at first sight. For one of them. "Well," he smiles, "I worked on it anyway."

Norm keeps a pen and a tire gauge in the front pocket of his Key overalls, which he wears over a gray, button-down work shirt embroidered with his name. Sometimes, he'll stop for a cup of coffee and some breakfast at Pinky's. Joerg, Steve, Larry, Carlson, Hootie, and the rest of the boys will all say "Hey, Norm!" while Betty takes a few minutes to sit down and talk to him. He'll eat. Pay his check. Grab a toothpick. Walk over to the *Journal* to say hello to Mr. Mainquist. Get in his truck and go back to the station, which is located on the west side of town, a few blocks away from Jensen Tire & Service, the station on the east side of town.

Norm is very quiet and very sweet. He gets frustrated when his words don't always come out right. "Damn stroke," he'll say, his voice a few decibels higher than a whisper. But he still drives his tan Chevy pickup, over to Formoso for Hamburger Night at The Barn, and into town almost every day for lunch at AnTeaQues.

He still likes to get his hands dirty, get them into those engines. Wrench on things. Even when Hoard's Oil is closed for business, Norm is there. "Until they carry me out feet first," he says.

Norm has lived here his entire life. He was a farm boy. Grew up poor, out in the country a few miles south of town. He rode a horse to school, had to learn how to become a jack of all trades. When he was a sophomore in high school, he took woodshop. One day, he was pushing a block through a wood joiner. The blade started to twirl. A little. Then a lot. Then it kicked out. When it did, it chewed two fingertips off his right hand.

Which didn't stop him from doing much of anything. Not from playing basketball, although everyone else thought he was nuts. Norm thought he was kind of nuts, too. "I didn't know how successful I'd be with stubs," he says.

But he hooked a rim into the side of a corn crib on his family farm and would take that basketball and shoot and shoot and shoot. And eventually, all that shoot-shoot-shooting with those stubs got him a 26-point average per game.

He wasn't sure how successful he'd be at owning a gas station, either, but he had vowed to take care of his new bride. So, when Norm got wind that the Standard Oil was up for sale, he bought the place. At closing time after his first day of business, he only had $15 more in his pocket than he had when he started in the morning.

"Not good," he says. "I was green as a gourd."

Norm worked seven days a week, 6:30 a.m. to 9 p.m., and mopped the floors every morning. Started changing oil and spark plugs and tires, pumping gas for twenty-six cents a gallon: Red Crown (regular) and Gold Crown (ethyl), which is basically high octane, like a 91. Sold ice-cold Coca-Cola from a cooler and Camels and Lucky Strikes from a display inside of his office, which looked like a little cottage with a peak above the door. He kept the joint clean. He kept the johns clean, too.

"Customers always appreciated that," he says.

Once a month, the Standard Oil rep would come by. He'd look things over, offer a tip or two about how to run a successful operation.

Always keep your business clean. No, it's not a good idea to bring your brother on as a partner . . . it never works.

Back then, the gas station was busy. Nonstop. If you wanted a quick route across Kansas, you were driving Highway 36, through farm towns and past cornfields. One lane east. One lane west. There was no interstate highway, no Flying J Travel Center or Cracker Barrel every twenty miles.

Highway 36 took people right through Courtland. Right past Norman's Standard. He worked fifteen hours a day, seven days a week.

"I didn't hire anyone to help me. Couldn't afford it."

When their son, Kevan, was born, the doctor charged Norm sixty bucks for the delivery. He and Doris had two more boys: Kris and Scott. Doris helped out a lot. She'd put the boys in the stroller, come down to the station, pump gasoline, keep the books, do whatever needed to be done.

"We couldn't afford to take family vacations. And when you have your own business, you can't let any Tom, Dick, or Harry run it when you're gone," he says.

When Highway 36 was rerouted north of town in '63, the steady stream of vacationing station wagons and all those Pacific Intermountain Express trucks were rerouted with it. Traffic was no longer coming right through Courtland. They weren't coming right past Norman's Standard, pumping a full tank, buying a Coke and some Camels.

"It was like someone turned the switch," he says. "I wasn't worried . . . but I was concerned." So, Norm diversified.

He began to sell tires. A lot of tires. The dirt and the gravel roads around Republic County were always good for chewing up tires. Back then, there were only eight different types of tires to choose from. They were easy to stock and sell. Not like today. Today, there are like, five hundred tires to choose from. Not so easy to stock and sell when you're a one-man band.

He expanded the business in '66. Started delivering oil. Built a new office and service garage. His old office, the one that looked like a little cottage, was sold to his friend Marvin Bergstrom, jacked up onto a flatbed, and taken to Marvin's livestock farm a few miles north of town, where it still sits today.

Norm kept on expanding. Over the years he switched from Standard to Sinclair to Amoco and then just started selling his own brand of gasoline. And as soon as Scott, Kris, and Kevan were big enough, they came to work at the station, too. After school. During the summer.

"We were raised here," Scott says. "My dad instilled hard work in all of us. He and my mom both put their heart and soul into the business." Scott took over in the late 1990s. When he goes on vacation to Alaska in a few weeks, his wife, Brenda, will be the one driving the 2014 Peterbilt with the 2,700-gallon tank to deliver fuel to the farmers who need it to run their equipment.

The gas pumps at Hoard's Oil are short and squat and mechanized, with analog dials that tick and spin as you pump: *.20, .30, .40, .50 . . . tick . . . tick*

. . . *tick.* If you want to swipe your card, you can pay at a pay station near the pumps, although no one has figured out it's there. So, most everyone still comes inside to pay, to say hi to Brenda and Scott. *Where's the boss?* Look for Norm. *Hey Norm!* Pet his dog, Boone. *Aw, good boy!*

Doris passed away in 2013. Cancer. She had worked right alongside her high school sweetheart for over fifty years. Norm still misses her. Every now and then, you can see his Chevy making its way down L Road, a dirt and gravel lane that runs past the old family farm, where only the barn remains, and into a small cemetery sitting on a bluff that is very green and very peaceful and dates to the early 1800s. Doris is buried there. On the back of their granite headstone is a laser-cut illustration of the station.

Norm still comes into the station five days a week. Right around 7 a.m. He still likes to mop the floors every other day. On the days he isn't mopping, he's sweeping. And if your truck is looking really muddy, he'll knock on your front door, offer to wash it for you, ask for the keys, and promise to bring it right back.

On his birthday, a lot of people came down to the station to celebrate it with him. Kevan, Scott, and Kris bought him a big sheet cake with blue and yellow icing. "Happy 82nd Birthday Dad!" They set off fireworks in the middle of the afternoon, right there on old Highway 36. Talked with friends. Ate birthday cake. And then the moon chimed in with a total eclipse of the sun. The photos ran on the front page of the *Courtland Journal* the following week.

Back in the shop, family-owned and operated for nearly sixty years, the phone rings.

"Hoard Oil, this is Norm . . . "

"I'm pretty proud of what he and my mom started," says Scott. "People say, 'You're lucky to work with your dad,' and they're right. My dad was my mentor. For Halloween, one of the kids dressed up as him. I had to go around the corner because it just made me bawl. There are not too many Norman Hoards left around here or in the world."

The Lutherans

" . . . if it is possible, as far as it depends on you, live at peace with everyone. Do not take revenge, my dear friends, but leave room for God's wrath, for it is written, 'It is mine to avenge; I will repay,' says the Lord . . . "

"In Romans 12, that's what Paul was asking, but it's difficult to follow, isn't it?" asks Al Urich.

Al is flattered when you call him "Pastor Al."

"Technically, I'm just a layperson," he replies, a smile on his face as if he's about to explode with joy into thousands of tiny little joy bubbles.

Al is blind. And right now, about thirty-five people are sitting in the pews, waiting for his sermon to begin at Ada Lutheran Church, one of four churches in Courtland. Although there are only thirty-five people here this morning, they're all sitting toward the back. Leaving a comfortable distance of about twelve pews between themselves and Al's message. Someone's kid is having a fit in the back row, and everyone else is trying to be polite, pretending like they can hear what's being delivered from the pulpit.

Since 1884, the church has sat on a foundation of Swedish heritage, Lutheranism, and limestone. Its spire stretches into the sky and houses a fourteen-hundred-pound bell that was purchased in the late 1800s for $279.62 from the St. Louis Bell Foundry and that arrived at the church on a stone rack during a time when all services and meetings were conducted in Swedish. *Si Guds Lam!* (Behold the Lamb of God!) Women and girls on one side. Men and boys on the other.

The building is located a few miles south of Courtland, down a dirt and gravel road that cuts its way past cornfields and wild sunflowers that dance in the breeze. The parking lot is a carpet of soft, short grass. In the cemetery, in the middle of the plains, sits a massive anchor across the grave of Mr. Mainquist's great uncle, Swan Anton Haggman. Born October 28, 1842. Died October 31, 1930. Member of the Grand Army of the Republic during the Civil

War. Before coming to the United States, Haggman had been a merchant marine in Sweden. Someone said the anchor came from his ship.

Ada Lutheran doesn't have a website, but it does have a Facebook page. They post bible verses and words of encouragement and other happy notes like, "Thank the Lord and sing praise. It's RAINING!!!"

Just like Pastor Sandra, Pastor Al is also aware of the outside assumptions that everyone in a small, midwestern farming community is going to church nine times a week and beating visitors over the head with bibles. "People see the Midwest as the bible belt. We have assumptions about people out there, too," he says. But he doesn't really think that the percentage of people in Courtland who attend church is a whole lot higher than national averages. "And I don't think it's because they're angry at the church. They're either bored by the service or don't want to sit there for an hour or their kid is in a basketball tournament on Sunday."

And even though a lot of people might not be attending church, he can feel the community ties that people still have with the church. It's weddings and funerals and potluck picnics. "We share a vacation bible school program with Covenant Church and there are kids who go to that who never come to church at either place. But it is a focal point in the community during June. It's just what you do right after school is out."

While Al is sure that none of the four churches in town are anywhere near full on a Sunday, he still thinks that people, even those that don't attend, see the church as having an important role in the community. "A kind of a foundation," he says. "It might be sort of a backstop in case of an emergency. Everyone went to church after 9/11, know what I'm saying? And churches are not at each other's throats here. It's just that people grow up with certain kinds of faith expressions and they go where they are most comfortable. And I think that's true in suburbs of larger cities and it's just as true in a small community."

There's a large tin can that is making its way up and down Ada's pews. The Noise Offering. Lutheran Good Gifts; gifts that will go to help their neighbors in need. As it makes its way down the pews, people toss in their currency, the kind that makes noise and the kind that doesn't.

Last Sunday, Ada received a total giving of $161. Of which, $36 came by way of loose offerings and $125 from contributions in sealed envelopes and folded, personal checks. The only two people that know who is contributing what amount are God and the financial secretary. It just keeps things simpler. You start knowing who is giving what and well, people start to feel bad about themselves. Or too good about themselves. It's just better to keep it all under wraps.

Ada also received another $1,600 in rent from the farmland it owns and $150 in basement rent, too. Both help keep the doors open. There are about seventy-five names on the rolls. On an average Sunday, you'll find about half of them sitting in the pews.

One of them is continuing to have a meltdown in the back row. The church is very warm and there is no air conditioning, so the front doors have been left open. A few people are using their bulletins as fans. Someone politely clears their throat, hoping to cue the parents that their kid is distracting everyone. The parents don't get the hint.

The next scripture Al reads comes from Jeremiah 15:15–21. "They will fight against you, but they shall not prevail over you, for I am with you to save you and deliver you, says the Lord. I will deliver you out of the hand of the wicked and redeem you from the grasp of the ruthless."

Psalm 26:1–8 is next. "Test me, O Lord, and try me; examine my heart and my mind . . . "

Followed by Romans 12. "Live at peace with everyone . . . do not take revenge . . . "

"Not exactly what we're used to hearing, is it?" Al asks, his hands moving fluidly across his notes, written in braille, as the wailing from the back raises a few decibels. All heads continue to face politely forward. One turns just enough to let the parents know that everyone else knows their kid is upset about something; a silent plea to spare the rest of the congregation.

"Because what does the world tell us?" Al continues, not missing a beat as the howling continues. "The world tells us, 'Don't get mad . . . get even!' Which sounds like a good idea. Especially when you're hurt and that hurt left a scar. Battle scars. And we tend to carry those battle scars around with us wherever we go. Some are fortunate and have allowed those scars to heal. But others pick at them. They reopen their scars. Become hostage to them."

"Don't get mad. Isn't that the part we just . . . can't . . . do?" Al asks as someone nods their head.

"Live at peace with *every*one," Al repeats. "Do *not* take revenge. We hear that and think, 'Okay, wonderful, see you next week,' but this is serious stuff. *Live at peace with everyone . . . do not take revenge.* This is the philosophy that first- and second-century Christians tried to live by. That's how I know that Christianity is a countercultural movement." No, don't get mad, he advises. No matter how much you want to pick at that battle scar, reopen it, get even. Just leave it. Live peaceably with all.

The kid in the back calms down long enough to reenergize and let out another howl. Someone coughs. A throat is cleared. Then another. Ever so politely. Mom finally takes the hint and the room is Al's again.

He remains at the pulpit for the offering—this one by way of a brass plate—and the prayers; for the church, the earth, the nations, and its leaders, for those in need, this community, and its ministry, giving thanks for all the saints who now rest from their labors, and commending into God's gracious hands all those for whom are prayed, trusting the power of Christ and the gifts of the spirit. Amen.

When the congregation rises to sing the sending song—"Lift High the Cross"—Al is escorted from the pulpit to the back of the church. The kid who's been throwing a fit has finally worn herself into a state of quiet exhaustion. A soft whimper, barely audible, signals a feeble attempt at an encore.

"Go in peace," says Al. "Serve the Lord."

"Thanks be to God," responds the thirty-five.

SPRING

Commodity Prices (per bushel)

	April 1920	April 1973	April 1984	April 2018
Corn	$1.33	$1.60	$3.45	$3.43
Wheat	$2.45	$2.41	$3.51	$5.28
Soybean	$2.68	$6.78	$7.89	$9.83

The Good-bye

Mikesell had been in on Friday morning, told Betty he'd see her on Saturday.

When he didn't show up in the morning, she thought it was odd. And when he didn't show up for lunch either, she knew something wasn't right. Everyone knew he hadn't been feeling very good lately. Mikesell never talked about it that much.

"Promise me you'll go to the doctor," Betty had asked.

"I will," he promised.

He had suddenly lost like, fifteen pounds.

"You need to go to the doctor," Betty told him.

"I will," Mikesell promised.

"He never did," Betty says.

The guys at Pinky's are handling it okay. A lot of them tried talking to him. He told a lot of them to mind their own business. They knew this was coming. They just didn't expect it to be this soon.

"He was a royal pain in the ass," Betty says. "But he was a good guy. Mikesell had a good heart."

The Morning Coffee: Friday

Joerg missed it.

The guy in the skirt. Big guy. Like, *huge* guy. Tattoos everywhere. Bushy black beard. Tall, too. Towering.

"In a *skirt*?" Joerg asks.

"Yep," Slug says. "A skirt."

"I was up late last night and thought I was seeing things," Betty says. But she wasn't. The guy was wearing a skirt.

"Who was he?" Joerg asks.

He was some trucker. A delivery guy maybe? He came into Pinky's around 6 a.m. asking for a tug. "I got my tailgate stuck. Grass was too wet," he said as he approached the table where Larry, Steve, and Slug were sitting.

"I'll be the tow guy," Steve finally offered, getting up.

"I've never seen anything like that," Slug laughed. "Never seen a man wearing a goddang skirt."

"An actual skirt?" Joerg asks again.

"Yep," Slug says. "A skirt."

"Not one of them Irish things?"

"Nope," Slug says. "Not a kilt. A skirt."

Joerg wanted to say something about the skirt or more than likely, what was under the skirt. "I don't want to make Betty blush," he says. Which makes everyone laugh. Because Betty doesn't even turn red now when the guys start talking about sex, sex, sex, and all the other things that used to make her blush.

"She's hardened over the years," Kenny says.

"I think she actually likes it," Joerg says. "She says she doesn't hear us, but she does."

"You're getting so much easier to ignore. Until your voices get loud . . . when you want me to hear. I might be old," she says, flipping eggs on the griddle, "but I'm not deaf."

Everyone is happy to have Betty back. Over the winter, she had finally found someone that seemed like they wanted to work, but that gal was *awful*. Just *terrible*. She couldn't even put her cell phone down to wait on Kenny. And poor Hootie; he ordered biscuits and gravy and got it thirty minutes later. She lasted a month. The farmers weren't happy.

So, Betty started coming into Pinky's at 5 a.m. again, getting her hockey pucks in the oven and the Bunn ready to begin brewing. Making sure there were eggs and sausage and toast on the griddle for whoever wanted it. Back to working seventy-seven hours a week.

"What's this?" Jim asks, turning over the white plastic cup as he sits down and rubs his eyes. He's got a five-dollar bill in his hand that he was hoping to get change for, but the cup is empty, and he's irritated about the damn Royals. They had a flyball soaring through the air last night and no one in the outfield acted like they could catch it.

"They need Cain back," he whistles as Carlson walks in the door with his friend, Eric Spain.

"Hey Spain," everyone says.

Spain's a full-blooded Cherokee Indian who lives down in Oklahoma, and everyone is surprised to see him this morning since Carlson had a big party at The Shed last night. No one expected to see them come into Pinky's for morning coffee or to see them in the morning for anything at all, actually. Not this early. But then again, no one expected Carlson to call Pinky's a few years ago when he rolled his ATV, either.

"Most people, if you're in trouble, you call 911," he says. "I call Pinky's."

He called at noon. Was out from under the ATV by 12:15.

"Have you seen them crossing 36 in the golf carts?" Larry asks.

"Yeah," Steve says. "Down in Scandia?"

"Yeah," Larry says.

"Yeah," Steve replies. "One guy used to cross in his motorized wheelchair. It's a miracle he wasn't hit. Won't be too long until someone gets creamed." He winces. His rib still hurts. He broke it when he rolled his ATV.

"I was chasing after a damn cow," he says.

Everyone just laughs. "Hell, Brownie," Joerg says. "Is there anything you haven't wrecked?"

"How many times have I gotten *that* call?" Larry wonders.

Dad? Steve would say. *Guess what happened?*

Where you at? Larry would sigh.

"You didn't call when you was thrown in jail," Larry points out.

"Yeah," Steve laughs, "'cuz I knew I'd stay there."

There's no point in asking what Steve was thrown in jail for because he won't tell you. But he will tell you about the Dodge 2500. Show you a picture of it, all burnt to a crisp.

"Transfer case blew," he says. "While I was driving it."

The Dodge is now a melted pile of twisted metal. He got a Ford to replace it. "We'll see how tough a Ford is," he says. His Ranchero is tough. It's *fast*. It's meant for drag racing. He and his son took it down to Kansas City not too long ago.

"Raised some hell," he says.

Which was incredible. Almost as incredible as the time Kenny got struck by lightning.

"July 5, 1964," he says. "It was 113 degrees that day. Judeen and I were up at Lov'll having a picnic. I was putting the basket in the back seat when one of those bolts bit me."

Since it was 113 degrees and he was only wearing swimming trunks, Kenny ended up with a burnt chest, half of his hair singed off, and a blown-out eardrum.

He and Judeen have been married for fifty-three years. Well, fifty-two and a half.

"As long as I don't die," he laughs, "we'll make it to fifty-three."

Everyone loves that story. Almost as much as they love the story about Joerg eating the worms. Someone at the bar dared him to do it. Who knows who came up with the idea? It was twenty years ago. But they dared him twenty bucks to eat some worms.

Okay!

So, they went outside, dug up some worms. "Like *this big*," he says, spreading apart his hands. "They still had dirt on 'em." He rolled them up, three or four of them, and ate them.

"You do some silly things when you get to drinking beer," he says.

But nothing was as silly as the guy in the skirt this morning. Although he was a good distraction from the rain that never came last night, even though the radar showed a big green blob heading this way, which got everyone excited.

"Hasn't been any rain since, what? September?" Joerg asks.

"It's bad," Steve says. "Real bad."

Some of the farmers are getting a little bit done. Got in a little bit of corn. Little bit of alfalfa. But the ponds are dry. The wheat's turning blue. Dust is blowing.

"It's worse south," Joerg says. "They got like an inch and a half near Wichita and it didn't do a thing."

Which is a shame. Because it's been raining on the West Coast. Raining on the East Coast. "Kinda forgets us good people here in the middle," Steve says.

There wasn't even that much snow over the winter. And they were supposed to get thirty snows. "The first day it snows on is how many snows you'll get over the winter," Steve says. "We got our first snow on November 30. So, thirty snows."

"It's an old wives tale," Betty says.

But it didn't snow thirty times. No snow at all for that matter. Maybe like, a *dusting* here or there, but nothing close to anything that would insulate those seeds and put just the right amount of moisture into the ground to keep them good and watered.

Steve was the first one this morning. Right around 5:30 a.m. Had a jacket on. Peeled it off after a while. Because always, a T-shirt. Never mind that it's 40 degrees outside, or if it's raining or cold. Always, a T-shirt. He thought that big green blob would turn into a good one overnight, but it just didn't happen.

"We got a puddle last night," he says. "We need six inches to fill our ponds. We got just enough to get the alfalfa to sprout and die. You just do what you do and go on."

"How are you doing?" he asks as Larry comes in.

"Not worth a damn," Larry replies.

"Oh, crap," Steve says, reaching for the Bunn.

The Bunn has finished brewing one pot, there's about a quarter of a pot left in another on the burner, and Betty's about to put her hockey pucks into the oven.

"Want me to feed your bulls?" Steve asks.

"No," Larry says.

"Sure?"

"Fat already."

It's so dry that Steve has been getting phone calls from farmers who want to buy his hay. Also not a good sign.

If someone's calling to buy your hay, it's because there's no carpet of grass in the ground to feed their cattle. So, you supplement their diet with hay until it rains and warms up and the grass grows again. And cows just milk better on grass, they say, so while a little hay isn't bad, a lot of hay is not very good.

In a dream scenario, Mother Nature would actually *cooperate* instead of working against everyone so they could get their seeds planted; alfalfa first, then corn, beans, milo, then wheat, then plant a double crop of beans behind that to make the most out of your land.

"Lookin' a little dry there," Hootie says, making his way over to the table.

"I was waitin' for ya," Steve says as Hootie fills his Styrofoam cup.

"Sluggo?" he asks next, holding up the pot.

"I'm good," Slug says.

"You can take more of that, Steve," Hootie says, emptying the remainder of the pot into Steve's cup.

"You missed a sight," Slug says.

"A guy came in wearing a skirt," they tell him.

Hootie smiles, shakes his head. "Well," he says, looking at the radar on his phone. "Another storm is heading east."

"Something's sitting on the Colorado border," Joerg says, looking at the radar on his phone. "But it's not moving."

Sure would be nice, to get some rain. More than the thirty-eight hundredths of an inch that Steve got. More than the puddle.

"One inch since September," Steve says. "The last time it was this dry was '92."

The lake will never fill again, the engineer had said as he checked the levels at Lov'll. Not in our lifetime.

"It flooded in '93," Steve says. "So much for that."

The Farmers:
Kenny Joerg

Joerg has the Titan trailer hooked up to his maroon Chevy 2500. From the ignition dangle a set of jangly keys attached to a short lanyard that says "I Love Grandpa."

He's got to haul about fifty thousand pounds of Black and Red Angus, seventeen head at a time, from a feedlot over in Jewell. Strictly steers and grass cattle. Seventy of them have been at the feedlot for the past couple of months. He got them at 600 pounds. The feedlot will get them up to 750, and the grass at Joerg's farm will round them out to 900. He needs to transport them all back to his thirteen hundred acres in Formoso, for a total distance of one mile north and four miles west.

They're at the feedlot because there hasn't been any good grass to graze them on. It's been hot. Dry. No rain at all. Nothing green and lush coming out of the ground.

"Goddamnit! My pond is dry," he says, driving past a brown, empty depression in the ground. "You know, those Okies call it a tank. They come up and look at our ponds and say, 'Your tank is running low.'"

The pond/tank is where the cattle get watered. Every single pond in Republic County is dry right now. "But then it gets just as wet as it gets dry, so you really can't stress about it," he says. "Drinking helps. It's a temporary fix, but nothing more than that. You really gotta keep it under control or it'll eat you up."

They all watched it happen to Mikesell. And they tried . . . they really did try. A handful of them sat him down, tried to talk to him.

"He didn't want to hear it," Joerg says.

Farming can be stressful, they all say. But it's a great way of life if you like doing it, they all add.

Joerg is a fourth-generation farmer, just like Hootie and Steve.

"I loved sitting in the tractor, stirring dust," Joerg says. "Out there by myself. Thinking about things for sixteen to eighteen hours a day. Day after day."

He can't do it anymore, though. It kills his back. Couldn't even get out of bed thanks to the compressed discs from years of riding in the Caterpillar D4, an itty-bitty thing that plowed 160 acres five feet at a time going five miles per hour. Back then, he and his cousin would switch off, plowing day and night to get a field done.

"You really don't have to stir the dust for sixteen to eighteen hours these days," he says, maneuvering the Chevy down the road. "Once you harvest the wheat, you spray the stubble that's left down with herbicide. The herbicide is expensive, but it'll kill the weeds and save moisture in the ground. They used to say that when you worked the ground, you'd lose half an inch of rain. So, it's worth it. Worth not having to plow to turn over the dirt, then two to three weeks later disc it twice. Then running the field cultivator twice. Then planting more wheat, then even more wheat, then wheat again, which wasn't good. The herbicide lets you rotate your crops, which *is* good. It helps alleviate bugs and diseases that can happen when three times in a row you plant wheat, wheat, wheat. No-tillin' changed everything," he says.

It also meant that he didn't necessarily have to hire a bunch of guys to help him or have ten kids, either. "I knew I could do it better anyway. I'm not good at giving someone orders. So, I did it all myself. Well, my first wife would drive the truck during harvest, so I guess I didn't do it all myself."

His first wife wanted a nice house and the white picket fence, and he just couldn't give it to her because it was the 1980s, and not much of anything was going well for a farmer in the 1980s. In the end, Joerg did end up getting her a nice house, though.

"As part of the divorce," he says, waving his hand.

He swings the Chevy into Green Farms, backing up to the steel pens where the Black and Red Angus are waiting, green tags dangling from their ears.

"No branding this year," he says. Two guys are already in the pens, trying to corral seventeen of Joerg's cattle into a walkway that will take them directly into the trailer. "Come on!" they urge, smacking their hindquarters with long, thin plastic rods.

"Get!" Joerg says, zapping one with an electric cattle prod called the Green One. One by one they hoof it into the trailer, huddling together as he shuts the door behind them, latches it, and adds the chain.

"Just in case," he says. The last thing he wants is his cattle to spill out onto the road. "That wouldn't be good."

The Chevy 2500 slowly lurches forward, the engine revving as it tows ten thousand pounds of cattle. It feels good today. The temperature says it's 72.

"Thank God," Joerg says to Max, who's helping him out this year. "Max farms what? How many thousands of acres?"

About four, Max replies from behind his Oakleys.

It irks Joerg that the outside world seems to be under the impression that the farmers out here are all getting rich, just rolling in the dough. "It's not true," he says. "We're in debt all of our lives. I didn't get out until three or four years ago during those good years I've talked about." He never thought it would happen. Took him forty-five years to crawl out of the hole. Now he has four hundred acres paid for. His cattle are paid for. Some of his equipment is paid for.

"A lot of guys just don't want to save," he says.

This means that when things go south, the only thing left to do is start selling off their biggest asset: land. Section by section.

When that happens, the town doesn't riot if another farmer puts in a bid to buy it. "It's actually a good thing someone wants to buy it. You're helping them pay off their debt. Otherwise, they'd have to sell two sections. You just have to be *really* smart about how you're spending. You can't spend yourself rich," he says. "And some of them don't want to pay income tax, either. So, the minute they're in the black, they'll buy a tractor or something, just so they don't have to pay income tax." Which makes no sense to Joerg. Or his banker.

"My banker always says, 'It's a good thing to pay taxes. It means you made money.' And what about Social Security? If you're not paying income tax you're cutting into your Social Security."

The house he owns, which sits one mile north and four miles west, is the one Joerg was born in. He grew up in that house. He and his second wife, Pat, were going to fix it up. Tear out some walls, do this and that. But that never happened. It was so strange. She had never been ill. Nothing. Then one morning, she just didn't wake up. Joerg spent the next month living in his man cave in the garage. On the inflatable mattress shoved into the corner under the University of Kansas wallpaper border.

"I'm a big KU fan," he says. "Not as bad as Jim, though."

He turns off Highway 36 and down a long dirt and gravel road, maneuvering his trailer through an open gate that sits across from his house, which itself sits unburdened by neighbors. He climbs out of the Chevy and stands at the rear of the trailer. Max goes on one side of the steel doors and Joerg goes on the other. As they open them, seventeen cows run onto 120 acres of grass that hopefully will be six inches high in about a week.

He'll do this three more times. Drive to the feedlot. Open trailer. Cattle-prod prodding. Seventeen cows in. Shut trailer. Down one road. Up another. Into his field. Steel doors open. Seventeen cows out and running into the grass. "Ornery buggers," he says. He has been kicked and charged at and knocked over and he won't miss them when they go to the Mankato Sale Barn in September. "Beef is up two bucks," he adds, checking his phone before glancing out the window. He loves it out here.

"I can't even stand driving down to Kansas City anymore. People drive like they're crazy. It's loud. It's just too much. I really don't like it at all." He likes his weekly golf game with Carlson, likes being semiretired, likes going to see his grandson play football on Friday night, likes seeing Steve, Larry, Slug, and Hootie for coffee in the morning. "Sometimes it's boring, yeah, but there's always something going on, even if it's not going on with me."

Not too long ago, he and Max were in the Chevy, heading west on Highway 36 when they came across an accident. A guy in a refrigerated box truck had flipped into a ditch, spilling his entire load. There were mountain oysters everywhere. They were breaded and everything.

"Some still frozen in the box," Joerg says. "Damnit! We could have had so many parties."

When the state trooper got there and did CPR on the guy, he made Joerg climb into the cab to make sure no one else was in the truck. There wasn't. But the guy who was driving it was dead.

"Maybe he had a heart attack or something, who knows," Joerg says, turning into the feedlot. "It was too bad. But damnit! Think of all those mountain oysters we could have had."

The Ladies

If you want THE REAL STORY, you don't go to Pinky's at 6 a.m.

"You come to AnTeaQues on Wednesdays and talk to the ladies," says Mrs. C.

Once a week. Nine to 11 a.m. Where two or four or seven or twenty of the ladies gather for a cup of coffee or tea like Cinnamon Plum, Ginger Hibiscus, or Earl Grey that they'll each pay a dollar for. There is no dirty white plastic cup to put their money in. But there is a glass jar.

"And we don't gossip like the men do," she says.

They exchange recipes. Talk about the grandkids. Where you can buy the best bras. But no gossip.

"If you're smart you won't. You never know who's connected in the community," says Mrs. C, balancing a baby on her hip. "Men can skirt out of that much better than the ladies."

The baby is Brooks. Brooks is Cindy Hedstrom's grandson, and Cindy will be at AnTeaQues this morning with the rest of the ladies.

Brooks is eight months old. He is very cute and very smiley and wearing a T-shirt that says "Little Squirt" with a drawing of a lemon underneath. He is one of the neighborhood kids that Mrs. C babysits because her retirement from a thirty-five-year teaching career didn't include knitting needles.

"Work here is never done," she says bouncing Brooks to a lull. "There's always something else that needs to happen."

For the men, that something else could mean anything: tending to cattle, fixing, planting, harvesting, or, if they're retired, helping someone else tend to their cattle, or helping them plant, harvest, fix something.

"I don't think there's such a thing as a retired farmer," she says. Carlson is retired. But he and Mrs. C had supper last night at 9:15 p.m. because he was busy doing something on the farm. "It's a rare man that can stop a lifetime career and just turn it into hobbies, golf, and travel. Maybe in the corporate world. But not a farmer."

The women really don't retire, either. Some of them had their own careers. Others raised the kids. Many did both simultaneously, on top of helping on the farm. On top of making meals from scratch and driving them out to the fields so their husbands didn't have to stop what they were doing and lose precious time.

"A lot of the younger ones don't do that," she says. "They're not taking meals to the fields like we did. And a lot more of the younger ones get frustrated and take a hike. But for most of us, you just put your big girl pants on and do what you have to do. And sometimes, that means be quiet and just listen."

Which can be hard. Really hard. Especially when you're frustrated, irritated, exasperated. When decisions are being made involving things that will affect you, too, and you're the last one to know about them. Like, for example, when no one talks to you about buying another New Holland T5 tractor when you were *thisclose* to having most of your debt paid off.

"It can be a chauvinistic environment," she says. "But you pick your battles."

It also gets lonesome. Very, very quickly. You might be having dinner together, but that doesn't mean you're talking about all the exciting things that happened that afternoon. By the time a farmer has time to sit down and have a meal, he's usually exhausted. Which means there might not be a lot of *How was your day, honey? What did you do?* conversation going on. Just because he got out of the combine to come into the house for dinner doesn't mean that he isn't still out in his bean field. Mentally, it never stops. Farming is not just their job. Farming is their life.

"You're a part of it," she says. "But only when you're needed." And when you are needed, the best thing you can do is be the calm in the storm, whether that storm is an illness, trauma, finances, no rain, or a freak hailstorm in June.

"You're the ocean. Either on top of the wave or under it," she says.

Your cell phone becomes your lifeline. Because while you might not have the time or energy to call a friend, you can at least *text* them. Feel *some* connection. *How are you feeling today? Can you make it to AnTeaQues on Wednesday?*

"The ladies meet for coffee one time a week," she says. "The guys meet for coffee six times a week. What does that tell you?"

When she finally gets Brooks loaded into her Jeep SUV and drives a few miles into town, it's just after 10 a.m. and seven of the ladies are already inside.

Pastor Sandra is here. So is Janet Nelson, a retired teacher; the one who got stuck in the snow in her driveway.

There's Gayle Hudson, who grew up in Courtland, enjoyed a career as an

RN, recently retired, and has been married to Jim—Pinky's morning crew Jim—for forty-three years. "The secret to staying married forty-three years? We both worked," she laughs.

And Cindy Hedstrom, Brooks's grandma, is also here, and promptly takes the Little Squirt from Mrs. C's hands. Cindy was the director of radiation at the hospital in nearby Superior, Nebraska, and is now retired. She is married to Lonnie, who farms north of town. They have ten grandkids. Cindy babysits many of them and attends every single one of their baseball games, which in the summer means she's never home at night. She has a ladybug tattoo on her ankle that she got for her sixtieth birthday while on vacation in Hawaii, likes to mow, and can drive the grain cart. It's nothing unusual for her to get a phone call in the middle of the day from Lonnie, who needs a part because something is not working right, which means she'll pile the grandkids into the car and drive about an hour south to Beloit to the parts store. "My day is always go-go-go."

Cindy also recently gutted a cabin. "By myself," she says. "Want to see the photos?"

The Cabin on 20 Road has modern farmhouse vibes with its covered front porch and galvanized metal backsplash in the kitchen and bathroom. Sleeps five, available for a hundred bucks a night on Airbnb, and enjoys glowing reviews. *This cabin was adorable!*

Jana is here too. She's also married to a Carlson, just like Mrs. C. So, two Mrs. Carlsons. Jan and Jana. "It's caused lots of fun," Mrs. C says. "People always ask, 'Why don't you change your name?' But we already did that! That's the problem."

Courtland, they all agree, is the most amazing place to raise your kids.

"Farm kids get shown whatever needs done. They know how to work and stay busy. Back in the day, most of the kids were riding a tractor before they were ten years old," says Cindy.

"At eight years old, Robert was put out on a tractor without a cab," says Mrs. C. "The worst thing was changing the law so that a kid had to be sixteen to work."

"Kids out here don't often get in trouble because there isn't time to. When they're not in school or helping on the farm they're in FFA, 4H, or heading off to baseball, football, volleyball, or some other practice. That's why the moms are so busy," Cindy says. "Running the kids to all this stuff because the men are too busy."

Regardless of where you live in the world, anyone with kids can relate to the minor havoc that the seemingly endless string of games, practices, and competitions can bring to the daily routine of a household. And while it might take you a few traffic lights and miles to get to the ballfields or gymnasium, more than likely you'll still be home in plenty of time to get dinner on the table, get the homework done, and put everyone to bed at the usual time.

Not so much here. Courtland isn't like your everyday American suburb, where ten others surround you and it's just a quick trip down the road to get to the ballfields. It's a long haul to get to those games, practices, and competitions. Forty miles here. Sixty miles there. Weeknights. Weekends. All the way there. And then all the way back. When Cindy says she's going to one of her grandkids' baseball games, a "close" one is a forty-mile drive.

If your kid plays tight end for the Pike Valley Panthers, you'll be driving an hour and a half east to Axtell to see him play under Friday Night Lights.

If you're grooming the next Mary Lou Retton, you'll be driving forty minutes south to Concordia, twice a week, for practice. When it's competition time, get ready to haul your little balance beamer 166 miles and two and a half hours south to Wichita.

Raising the next LeBron James? Weekend tournaments can be in cities that are a three-hour drive.

And if their after-school activities are taking place during harvest or any other busy farm season, most of the women are driving their kids alone. Although, some of the women say that the next generation of farmers in Courtland are getting into the habit of powering down the tractor even when there's still a few hours of work left to be done, just so that they can be cheering on the sidelines, too.

For the women, both the younger and older generations, none of this seems like that big of a deal because it's what they're used to; it's what their parents did for them when they were growing up. Many outsiders see the remoteness, smaller schools, and driving eighty miles to see your kid play baseball as disadvantages. But many in Courtland will say that all you have to do is turn on the evening news to see how the rest of the world and their oasis of convenience is working out to realize those "disadvantages" are quite advantageous. Between the school shootings, the road rage, and day care that will set you back $1,500 a month per kid? What's there to miss out there?

"It's why we're still seeing young families coming back to Courtland to raise their kids," says Cindy.

Mrs. C, Cindy, Janet, Jana, Pastor Sandra, and Gayle are also very much aware of the misconceptions that people outside of a small, rural town tend to have about the women who live there.

"Like we're not cultured. A little backward."

"We listen to country music all the time."

"That we sit around and knit all day."

Most of the women here wouldn't have time for a knit-purl even if they wanted to. There are kids to raise and jobs to go to, many of which are their own businesses that have nothing to do with farming.

Jenny Russell owns JenRus Freelance, a digital marketing firm.

Sherie Mahin operates a day care from her home on Washington Street.

Shanna and Michelle Lindberg own Soul Sister Ceramics.

Shannon Langston and Linda Swanson keep the doors open at AnTeaQues.

Christy Newman is one of the top producers in the country for Mary Kay and has sold enough products over the past eighteen years to earn six diamond rings and seven Mary Kay cars.

It's funny to all of them, that people think they just sit around and knit. "Oh well," says Mrs. C. It's all about rolling with the punches. Being flexible, really. Because if you want to survive out here, you have to be flexible.

"You can get up in the morning and think you have a plan," Cindy says. "Well, if you're married to a farmer, your husband or son might call and you have to run someone to a field, get parts, give them a ride somewhere else. You are always at their beck and call."

Because even with modern technology, farmers go from sunup to sundown and usually a few hours more. Which usually means so do you.

"You can spend hours fixing dinner for your husband and sons, and then be the only one eating it because none of them can take a break and join you," Cindy says. "No big deal. You just put it in the fridge."

Because there's so much riding on that crop. On that cattle. If you lose a beef cow, there goes your paycheck. If you lose your wheat, there goes your paycheck. And it's not just your economy that's at risk. Because even with the thinking-outside-of-the-box ways to generate income out here, when you've only got 285 people living in your town, your economy is everyone's economy.

And it never ends. Not even when it's supposed to. A retired farmer? Hilarious. Cindy's dad is eighty-nine years old and still tagging cows.

"It'd kill him if he had to stop," she says.

The Entrepreneur

Jenny Russell's got her MacBook Pro flipped open, emails that are pinging, three interns working behind her, and now, an iPhone that won't stop ringing.

"Hey, Owen? I'll call you right back," she says, placing her phone down. "My son," she explains, rubbing her forehead. "I think he's bored."

There's a large bottle of Germ-X, a packet of Extra Long Lasting Spearmint gum, and a pile of folders stacked next to the Mac. Behind her is a sign. "Welcome to the 66939." She is wearing a colorful sundress, black sandals, and gold statement earrings, and her desk faces a wall of tinted windows that stretch from floor to ceiling, which she quickly glances out of before firing off an email.

"It's been one of those mornings," she says, hitting send.

JenRus Freelance was born in 2008, right after she gave birth to Owen. And her company has a laser-sharp focus on rural economic development. JenRus is who you are calling for help with digital marketing, search engine optimization, public relations, grant writing, and whatever else you need to make sure your rural business is running like a well-oiled machine. Her biggest accounts include Republic County Economic Development, Jewell County Economic Development, and now, the Swedish-American State Bank, right down the street. The interns are here for the summer and are all being paid for their time thanks to a grant from the Dane G. Hansen Foundation. Luke Mahin was her first official hire, recently named a partner, and there's a quote from him on the JenRus homepage: "Nothing is a commodity we have in rural Kansas. No traffic. No bad air. No crowds. 'Nothing' is an amenity."

"Nothing ever compared to here," she says. "We wanted to be here."

"We" is Jenny and her husband, Jay, who works at the Swedish-American and farms part-time. They have two kids, Owen and Alyssa, just built a house north of town, and spent three years trying to figure out how in the world they could make it work in a rural farm town with only 285 people.

"Jay would love to farm full-time, but that's not happening. It's too expensive. And when you're rural, you have to do multiple things to make it work," she says. "You just gotta do what you gotta do. But I totally get that it can be hard to make concessions to work somewhere that you're overqualified for."

When someone has one of those "it's gotta be better than this" epiphanies and decides that the hour-long commute, $1,800/month rent, and overall feeling of dread that occurs every time they step into the office just isn't worth it anymore, realizing what those concessions are usually puts the ki-bosh on renting the U-Haul. The trade-off for going from the manic chaos of a metropolitan city to the peaceful, slower pace of the rural countryside is that there's probably going to be a pit stop on the corporate ladder you're climbing, and it might involve working for tips. Which can be a hard pill to swallow, no matter how much you hate your current boss. "If you move here, there's a chance you will have to immerse yourself into the community and take a lesser job for a while until something opens up, mainly because a lot of jobs out here aren't advertised," she says.

But let's say that you're just sick of it all. You've had it! You want to be "Rural by Choice." If you're gung ho about moving to Courtland and aren't living off a trust fund, you'd probably be wasting your time logging onto Indeed.com or trying to hook up with a headhunter.

"Your best bet is to talk to people here about your skill sets. You wouldn't believe how many times someone has said, 'Oh, you do that? My cousin Jake is looking to hire someone who does that.' You can talk to the chamber of commerce. If there's a business in the area that you're interested in and it's run by an older person who's ready to retire, ask if you can shadow them and talk about a possible succession plan. I'd even talk to the banker . . . bankers always have the inside scoop on everything in a small town," she says.

You can also log on to republiccountykansas.com and click the "Jobs" tab. Jenny and Luke stay keyed into all the rural communities in Republic and Jewell Counties. They have conversations. Catch wind of jobs. Read the local newspapers and listen to KREP 92.1 FM for jobs that they can post on social media.

"We actually have jobs coming out of our ears and not enough people to fill them," she says. Jobs like technology directors, dietary technicians, bankers, teachers, parts salesmen, custodians, service technicians, pizza chefs, baristas, truck drivers, cashiers, waitresses, equipment operators, as well as RNs and LPNs with $5,000 sign-on bonuses. The problem is the pay. While the cost of living can be lower here, that doesn't mean that $13 an hour is enough to keep the average 401(k) going strong. There's also the issue of health benefits, which aren't always part of your compensation package. Probably not a big deal if you're in your early twenties and holding a crisp diploma in your hands. But if you're mid-career, the idea of sacrificing retirement packages, saying good-bye to pensions, and making less money than your college-aged kid can be enough to keep you in the rat race, regardless of how miserable you are.

But there's a lot of room to get creative in a small town. "People always said, 'Oh, why would you need something like a coffee shop in a small town? It will never survive.' And yet another one just opened in Belleville and has been doing really well, and Belleville is a town with less than two thousand people."

Coffee shops are sprouting up in a lot of rural Kansas corners. Fresh Seven Coffee in St. Francis (population thirteen hundred) started in 2012 by selling small batch, freshly roasted coffee, and espresso from a trailer attached to a pickup truck that the owners parked on the main drag. It got so popular that they expanded into a brick-and-mortar building, which is usually going full tilt and always gets rave reviews. *I love the urban, artsy vibe!* Now you can buy bags of their seasonal and organic coffee beans, sourced from all over the world, at locally owned shops scattered throughout the state, like Soul Sister Ceramics.

Jenny's mind is always thinking one step ahead because she gets the economic challenges of living in a rural area like Courtland, even for her own business. But she wouldn't exactly lump those challenges into a category marked "Disadvantage." It's one of the reasons she wanted to expand the Jen-Rus office. The old one across the street was getting cramped. There wasn't enough room for Jenny, Luke, and the interns anymore. And there wasn't enough room for the ideas Jenny had to grow her business, either.

She set her sights on 301 Main, a building across the street. The building where the Mayor's family sold farm implements in the early 1900s, and later, Whirlpool appliances. "People will tell us, 'Oh, my grandpa bought his first tractor here,' or 'My dad bought our first dishwasher here.'" After the Mayor retired, the building was sold, used for one thing and then another, sold again, and used for storage. Jenny realized she was running out of space in the old office, asked the owner of 301 Main if he'd consider selling it.

"He was just using it for storage, because the whole reason he had bought it was so that it wouldn't fall into disrepair," she says. "A lot of people do that here."

The owner thought about her offer. Said yes.

"We went half and half with Ag Marketing partners, the commodity broker in town, who we shared the other building with," she says. "So, we both split the cost of buying the new building and also, the cost to renovate it."

When it was time for the hammer to swing, Jenny immediately called Bryan VanMeter, just like Shanna and Michelle when it came time to renovate the old gas station into Soul Sister Ceramics. "He gets my crazy a little," Jenny says. He exposed brick, installed industrial lighting, poured a concrete floor. There's no indication that this is where dad bought the family's first dishwasher. The building that is 301 Main is sleek. Modern. The kind of space most people would expect to see in cities with commuter trains and martini bars, not tucked in between cornfields.

Jenny has plans for the raw space in the back of the building, too. "We could renovate it into an apartment because lack of housing is a huge issue in Courtland. There just isn't much that's available. Or, we could rent it out as an Airbnb," she says. "We'll have to see."

Her mind is always thinking about expanding, growing; both JenRus Freelance and Courtland. It's why JenRus created a new division, 314 Graphic Design, which can handle your website design, print design, and branding. Why they just hired Josey, a professional photographer, and videographer who can add a visual element to the client experience. Why Jenny created coworking space at 301 Main.

"People out here are finally 'getting' the idea of remote work and telecommuting, and really, it's a natural by-product of the 'rural and remote' initiatives that are gaining in popularity," she says.

In the common space that JenRus and Ag Marketing Partners share is a modern kitchenette next to an open conference room, adjacent to two closed offices with sliding barn doors. "These are two of our coworking spaces," she explains. "We rented both pretty quickly. One of the girls sells leggings. Must Love Leggings. Have you heard of them? They have all these wild prints and crazy colors. She has a website and Instagram and sells them online. I'll see her carrying armfuls of orders out all the time. She ships them all over the place. It's crazy, to think that a business like that is based right here in Courtland, Kansas."

Also available are four, open concept coworking spaces that each rent for twenty-five bucks a day, a fee that includes tapping into the WiFi, using the printer, and helping yourself to the Keurig. "If you want those spaces for more than a day, we offer a special rate for a one-year commitment," she says. "You can rent the conference room, too. And it doesn't have to be work-related. We've had people rent it for parties."

She checks her phone and her emails. It's almost noon; she got in early today, but her day isn't even half over. "Last Tuesday was the first time I've been home at night in two months," she says, hitting send.

"Is it tough to live in a rural area like Courtland? Yeah, it's tough. If you don't have vision in a rural area, you're gonna be hard-pressed to make a

living here. But the internet has changed what we can do and how we can work here. I mean, it's not apples to apples compared to working in a large city, but our costs are low, and you just have to ask yourself, 'What's my time worth?' My commute is less than ten minutes with no traffic and no lights. I can bring my kids to work if I want to."

Her phone pings again. Her eyes quickly scan the message, and she fires off a response.

"My goal is to be able to hire a lot of people and make this the best place I can," she says. "I want to make places like Courtland more relevant again."

The Day Care

The kids all come in around 7:45 or 8 in the morning, sometimes as early as 6:30, and they'll stay here all day. Until like, 5:00. Maybe later. "My cutoff is six," says Sherie Mahin. "That's late enough. And it's usually my own son who shows up later than that."

Right now, there are four day cares in town. It was down to two. "That was bad," she says. But now it's up to four again. "So much better." All are home-based.

Sherie Mahin Day Care Home is one of them. She has a maximum capacity of ten kids, is licensed and certified, and has been providing day care for twenty-nine years out of her home on Washington Street, which has a big yard and tidy landscaping. She is trained in CPR and first aid and emergency evacuation planning. "You have to write up all these charts and put them up somewhere. Where are you gonna go if there's a tornado? Where are you gonna go if there's a fire? Where are you gonna go if there's a flood?"

Sherie has watched babies get old enough to go to kindergarten who then go to high school and ask her to come to the graduation ceremony.

"Longevity in day care doesn't always happen," she says. "It's not a high-paying job in towns like Courtland. Here, the pay scale is low."

Sherie used to do a per hour, per kid deal. No contract. Just on faith. And it was fine. Until it wasn't. When she started getting the "Oh, I don't need you to watch him today. He's going to grandma's house," calls and the "Oh, I don't need you to watch her this week, we're going on vacation," calls.

"People would just call, last minute, to tell me that they wouldn't be bringing their kid over," she says. Which was irritating. And kinda inconsiderate. "I never knew what I was going to be doing each day, or even what I was going to be making each month. And I need to know how much I'm making every month. I need a guarantee."

Now she has the parents sign an annual contract. It's flexible, though. "I tell them, 'Look if something changes, just let me know and we'll figure it out.'"

Sherie charges $2 per child per hour and $2.50 per baby per hour. "I'm on the cheap side," she says. "In this area, just because of the pay scale, you don't make enough, but if you jack your price up too much, you're not going to make anything."

So, for about $750 a month, you'll get two kids watched for nine hours or so, five days a week. "In places like Kansas City, it'd be between $800 to $1,200 per month for one kid," she says. Hardly anyone complains about her rates, but occasionally there is someone that does. "I tell them, 'You don't know what high is. Go to a bigger city and see what they'd charge. I am not high.'"

Sherie loves kids. But it is not easy looking after five or six of them Monday through Friday for up to ten hours a day. "I am a cook, cleaner, snot wiper," she says.

Sherie enrolled in the Martin Luther King Jr. Food Program, which gives her money to help feed the kids in her care, and the training that's associated with it counts toward the twelve hours per year she needs to keep her license current and active. About three times a year, a social worker from the food program pops in to make sure Sherie has all her menus written out for the week. Things like hamburgers and baked beans. Carrots and mandarin oranges. Toast and milk. "It used to be we could give formula until they turned one, whole milk until they turned two, then 2 percent from then on. But Mrs. Obama changed that. She said that kids were getting fat. From the milk, though? Are you kidding me? What about the junk they eat all day long? Anyway, we had to switch to 1 percent when they turned two years old. Which is terrible. What are they getting from 1 percent? It's so watered down."

They also do a head count. And if you have more kids running around than the State of Kansas allows, you get turned in. Way back when it was a free for all. As many kids as you could handle. Now, there are rules. Options, actually. Four of them. "I'll read them to you right off of my license," she says. "Okay, Option A: if you have zero children under eighteen months, you can have seven that are eighteen months to five years old and three that are school age."

"Option B: you can have one baby under eighteen months, five that are eighteen months to five years old, and four that are school age."

"Option C: two babies under eighteen months and four that are eighteen months to five years old and three that are school age."

"And Option D: three babies and three that are eighteen months to five years old and two that are school age. Oh, and you have to count your own children, too, until they turn twelve."

Right now, she's at Option A. "No babies," she says.

Monday through Friday, Sherie is go-go-go. Cooking meals and pouring milk and helping with homework and drying tears and wiping snot. "By Friday night, I'm ready for a beer," she says. She likes to get the kids outside during the day. Walk them around town. Get them comfortable with talking to people. "Actually *interacting* with them. What a concept, right?"

She likes to walk them toward Main Street and past Pinky's, so the kids can give high fives to all the guys sitting on the Liar's Bench. "They *love* to give the guys high fives." Then they walk down to the post office. Put mail in the slot. They go down the street and stop by the Swedish-American. "They always give us cookies. On Friday, they make popcorn."

She'll take them to 301 Main to see her son, Luke, and Jenny, and the interns at JenRus. "Those windows are so dark that we can't see in. So, they'll press their faces up close and try not to smudge the glass. Jenny always says, 'We look forward to seeing these kids every day!'"

They'll walk back to the house around 10:30, and Sherie will start cooking lunch while the kids watch Sesame Street. Lunch is at 11:30. Storytime around one. Then, a nap. "Until about three . . . or whenever they get up." They'll eat a snack, go to the mini-park or the swimming pool. She'll help put on swimsuits and swim diapers and apply the SPF to prevent sunburn. Sherie loves taking the kids outside. Getting them out of the house. "It's good for them," she says. It's good for Sherie, too. "I need adults to talk to."

Sherie will do this Monday, Tuesday, Wednesday, Thursday, Friday. "No weekends," she says. "Well, my kids usually find things to do on the weekends, so I have my grandkids coming over and spending the night," she says.

Finding day care in Courtland can be tough. "Especially if you're a newbie," she says. A lot of people end up calling Luke for advice. "Not because he's my son. Because he's with the Republic County Economic Development office," she says. Luke will get them in touch with KansasChildAware.org. He'll give them the website, the 800 number. ("Speak with one of our knowledgeable Resource Specialists!")

"You can also just beat around the bushes and ask around," she says. "Talk to people at your new job or your church to find out who has openings. Sometimes all four of us are full. It's that bad."

Right now, Sherie is full. And even though she's pushing strollers and pouring milk and wiping tears and helping out with homework five days a week, she rarely takes a day off.

"If you're your own entity, you can't find just anyone to take your place,"

she says. A substitute has to be licensed, certified, have all their vaccinations up to date.

"I feel bad for people. I do. It's why I hardly ever take off. If I'm on vacation, who is watching the kids? One of the other gals who runs a day care in town is about to have a baby and will be taking six weeks off. I told her, 'Girl! You should have planned that so that you would be giving birth in the summertime.' And that's the risk you run out here. What do you do if your day care provider goes on maternity leave and they shut down for six weeks? It's not an easy fix. That's when you have to call grandparents, neighbors, or friends to help. And those people aren't going to be licensed. So, it's gotta be someone you trust."

The Ranchero

The Ranchero 500 came from Missouri. Rigged up with a three-speed on the floor and a bumper sticker in the back window: "GET IN. SIT DOWN. SHUT UP. AND HOLD ON!"

"My son found that," says Steve Brown.

The Ranchero is white with red stripes running up the center of the hood. Six hundred turbo now. Steve wants to jack it up to 900. He keeps it in a garage, right there on the north side of town. Easy access when he feels like blowing off steam.

Two handprints are visible in a layer of dust covering the dashboard. "Probably from my wife when I took her out yesterday," he says, maneuvering the Ranchero slowly down Main Street. It's growling. Low. The smell of gasoline clinging to everything in the cab. The rain that Steve, Larry, Carlson, Kenny, Hootie, Slug, and Joerg were praying for finally came . . . and then, wouldn't stop. Three days of nonstop rain. Three days of big green blobs on the radar. Which turned their fields into quicksand, and now no one can get their equipment on the dirt, which means that corn planting has officially ground to a halt.

He pulls to the edge of Main, right past the last house in town; nothing but Highway 36 in front of him, and cornfields on either side. A quarter-mile stretch. The perfect drag strip. He puts his foot on the brake. Puts the other one on the gas. Rear fishtailing. Tires squealing. And then, launches. The Ranchero fishtails left. Fishtails right. Straightens out just beyond the big hay bale stacked by the side of the road. Hits 60 miles an hour . . . 90 . . . 110. And then . . . nothing.

"Fuck. I think I dropped the transmission," he says, the smell of burning rubber filling the air. "Shit," he says, trying to throw it into third again. "Damnit!"

Puttering at ten miles an hour, closing in on Highway 36. Hand on a sterling silver shifter, finally catching third.

"There it is," he says.

He rolls to the stop sign. Looks left. Looks right. One foot on the brake. One foot on the gas. Rear fishtailing. Tires squealing. And then, launches. A full circle. Then another. Then another. Right in the middle of Highway 36. Tread marks burned into asphalt that'll still be there six months later.

Rolling back down Main Street, a low growl heading toward Freedom. Comes to the intersection. Looks left. Looks right. Foot on the brake. Foot on the gas. Rear fishtailing. Tires squealing. And then, launches. A full circle. Then another. Then another. Right in front of Pinky's. People staring out of windows. Stopping on sidewalks.

On a gray, overcast Wednesday in the middle of the afternoon. After three straight days of rain. When he and Larry, Carlson, Kenny, Hootie, Slug, Joerg, and every other farmer in town would rather be out in the fields. Running equipment. Getting their corn under the dirt. But they can't. So, they wait. Find something else to do. Until it's time to start farming again.

"Oh, Mylanta," he says, staring at the tread marks burned into the middle of the street. "Welp, everyone will be bitchin' about this on Facebook. Everyone."

The Date Night

"They told us to bring a snack," Jennifer says. "What do you have?"

"Chips," Luke replies. "And salsa."

"Do you *have* salsa?"

"Yes."

"Do you have chips that aren't open?"

"I'm not sure."

"You can't show up with an open bag of chips! It's weird!"

"It's not weird."

"It is weird! And that salsa is old! You cannot pack that. Pack something that's not used. Ugh!"

It's Saturday night. Date night. No beer festivals or ski trips or concerts this weekend. Nothing in Nebraska or Colorado or Kansas City. So, it's a toss-up between playing Booray at Ashley and Dave's house at 7:30 or going to the Lazy Horse Winery, which is like, an hour and ten minutes away.

"No, it's not. You make it in forty-five," Jennifer says.

"Well, whatever; we can go and get woodfire pizza. I like the wine better, though," Luke replies.

"I like the wine better," she agrees. "Better than the beer."

"The pizza is expensive."

"Superior Winery sells frozen pizzas for like, eighteen bucks!" she says.

"Well, compared to that it sounds good. But otherwise, it's expensive," he replies.

"Do you have money?" she says. "Ashley said to bring money for the game."

The drive to the winery would have been fine, but it's gray and kinda cold outside, and they're just not in the mood. Jennifer and Luke have never played Booray. They've never even heard of Booray. But Ashley and Dave are part of a group that plays cards, and one of the couples had to bail tonight. So, they invited Luke and Jennifer to fill in.

"Are we seriously driving to their house when it's right around the corner?" she asks.

"Do *you* want to carry the cooler? And it's also raining."

"We'll drive," she says.

He and Jennifer load the cooler into his SUV and circle the block. There are already a handful of cars parked outside of Ashley and Dave's house. It is red with white trim, has a covered front porch, a nice front yard, and looks like something that would get a lot of likes on Instagram. Ashley grew up in that house. Now, she and Dave are raising their two kids there. Ashley's parents, who are also part of the card club, live behind them in a log cabin. They tell everyone who is coming through the door to grab a plate and eat, eat, eat from a massive spread of potluck on the kitchen island.

The Mayor is there, but probably won't be able to stay long. "I'm on call," he says. "Tibbetts-Fischer has another one for me."

Carl is there. Served in Vietnam and then Saudi Arabia and most recently, as the auctioneer for the 5 lb. Art Auction at the Courtland Arts Center. Forty-seven people attended and raised almost $3,000 for the annual summer art camp by bidding on everything from legitimate art to weirdly packaged mystery gifts, the only common denominator being that they had to weigh five pounds.

"I thought there were going to be younger people here," Jennifer says quietly over the chip n' dip.

"It's a mix," Luke whispers back.

After everyone has had plenty to eat, eat, eat, the group splits in half. There are five people in the dining room with Luke, five in the breakfast nook with Jennifer, and a lot of Booray rules to explain to both of them.

Like: "If you stay in and don't take any tricks you have to match the pot."
And: "You always have to play any card higher than what's been played."
As well as: "You have to follow suit. If you have a club, you have to play it."
So, basically: "Big cards in any set are good."

"I have no clue what's going on," Jennifer says, sipping a beer wrapped in a koozie that says "Love You Till the Cows Come Home" as the group tries one last time to explain it.

"Booray is kinda like that game . . . the poker one that everyone plays?"

"Texas Hold'em?"

"Yeah. Kind of. But not exactly. So, I guess not. It's just . . . Booray."

Each of the chips in the Booray game is worth twenty-five cents. The biggest pot ever won during card night was like eight or nine bucks. Ashley won it.

Money Britches!

"It feels a little bit like poker," Luke says as Ashley deals. "But I told them that if Jennifer is better at this than me then I won't play."

When Luke was single, he and some of his friends used to have a Poker Night. They'd drive half an hour east to play with some guys over in Cuba. But then everyone started getting married and having kids and that was the end of that. This is why, about every other day, people want to know when Luke's going to pop THE QUESTION.

"*I haven't gotten my invitation yet!*" they hint. Hint, hint.

"*Do you have a ring packed?*" they ask whenever Luke and Jennifer go on vacation. Hint, hint, hint.

"*Okay, so when are you two getting married?*" they push when they get tired of hint, hint, hinting.

"Next week," Luke will tell them. Always, *next week*.

Some people probably think that living together is living in sin, especially the Catholic church he and Jennifer attend in Belleville, but Luke doesn't really feel bad about it.

"Economics and lack of housing is why I don't feel bad about it," he says.

And he did finally pop THE QUESTION a few months later.

"So," everyone immediately wanted to know. "When are you gonna have kids?"

A few weeks after she got the ring, Jennifer drove an hour south to Downs, Kansas, and said "Yes to My Fairytale Dress" at Schoen's Bridal World. They registered on Amazon and had engagement photos taken by Josey, who works with Luke at JenRus. Photos that included Gus, who sported a brand-new plaid handkerchief handmade by Jennifer's mom. The photos of Gus and his sideway glances got a lot of likes on Facebook and Instagram. Way more than the photos of Jennifer and Luke, looking very cute and very in love under a very beautiful Kansas sunset.

"Ridiculous," she says.

The Body

"Duty calls," says the Mayor, flipping his flip phone shut.

It's Saturday night. Nine thirty. The Mayor is in the middle of drinking a scotch on the rocks at the Booray game at Ashley and Dave's house, where Jennifer and Luke are finally starting to get the point of the whole *you always have to play any card higher than what's been played* thing.

He has two stacks of chips in front of him. A good hand. And now, a body to pick up in Salina that has to be driven to Hebron, Nebraska, to get embalmed.

"We'll stop at McDonald's," he says. "Get something to eat. The people I'm picking up don't complain if we stop at McDonald's. They don't say much of anything, actually . . . "

Might as well. It will take him an hour and a half to get down to Salina and even longer to get up to Hebron. It'll be five o'clock in the morning before the Mayor gets back home to Courtland.

It keeps him busy during retirement, this duty. The calls come morning, noon, during Booray, at 2 a.m. Whenever.

It's why he wore the Dockers, button-down shirt, and a sport coat to the Booray game. You just never know when you're going to get the Call.

"The Death Call," he says.

He gets another one three days later. This time, to transport the body that he took up to Hebron back down to a crematorium in Salina, and he'll do it in a gray, late model Chevy minivan with 105,000 miles on the odometer.

Randy is one of the shareholders of Tibbetts-Fischer and the owner of the Chevy van. He and the Mayor are golf buddies.

When you retire, you're going to come work for me, Randy had informed him.

The Mayor figured he'd be helping with the funeral service. Getting people to sign the guest book. Offering sympathetic smiles and sincere condolences.

Uh, no, Randy informed him. You're gonna help with removals.

Removals can take place anywhere. From homes, nursing facilities, hospitals, hospice care; wherever you die is where you need to be removed from. Which can get sticky when there's a lot of you to remove.

"It's why we like little people," the Mayor says.

And whether you weigh ninety pounds or four hundred, when you're dead, you have to get to the funeral home somehow. Which is when Randy will pick up the phone and call the Mayor.

"Are you in a condition for driving?"

"Yeah," the Mayor will reply.

He'll get an address, fire up the minivan, and get moving with the removal. The one he's driving today had been in the mortuary refrigerator at Tibbetts-Fischer because it took a little while to get all the paperwork filled out, signed, and filed. This is a normal process, one that can take anywhere from no time at all, to so much time that you wait out your final moments above the ground in a refrigerator.

In the back of the van is a cardboard box. A very long, impressively sturdy-looking cardboard box, inside of which is the body.

"It's a cremation container," he clarifies.

Scrawled across the top in thick, black magic marker is the only important information left about the person inside: name, date of death, funeral home, funeral home location. It doesn't matter if you were a multimillionaire or living under a bridge. When your time's up, everyone gets put into a big cardboard box.

"Cremation container," he corrects.

The cremation container costs thirty bucks and comes with a very tight lid. There are two plastic handles at the head and the feet so that it can be pulled, pushed, or carried. The box is one-size-fits-all, and if the person inside isn't exactly petite, they sometimes use tape to keep the lid shut.

The Mayor adjusts the van to the speed limit on Highway 81, attempts to put it in cruise control, realizes cruise control isn't working and puts his foot back on the gas. He likes short-distance hauling. Some people will drive all over the place, but the furthest he'll go to transport a body is about two hours south to Wichita. Any further and his back starts to hurt thanks to three surgeries and too many years of lifting appliances for the family business.

He has no idea what would happen if he got into an accident with a body in the back of the van. "Good question. I don't know. It never happened." He's never gotten pulled over and wouldn't have a good excuse if he did. "What am I going to say? I'm in a rush to get to the crematorium? What's the hurry?"

He's never been weirded out by anything, although transporting small boxes will get to him. "Young people are the worst," he says. "Older people have lived their lives. Had a good life."

About halfway to Salina, he flips open his phone, scrolls down to the number for Mortuary Crematory, and dials.

"Good morning, this is Tim with Tibbetts. I'm in Concordia heading your way with some work for ya . . . "

The Mayor doesn't really care if he's cremated or buried when he dies, because really, why would he care? He's dead. Randy has big plans for him, though.

"He wants to put my remains in a fish bobber, one of those red and white ones. Or, a golf ball."

A lot of funeral homes have someone that works full-time transporting bodies, but the Mayor only does this part-time even though he's pretty much on call 24/7. "I've hauled, oh, maybe fifty to a hundred bodies over the course of two W-2s." His schedule varies. Sometimes he'll go days without getting the Call, the busiest he's been was transporting three bodies in one week, and once he had a double delivery and had to stack the boxes.

He really doesn't remember much about the first body he transported, and the best part about the job is feeling like he's helping people. Making everything right for them at the end of their road.

"Most people who know me can't believe I'm doing it," he says. "They all want to know if I *like* doing it. Well, if I didn't like doing it, I wouldn't be doing it, I guess."

He takes the exit for Salina and turns left at the light. He drives past strip malls and into a residential neighborhood where kids are riding bicycles and moms are pushing strollers. He pulls the minivan into a partially fenced parking lot surrounding the back of a nondescript building with three garage bays and faded yellow siding. "Mortuary parking only. Unauthorized cars will be towed." The Mayor backs the minivan into one of them just as the door slowly starts to open.

Standing inside is the funeral director, wearing a crisp, white button-down shirt and a red and blue tie. He wheels out a mechanized lift and helps the Mayor lift the box onto it, rolling it back into the crematorium, which looks like your dad's very clean garage. Close to the wall is a large, shiny metal box.

"That's the cremation chamber," says the funeral director.

With the press of a button, the chamber will be preheated to somewhere between 1,400 and 1,800 degrees and in one to three hours will make good on the whole ashes to ashes thing. At the foot of the chamber is a black metal container filled with things that look like old, rusted car parts that are really all the screws and plates and rods that were holding people's bones together.

Before leaving, the funeral director hands the Mayor a new cardboard box, still in need of assembly, which he then places in the minivan to take back to Tibbetts-Fischer. He adjusts his seat. Gets back onto the highway and hits cruise control, then remembers cruise control isn't working. He puts his foot on the gas, flips the visor down, and settles in for the drive.

Transporting bodies hasn't made the Mayor philosophical about life and death. It doesn't fill him with inspiration or despair or make him panicky about creating a bucket list. He doesn't bother wondering about when it'll be his time, when he'll be making his final ride, in a cardboard box that costs thirty bucks and is placed in the back of a gray, late model Chevy minivan.

"It's just a job," he says.

The Transplant

"I have no idea why they call me the 'transplant.'"

Dan Kuhn thinks this is funny; the fact that he's been living in Courtland since like, 1979, and has been president of the Courtland Pride Club for over twenty years, but people still call him the "transplant" just because he was born in Ohio.

He and his wife Kathy own the Depot Market. Farm fresh produce and the only one of its kind for a hundred miles. A rainbow of zucchini, asparagus, tomatoes, cherries, green peppers, and peaches sitting tight in bins displayed in front of shelving lined with jars of golden honey and amber syrup that's been poured into glass bottles shaped like a maple leaf. "U Pick Blackberries!" reads the hand-painted sign outside, where you can get a pint or a quart of berries that are perfectly ripened and melt in your mouth.

The Depot Market is very cute, radiates Norman Rockwell vibes, and is hard to resist while speeding along Highway 36, so most people don't. It has a red door and batten siding painted periwinkle blue with bright white trim. Outside are giant farm wagons filled with homegrown ripened watermelons or color-coordinated piles of fat pumpkins and knobby gourds arranged next to the door.

The whole thing started with some apple trees, even though orchards aren't a dime a dozen out here. Farmers in Courtland have the land to grow them. They kinda have the weather. But growing apples isn't really their thing.

"LABOR-INTENSIVE!" the farmers say.

This is because you can't roll your combine over an acre of apple orchards and expect things to end well. Someone has to be out there picking the apples one by one by one . . . by hand. And because it is so labor-intensive, most farmers don't hesitate to say, "Pass." Especially when you're already spending

eighteen hours a day, seven days a week, babying a thousand acres of wheat, beans, sorghum, and corn, in addition to your four hundred head of cattle.

Dan went to the University of Kansas and studied the classics. He spent a semester in Inishbofin, Ireland, a remote island off the coast, where he learned a poem a week and started getting dreamy about rural life. "I was a city kid," he says. "I didn't have any farm background. I didn't have any family who had land. It was just nuts. Stupidly idealistic."

When he returned from Ireland, he shipped off to Alaska to work on the pipeline in the summer of '75 and '76. Got some money in his pocket. Started thinking even more about his stupidly idealistic ideas. Like, Jonathan apples. He couldn't stop thinking about Jonathan apples. *With all my heart I would like to raise a family in an orchard in Kansas,* he thought. So, he figured he might as well rent a few orchards in Manhattan, Kansas, just for two growing seasons, just to see how things went.

And things went okay. Which meant that all the stupidly idealistic ideas began to seem not so stupid after all.

While he was studying crop protection at K-State, the phone rang. It was a buddy who lived two hours northwest of Manhattan in some little farm town named Courtland.

Come up and visit!

"Okay," Dan replied. So, he fired up his green, 1969 Chevy Pickup that he bought for $1,700 and drove two hours to Courtland, which was very rural and remote and vast and just felt like . . . freedom. "I remember driving around thinking, 'I can do whatever I want here.'" And it was kind of a weird feeling because farming wasn't such a hot endeavor anymore.

The early 1970s had proved to be intensely lucrative years for the American farmer. Grain exports had soared on the heels of a surprise demand from the Soviet Union, which caused US farm incomes to spike 50 percent above the national average. As a result, banks started getting looser with their funding, approving more loans for farmland purchases, around the same time that interest rates were conveniently, and appealingly, low.

This enticed existing farmers, and all of the would-be farmers, to make land grabs, buying more acreage while taking on massive debt, all under the assumption that the good times would continue to roll: commodity prices and land values would remain high and interest rates would remain low. The boom did not last very long. Within a few years, the bubble was bursting with the rumblings of a catastrophic economic avalanche that would come to be known as the 1980s Farm Crisis.

Between 1973 and 1980, four embargos had been placed on our agricultural exports. The first came in the summer of '73 when a ban was slapped on all exports of soy and cottonseed products to counter high soybean prices and concern about our domestic supply. The second and third embargos came in '74 and '75 when we put a delay on sales to the USSR and then the USSR and Poland due to droughts. By 1976, South America suddenly emerged as a major soybean exporter, giving us a run for our money, around the same time that the value of the dollar increased, world economic growth slowed, and our farmers were having bang-up years of production. The fourth, final, and infamous embargo came when President Jimmy Carter decided to put a partial halt on grain sales to the USSR— punishment for the invasion of Afghanistan—resulting in a massive blow to the American farmer's bottom line.

Then, the Federal Reserve tried to rein in inflation to deflate interest rates that had spiked as high as 21 percent on bank loans for major purchases like houses, which in turn caused the value of farmland to tank 40 percent in Kansas, after seeing land values surge as high as 200 percent in the 1970s and plummet up to 60 percent throughout the rest of the Midwest.

By the time President Ronald Reagan lifted the embargo on grain exports to the USSR in 1981, our commodity prices were already going south, we had produced way more than we could sell, and farm debt was beginning to bloat, spiking to $216 billion by 1984.

Then came the massive, widespread bankruptcies, foreclosure of family farms, and horrifying news stories about farmers who got so depressed, they cocked the barrel of a .22 and put it to their heads, sometimes after killing their family members as well as their bankers. The economic crisis spread like a disease; affecting suppliers in fertilizer, seed, and farm machinery sales, the railroads that hauled agricultural products, the mills that processed products, and the shippers that shipped it. One domino into another. Rural banks closed. Schools closed. Local businesses went bankrupt. And then, entire towns began to disappear. Experts dubbed it the worst economic crisis since the Great Depression.

Things got so bad that in the spring of 1985, droves of farmers rode their tractors all the way to Washington in protest, descending on the White House and driving black crosses into the ground in front of the USDA building that represented each farm foreclosure or suicide victim. The rapid decimation of the American family farm would be immortalized by John Mellencamp in his Top 40 hit, "Rain on the Scarecrow." In an attempt to cauterize the wound, President Reagan made drastic reductions to the prices of our agricultural products to try and stimulate foreign demand and reduce our surplus and offered farmers the opportunity to borrow money from the government, pledging their crops as collateral, but the mass exodus of Small Town USA continued.

"Oh, gosh, but not me," Dan says. "I *wanted* to be in a small town. How nuts."

By the time K-State had handed him a degree in 1979, Dan had packed up his then-wife—who was also pregnant with what would be their first of seven kids—and headed to Courtland. He got a job managing thirty acres of apple orchards three miles north of town. "When I moved here, I wasn't so much about the town of Courtland. I was all about farming and rural life. It took a while for the town to become an object of my affection."

North Central Kansas was very hot and very windy with very fickle weather. "Not a very good meal ticket," he says. "I really loved growing apples. It was an adventure. Some years were really good and some really sucked . . . but it was a thing I knew how to do."

He started planting more. Things like tomatoes, zucchini, asparagus, peppers, and sweet potatoes. Eventually, things started to ripen and grow, and in the late eighties, he had an epiphany.

"We had been selling apples a few miles north of town, and I was smart enough to know we needed to be retailing as much as we could, and to be on a federal highway was ideal. So, I bought an acre of land next to Highway 36. And one day, I was driving through town and saw that old train depot, which I had seen hundreds of times before, and thought, 'Wouldn't that be cool?'"

The old depot he was falling in love with was vacant, falling apart, and propped up on concrete blocks. A fading beauty born in 1888 to the Atchison, Topeka, and Santa Fe Railway Company, which used it as a depot for passengers waiting for a shiny Super Chief engine to come chug, chug, chugging down the tracks, which they did for almost a century. But then people became enamored with the interstate highway system, grew tired of the chugging engines, and stopped riding on the railroad. When that happened, the depot was shuttered and abandoned.

So, Dan bought it for $3,500.

He hired a father and son team to move it. Another $3,500. They took two days to jack it up and load it onto a flatbed, then lifted all the cable TV and power lines along Main Street to transport the old depot 1.2 miles north to the acre of land Dan had bought along Highway 36.

"They drove about one mile an hour. Probably less than that," he says. "The dad was pulling one Winston after another the whole way."

When they got to their destination, they set the old depot gently down on the newly constructed foundation, wiped the beads of sweat off their brows, lit a celebratory Winston, and waved good-bye. And while Dan got to work getting the building wired and plumbed, tearing off lath and plaster, and replacing all the windows that had been broken over the years, members of the Courtland Pride Club volunteered to scrape layers and layers of peeling paint before giving it a fresh coat. Three months later, the Depot Market was open for business.

"I thought we'd cut a fat hog in the butt," he says.

When their first day ended, he had sixty-five bucks in the cash register.

"Not exactly a fortune," he says. But it didn't send him running for the hills, either. He was already kinda used to life not exactly taking you from point A to point B without a few twists and turns and detours along the way.

Dan and Kathy had first met when they were lab partners in a fruit science class at K-State. It was those blue eyes, she'll say. That dark hair. "He was full of life. And all he talked about was how he was going to get married, live in the middle of nowhere in a house with no electricity, and grow apples."

After the semester ended, she didn't see Dan again until fifteen years later. At the time, she was working in Kansas City for a hardware company that owned eighty stores and bought a lot of pumpkins from some guy named Dan Kuhn.

I wonder if that's Dan from K-State? she thought to herself.

It was. And soon, they were talking on the phone almost every day, filling orders for the pumpkins he was growing; which they continued to do for the next twelve years, during which Kathy dated a few guys who were just . . . OK.

Why can't I meet someone like Dan?

But she didn't. Which turned out to be a good thing. Because a few years later, Dan and his first wife divorced. And a few months later, he asked Kathy out on a date. It was August 2005. One year later, they said, "I do."

"I dropped my family, friends, a great job, and moved here," she says. "My parents still say, 'When are you gonna come back to Kansas City?' I don't think they get it . . . they've only visited here twice."

The Depot Market employs thirty or so people when they're in full swing for the season, which runs from sometime in June until sometime in October, depending on how finicky the weather is and how much growth is happening during the growing season. Most of his employees, the ones who are out there handpicking the apples and the watermelons and the pumpkins, are Mexican; documented visa workers. Of the 285 people in town, only two made it known that they weren't too happy about their seasonal neighbors.

"Many in our community are fond of the Depot and can put two and two together that all those vegetables have to be picked by someone, and probably not by anyone local," says Dan. "Most Courtlanders see that they are peaceful men, and marvel at their hard work in tough weather conditions. People who work hard in rural communities are respected."

It's not like he hasn't tried hiring locals. He did at first. And at first, it worked. But then, it didn't. He ended up with the same deal that Betty did at Pinky's and Shannon and Linda did at AnTeaQues. "Locals doing manual labor became fewer and fewer," he said. So, he started hiring Mexicans, who were happy to take the job. Dan pays them $14.30 an hour and covers their travel to and from Mexico. While they're working for the Depot Market, they stay at one of the three houses in town that Dan and Kathy own, do their grocery shopping once a week at the Walmart located twenty-eight miles south in Concordia, and then send the rest of the money back home to their family.

Most of his workers keep to themselves while they are here, but when they pop into Pinky's to grab a Mountain Dew out of the cooler, all the morning coffee guys wave.

Hola!

"I wish there was more interaction between them and the community, but language and culture are a tough barrier to overcome," Dan says. That's not to say it never happens. Every year, the Depot Market hosts a fall festival; pumpkin decorating and face painting and sometimes live music, but always a meal. Sixty people usually show up. A few years ago, Dan's Mexican workers volunteered to cook the meal. They went grocery shopping, bought all the ingredients, and 200 people in a town of 285 showed up asking for seconds. "It was a miracle we didn't run out of food."

Almost everything that people buy at the Depot Market is grown locally or made locally: fruits, veggies, honey, cheese, farm fresh eggs for $2.99 a dozen. Kathy came up with the idea for slushes that churn in a machine behind the counter: flavors like strawberry and peach. One hundred percent fruit. She also started selling homemade ice cream, making small batches, and using ingredients like Ugandan vanilla beans that she hand cuts on a butcher block and heavy cream for flavors like Coffee Caboose and Maple Nut.

And the retail side of the business is good, but the demographics and remoteness of Courtland are what inspired him to expand into the wholesale market. Pumpkins are his biggest crop.

"We loaded seven semis in one day," he says.

And the whole apple-growing thing, what Dan used to dream about when he was at K-State, ended in 2003. Things were just changing. Back in the eighties, most of the women in town were into the idea of farm food storage, canning anything they could into mason jars, including lots and lots of apples.

"In the span of ten years, the women that were canning weren't anymore. They were in rest homes. And the younger generation wasn't interested in staying at home canning apples. They were interested in having a career. It was a real cultural shift," he says.

The apples they sell now are from Missouri. But that's about to change. Dan and Kathy are getting into high-density apples; a less labor-intensive and more sustainable, efficient, and profitable way of growing them. "We've had all of these younger people coming in and saying, 'My grandma used to bring us to the orchard when we were a little kid and we'd go home and make applesauce and I have the fondest memory of that.' So, that's what we're trying to bring back."

They're also into agritourism with the u-pick blackberries and the corn maze and the pumpkin patch in the fall.

Kathy and Dan love rural life. Being close to nature. "That rhythm," he says. "It's artificial in the city. You're not aware of the wind blowing, the sunsets, the birds, the changing of the seasons. It's a great thing to be close to nature . . . but it's also a bad thing to be close to nature. Bugs. Mud. But we're all living it together."

It's like a song, he says. The harvest, the planting, the weather.

"You do what the weather lets you do," he says. "There's a lot of freedom out here, but it's all dictated by the weather. It's like a cosmic dance that you all do together. Super busy. Super not. Everyone in it together. It's a beautiful thing."

It's the human relationships they like best about living in a small, rural town like Courtland. "You can't throw people away. You can't be anonymous . . . which is one of the greatest things about living here and one of the worst," he says. "But you also have a much greater level of trust than you do in a big city. You have to be accountable. This is why you generally trust people more out here. If you have trouble, people will help. There's a great deal of patriotism and a love of the community. There's a sense of pride here, which is strange, because really, what do we have? It's just a little cow town. It's like the rich kid that gets everything for Christmas but takes it all for granted, and the poor kid who just gets one thing that he really, truly treasures. Well, who's richer?"

The Morning Coffee: Saturday

With the right weather, everyone could be out planting corn. All they need is a good rain, but not too much. And a little bit of sunshine, but not so much that it removes all the moisture from the rain.

They could use a good rain to fill the ponds. A real gully washer. Even if the rain moves the dirt around and they have to hit the fields with a hiller to clean out the debris between each row of corn. It'd be worth it to get a gully washer and a 70-degree day.

"I want to start planting Thursday," Slug says, sipping his coffee.

"Good luck," Steve laughs, peeling off his coat. Gray T-shirt.

They're supposed to get rain tomorrow. Good and bad news. Good for the pastures and the ponds. Bad for getting the corn in the ground. All the drizzling rain did from the past few days was wet the thick layer of dried, cracked topsoil and turn it into mud. Just enough to cause the wheels of the tractors and planters to sink and get stuck. What they needed was a good rain to seep deep into the soil and get it ready to be planted.

If Steve doesn't plant his corn today, he'll go feed the cattle. String some electric fence. Drink coffee. Work on the planter. No plans for the Ranchero. It's back in the garage.

"I'm not going to plant until Slugger does," Steve says. "He doesn't make a mistake. You know, if I had gone on and done what I really wanted to do, I wouldn't have to worry about the damn corn."

What Steve really wanted to do was join the Marines. But he didn't. "My father and my fiancée are why I didn't," he said.

He could have worked for the state, too. Or got a job making fifty bucks an hour working construction. But the union. Telling him what to do. *You can't work on that equipment, only this equipment.* "Fuck that," he says. "The union was great at first but then it just became a bunch of bullshit."

"You know," Joerg says, "those bricklayers make a hundred grand a year."

"No doubt," Steve says.

"And those crane operators?" he adds. "In one of those sky highs? A million a year."

"Oh, easy," Steve agrees. "If they can find someone to work in them."

"This younger generation; they want everything handed to them," Joerg says.

"No doubt," Steve says.

"And they don't realize that the government is eventually going to run out of money, that it's the middle class that's paying for all those things they want handed to them."

"Absolutely," Steve says.

Most of the farmers here have told their kids to go out and try something other than farming. Steve did. And Joerg, his kids graduated in the eighties, when things were *really* bad. He didn't want his kids to go into farming, either. Slug's son likes to farm, but being a farmer didn't work out so well, so instead, he drives a semi-truck hauling grain.

"I told them to get educated and see the world. Farming will always be here," Steve says. He doesn't lie awake at night, worrying about whether the fifth generation of Browns will take over the family farm when he retires. And right now, between getting rain but not enough and worrying about sunshine but not too much, he's not in the mood to wax poetic about the strong minority that is the American family farmer. "There's always some dumb idiot who wants to farm. It'll all be corporate one day anyway."

Steve, Larry, Slug, Hootie, Kenny, Joerg, and Carlson don't need to see the statistics because they are the statistics.

"The corporate farms have gotten bigger and bigger while the family-owned farms are becoming fewer and fewer."

"Yeah, because it costs too dang much to farm."

"You can't compete with them big guys."

"You used to be able to own a thousand acres and make a good living. Now, a thousand acres is considered small."

"You really have to grow up with farming to want to be a farmer because 90 percent is learning the work ethic. It's a way of life more than anything."

"Hard work used to get you something. It used to get you somewhere. Not now. It takes too much money to do it."

"They say that the pill and the tractor was the downfall of the country. The tractor because it took out the horses and the handwork that went into farming."

"Want to know why no one wants to live here?" Kenny asks. "We don't have a single shoe store in Republic County."

"What about Walmart?" someone asks. "Down in Salina?"

"That's Cloud County," Steve says.

"Not one shoe store or one clothing store," Kenny continues. "It's why city women don't want to live here. We were down at Walmart last weekend and you could barely move, it was so crowded. Everyone would rather haul it down to Salina to go shopping than buy anything local."

This is because there *are* no clothing or shoe stores to shop at locally. Not in Courtland or anywhere in Republic County, really. Because when a cold snap catches you off guard in the middle of August and you realize you didn't pack anything more than T-shirts, everyone will direct you to the closest option: the Dollar General, twenty miles east in Belleville, where you can grab a hoodie with the Republic County High School Buffalos logo on the front for fifteen bucks. Your only other option *is* to haul it down to Salina, an hour and twenty minutes away. This is why Jennifer used to come up with all sorts of excuses to drive there; so she could actually see/touch/buy outfits and shoes. Cute stuff.

"I guess most of the women are happy living here, though," Joerg says.

"Ehhh," Steve says, tipping his hand side to side.

"I don't think city women would be happy here. Not every woman is happy on the farm," Kenny says. "But most women have their own careers now anyway."

"My wife worked as a nurse in Belleville," Joerg says. "She made thirty an hour which was seventy-five grand a year. Plus insurance."

"That money helps when things are bad for us," Kenny says.

"Definitely," Joerg agrees.

"But some women don't work because they want to help the farm survive. Some women work because they want their own thing," says Steve.

Some women also want the conveniences that they take for granted living elsewhere, like having a grocery store that's not twenty miles away and closes at 7 p.m. every night and an ambulance that doesn't take thirty minutes to get to their emergency.

"Well, it takes a few minutes to just start it up," Don, who just retired from a career as an EMT, explains.

The ambulance is coming from the Republic County Hospital in Belleville, which, like the Dollar General and the grocery store, is twenty miles away. And while there are no traffic lights or stop signs along Highway 36 between there and here, depending on where you live in town, there might be a set of railroad tracks that can keep your emergency vehicle waiting in the middle of your emergency.

"That happened only once," Don says. But still. So, if something bad happens, chances are good that you'll just have to wait. And if you really live far out in the country, on one of the dirt and gravel roads like Jade Road, you'll just have to wait some more.

"You only die from two things," Don says, trying to be reassuring. "Cardiac arrest or respiratory arrest. Everything else can wait twenty minutes. And I honestly believe that people will do the best they can when they find themselves in an emergency. They can get pretty resourceful."

He still gave out his cell phone number to almost everyone in town, because when you're bleeding or in severe pain, it might be hard to remind yourself that if you are breathing and your heart is beating, you're good.

"You can always call your neighbors, too," he says. This is because there are a surprising number of nurses floating around. So yeah, got an emergency in Courtland? Call 911, then the neighbors, then Don's cell, and if he's not out on the Harley enjoying the retired life, he'll be there ASAP.

"Here's the thing: if you live here, you know what to expect. So, like in the case of a woman being pregnant, when you go into labor, you don't wait. Women here go to the hospital as soon as they feel something happening. Some of them choose to go to OB/GYNs all the way down in Salina, which is over an hour away. You know that you're not going to have the same kind of conveniences that you have somewhere else, right? We give up certain conveniences for certain privileges," he explains. "Like, not having to lock our doors at night."

Out here is not for everyone. They all agree on that. And neither is farming.

"We had some really good years," Joerg says.

Like back in 2012 and 2013. The drought pummeled most of the Midwest, which wiped out most of the supply. *That was a damn shame.* But then, a silver lining: demand. Lots of it. Wheat and corn trading for $8/bushel.

"Hell, beans were close to $18/bushel," Steve says.

Not like now. When everyone's getting beat to hell with low commodity prices, with the cherry on top being the staring contest between the United States and China over tariffs that began with imported steel and aluminum and got very interesting when China slapped a 25 percent tariff on American soybeans. Which is going to hurt. In 2017 alone, China bought 60 percent of our soybeans; a $12 billion chunk of change missing from the agriculture industry's wallet.

"*Horrifying,*" the headlines scream. "*Devastating to American farmers.*"

"There will be some winners and some losers," Joerg says. "Probably some short-term losers, but in the long run, we'll be alright. It's worth it to even the playing field."

"Tariffs or not, people are in trouble *right now*, because the market has been so bad for years," Steve says. "Another guy bowed under. Actually, two of them. Both had to sell a section."

"Which is why it's *so* important to be smart. You *really* have to be smart," Joerg says. "Thank God, though, it isn't as bad as it was in the eighties. When interest rates were like, 18 percent."

"That happens now," Steve says, "You might as well close the door."

Interest rates are at 6 percent now.

"Six isn't bad," Joerg says. "But you have to learn to put money away for a rainy day."

"Diversify, big time," Steve adds.

Diversification became a thing in the aftermath of the eighties. When farmers were advised *not* to put all their eggs into one basket. Literally. Planting twelve hundred acres of corn? Better get some cattle to offset a commodities market that's in a tailspin.

"And don't try to keep up with the Joneses by trading in your tractor every year," Joerg says. "This market can change in an instant. You know those steel and aluminum tariffs have caused the cost of everything to start going up. If a pickup or vehicle goes up two to three hundred dollars, a tractor will go up five hundred to a thousand," he says.

The market, the weather. The tariffs. The high cost of operation, the low profits from yields. No one in the farming industry has any problem understanding why there aren't a lot of younger guys who are willing or able to embark on a lifelong career that tends to operate like a roll of the dice.

"I didn't know enough about farming. That's why I got into it," the young farmer admits. "Plus, I helped my dad when I was younger, so that's probably how I got the bug." And he really did try the real-world thing. After he got his degree in wildlife biology, he took an internship for six months just outside of St. Louis. "It was all I could handle," he says. "No regrets. None that I want to admit yet. Because we're pretty happy here with the kids."

"How much rain did you get out at your place?" Steve asks, checking the radar.

"I got fifty-five hundredths," Don says.

"I didn't put my gauge out," Slug says. "I have to remember where I put it."

"I got sixty-nine," Joerg says. "My favorite number. But anyway, back to the tariff . . . "

"How come you're being so nice?" Betty accuses Joerg on her way to the griddle.

"I'm not! I'm being . . . myself!" Joerg replies innocently.

"Yeah, right," Betty says. "You're *behaving*. That is *not* yourself."

Joerg has about thirteen hundred acres. He used to have an additional two thousand he shared with Carlson. "I backed off of that," he says. "Hell, I'm going to be seventy-five years old. I got tired."

Tired of fixing fence.

Tired of wrestling cattle.

Tired of the market, the weather. Because always; the market, the weather.

"Tell the real truth," Don says, "You want to drink and play golf."

"I do," Joerg says. "But I'm not a fan of Tiger Woods. Not because he's black! Because of things he's done."

"I can't believe you," Betty says, shaking her head as she cracks open some eggs. "How good you're being."

"You bring out the worst in me!" Joerg says. "You're seeing my true self now."

"I might try to plant my corn today," Steve says, changing the subject again. "Although I know it's not gonna work. The ground is still too wet."

"To be or not to be," sings Jim as the front door swings open. "That is the question!"

"The Pollock's here," someone says.

"And the democrat," says someone else.

"Hey now," Jim says, heading over to the Bunn in his KU T-shirt.

Stupid Jayhawks! Get a new shirt, Jim!

"Oh, shut up," Jim says, refilling everyone's mug.

"Sign the book!" Steve says, pointing to the List. It's Don Long's birthday.

He's not here yet. But he usually comes in at eight, so no one is worried that he won't pay the coffee tab.

"You know what his nickname is?" Joerg asks. "Dong Long."

"Stop," Steve interjects.

"What?" Joerg asks, all innocent again. "He hates it when we call him . . . "

"Just stop," Steve interjects again.

When the door swings open at eight, Don Long walks in and everyone starts yelling.

"We need another tablet! This one's full!"

"Thanks for the coffee!"

"Happy Birthday!"

"Twenty-nine and holding?"

"No one was worried that he wouldn't show up and pay the coffee tab," says the other Don. "We know where to find him. And besides, Betty would kick his butt if he didn't pay."

The Average Sunday

Betty's got two deep fryers in the commercial-grade, stainless steel sink, scrubbing them clean with a big, wiry, silver scouring pad, a few feet away from the sticker on the kitchen door that says "Men are from Mars, Women are from Genius." The front door is locked. Somebody will still knock on it and want a Pepsi or a Snickers and Betty will let them in even though she's closed because it's Sunday. Everything on Main Street is closed on Sunday.

QVC is on the television hanging above the coffee maker. *Sundays with Carol and Dan* is on until noon.

"Amazing!" The hosts exclaim as a Shark IONFlex DuoClean sweeps up a row of Fruit Loops from the studio floor. "Six easy payments of $29.94."

Yesterday afternoon, when the guys came in to get a snack, *Little House on the Prairie* was on the television. Someone got sick and tired of what the weatherman had to say, and the Hallmark Channel seemed like a good alternative. Anything but the news. As soon as Betty's son, Ricky, left for Afghanistan, she stopped watching the news.

"I couldn't handle it," she says.

Ricky just retired from the air force after twenty years. Now, he just works for them. Which is why he's in Afghanistan and QVC is on instead of CNN, or MSNBC, or FOX.

When Ricky told his mom he was joining the air force way back when, she asked, "You know what you're doin'?"

Don't get her wrong; she was very proud of her son. She was also very scared. But she got it. He wanted out of Clifton, Kansas; was tired of seeing the same five hundred people doing the same things all the time. When Ricky joined the air force, he did and saw things that he never would have been able to do otherwise. Like, go to the Philippines. Germany. Twenty years of serving his country, although he doesn't like to talk about it.

Dad, did you ever shoot anyone?

"He won't talk about it when his kids ask that question," she says. He never talks about any of it.

Ricky was supposed to be in Afghanistan for ninety days, but he'll be leaving soon because his wife found a lump in her breast. Pastor Dwight at Living Waters and Pastor Jake at Covenant is keeping the two of them on their prayer lists, which is nice because it's hard to find time to go to church since Betty comes into Pinky's on Sunday to clean.

"Who knows?" she says. "Maybe one of these days that will change."

Betty is worried about Pinky's. Business hasn't been good because the market, the weather; everyone is getting beat up right now. It's just been so slow. And there's so much she'd like to do to the place.

She *really* wants to reopen all those fourteen rooms upstairs. Since there are only two bathrooms, she dreams about turning seven of the rooms into nice-sized bathrooms.

"A bathroom for every room!" she says.

But she never did hear anything from the historical society, she doesn't have three hundred grand to renovate the upstairs, and Wayne didn't seem too hip on the idea, so, oh well.

"I can dream," she says.

People keep telling Betty that she needs to take a break from Pinky's. Get away for a bit. "But what am I going to do?" she asks. She doesn't drink. Doesn't play cards. Doesn't drink coffee. Doesn't knit. She likes it here. Doesn't always like working seventy-seven hours a week, but what else would she be doing? Retirement was boring.

"Pinky's is a part of me if that makes sense," she says.

Sundays haven't been the same since Mikesell died. Everyone has their own opinion on what happened, but, really who knows?

Betty misses him. "I miss him a lot."

When Betty closed Pinky's in the middle of the day to go to his funeral, worrying the entire time that she smelled like a French fry, she managed to keep it together until she watched them close the casket.

"That's when I lost it," she said. It didn't even *look* like him in there. "He really tried," she says. "When he was sober, he went to every one of his kids' games. He was so proud of his kids."

Betty gets it. She's so proud of her kids, too. Proud of Ricky for serving his country. Proud of Tammy for working four to six jobs to put her kids through college. Proud of Shawn for being the head of maintenance at the company he works for.

And she was proud of her foster kids, too. She never counted how many she had over those seventeen years. All she ever wanted to do was give them a home and the love they deserved. Some of it was good. Her foster daughter

Mary went to nursing school. Became an LPN, then an RN, and is now going for her master's.

Some of it wasn't so good, though.

Taylor committed suicide. And one of her other girls, the one who Betty felt wanted to be loved more than anything, eventually found an older man who swore he *would* love her more than anything. Then, he killed her.

And eventually, Betty got tired of having a knife pulled on her and being shoved against the wall by some of the kids she was trying to help, tired of feeling like the system was more concerned about money, that they didn't care about the kids who were falling through the cracks. When she started fostering kids seventeen years ago, she got $15/day per kid. When she stopped fostering kids, she was only getting $18/day per kid. Three bucks more than she got seventeen years ago. Because the system, excuse her French, has gone to hell.

"It's not about money," she says, "but that's ridiculous."

Even now, it's not about money. "I live on the tips I make," she says. "Every dime I have gets put back into this place." Her retirement, every bit of her life savings, has gone into Pinky's. So, when people tell her to take a break from it, to get away, where in the world do they think she is going to go? "I have nothing else," she says.

If things don't pick up, she doesn't know what she's going to do. She might have to tell Wayne to sell the place. Figure out something else. "My shoulders are sagging right now," she says. "But thank God it's not up to me. It's up to God. And it will be okay."

Wayne tells her all the time that she wears her heart on her sleeve too much. That she's too nice for her own good. Because as soon as someone needs help, Betty will bend over backward to give it to them. She did for the father of the little girl she had fostered. He needed a car. Betty cosigned the loan. "That was stupid," she said. Because the father stopped paying for the car. And then the bank called. "I took the spare key down to them and they repossessed it."

And she's still kinda worried about the brewery that the Mahins are opening down the street. "I'm worried it'll cut my throat," Betty says. "But it'll all work out."

She loves it here, but no, it's not perfect. Even in a town of only 285 people that would go to bat for you, some will take advantage of you.

"Someone, who shall remain nameless, who also still comes into Pinky's almost every morning for his coffee, and was just in yesterday afternoon, owes me a thousand bucks. And he won't pay it because he says I pad his bills and insists that he doesn't owe me that much. He gets away with everything. I've seen it happen over and over and over again. And I don't understand it," she says. "But the funny thing is that I still *like* him."

The Morning Coffee: Monday

No one planted any corn yesterday.

"Maybe today if I can get the tires on my planter. 'Bout flat," Steve says. Despite a very cold 40 degrees outside, he is wearing another gray T-shirt.

"How's it workin'?" Larry asks.

"What?"

"Planter."

"Still in the building."

"Hmmm."

"Wasn't no one runnin' yesterday. Everyone was sittin'."

"I'll be damned."

"They're sayin' rain at noon."

"Yeah, they're talkin' rain again."

"I need about another half inch. Drove the whole fence on the inside. Saw two plants, two little leaves. Did a u-ey and left. The only ones runnin' in the field weren't doin' shit."

"Need any?" Slug asks, going straight for the Bunn.

"Nope," Larry says.

"Fine," Steve replies, holding up his Styrofoam mug.

It's 5:55 a.m. Betty is behind the bar at the register, counting money. There's an 80 percent chance of rain that just got dropped down to 60 percent, and all anyone can talk about is how much they need this rain to keep it goin'—until Slug mentions the liver and onions.

"They're serving it at noon over at The Barn today," Slug says.

"Oh yeah?" Steve asks.

"Yeah," Slug replies.

"Might have to head on over," Steve says.

Larry might head over, too. Liver and onions sound good. "Tastes good," he says. People don't know what they're missing.

"You go to a restaurant and they say it's Grade A, Number One Angus Beef bullshit when it's probably a chunk of fucking Holstein and you don't know it," Steve says.

"When that hide is off you don't know what it is," Larry agrees.

Joerg is worried that there's a hole in his fence somewhere that his cattle are going to get through.

If Steve can't get to planting, he might string some fence. He took the Ranchero out yesterday with his wife. "I was nice," he says. "Real nice. The only time she screamed was when I reared up and dropped the front end on 36."

"I wish you'd do that after the corn and beans were planted," Larry says, giving him a look.

"No one was runnin' yesterday!" Steve insists. "Maybe I'll go castrate some bulls today." Pick 'em up, drop them on their side. Knee in the flank. Knee in the neck. Top hind leg forward and let the other guy do his business with the razor. "I've castrated nine hundred pounders," he says. "They make good sandwiches. Mountain oysters. Delicious."

"I'm telling you, they were all over the damn place when that truck crashed on 36," Joerg says. "Think of all the mountain oysters we could have had!"

"Well," Don says, taking his seat at the round table. "How was Colorado?"

"Good," Larry says. "All I hear on the radio is how bad the wheat is. There was only a five-mile strip from here to Pueblo that didn't look good. But the ponds . . . so many of 'em are dry. Almost every pasture between here and Pueblo, the ponds are empty. I saw two dead critters that had just sunk in the mud."

"Eighty percent chance of rain today," Don says.

"They just dropped it down to 60," Steve replies.

"I lost my cap, too," Larry says. "Pisses me off royally."

"Sure you got another one," Steve says.

"Not with Courtland, Kansas, on it," Larry scowls.

"Since no one was doin' shit yesterday, if the weather cooperates, we'll try and plant today. Maybe tomorrow," Steve says.

Slug is still planning for tomorrow. Kenny *might* plant today. And everyone will try not to fall asleep while they're planting.

"Everyone has fallen asleep at one time or another while planting. You wake up when you hit something," Steve says.

Larry woke up just before he plowed into some trees down by the river. It happens.

"You know when you're drivin' your car and you hit those rumble strips?" Larry asks. "Well . . . same thing. Or when you're driving to Belleville and get to daydreaming and manage to blow past Scandia without realizing it? Same thing. Which is bad. Especially with all those damn golf carts crossing the highway."

And no, just because your tractor or combine or whatever has GPS doesn't mean you can just take a snooze while it does the work for you. "GPS doesn't see shit," Steve says. "It doesn't see pivots, poles, trees. Plug those coordinates in and it'll drive you around the world, but it will get caught up in anything standing in its way."

"The hardest thing about GPS is sittin' there, watchin' them tires swayin' and not grabbin' the wheel," Larry says. "Then, you look behind you and see all those rows perfectly straight. Amazing. Just amazing. You know, technology is great, but the equipment is so damn expensive now. Hell, you'll pay the same amount for three combine heads as you did forty years ago for all your machinery. And the rules and regulations?"

"Shit," Steve says, shaking his head.

"All happened when the Dems got in," Larry says.

"I remember drinking milk right out of the tit," Joerg says. "That was kinda rude . . . teet. The neighbor girl always wanted me to squirt it right in her mouth."

"Hell, I used to drink it straight from the bucket, right after the cow put its hoof in it," Kenny says.

"Things are different now. When I came here in the summer of '74, everyone had a farrowing house and hogs," Don says.

"There's just five in Republic now," Slug says. "Eastern part of the county."

"Margins got so small. All corporate now."

"Same with the eggs."

"Can buy them cheaper than you can raise them."

"You can go to the store and get Grade A Jumbos for eighty cents. They still callin' for rain?"

"Down to 60 percent chance."

They need the rain. Bad. Something that does more than get the fields all muddy. They need to get those ponds filled. They're so low. About three-quarters empty. Steve looks at the radar again. Something's coming. "Sonovabitch is movin' real quick," he says. There's a yellow blob over Osborne. Everyone's hoping. Everyone remembers '92, how dry it was, what that engineer said. *Lake will never fill again. Not in our lifetime.* They remember how wet it got in '93, how it flooded.

"No one ever saw him again," Steve laughs.

But even if it doesn't rain a drop from now until June, they'll still plant their corn. You still plant even if you're worried that whatever you put into the ground is going to wither out and die. Everyone does.

"Sometimes you hit, sometimes you lose," Steve says.

"You just have faith," Larry says.

"When we need it," Steve agrees, "it will rain."

The Memories

Norm Hoard is about to pull out of the gas station in his brown Chevy Silverado when he stops abruptly and throws it into park.

"Need to get my passenger," he says, slowly opening the door. "Boone!"

His chocolate lab runs over and jumps into the backseat. Norm climbs back in and pulls out onto old Highway 36; heading a few miles west before turning north on 20 Road, dirt and gravel spitting out from underneath rubber treads, rolling over railroad tracks, past pastures with Red Angus grazing and pivots sitting idle in the middle of brown cornstalks that have been shredded down to stubs. Dry fields; fields that should be getting ready for new corn to be planted, but always, the weather.

"Just another mile," he says, eventually turning the Chevy into the Bergstrom's sheep farm. "Well, there it is."

It's sitting at the end of the gravel lot, in the shadow of towering metal grain bins. A little cottagey looking thing; a miniature house with a peak above the door and two windows. The original Standard Oil office that he bought when he was nineteen, right after he married Doris.

"If these walls could talk," he says, opening the door. "A lot of bullshit went on!"

He kept the pop machine that sold Royal Crown and Coca-Cola against the wall to the left. In the summer, they'd move it outside so people traveling by on Highway 36 could grab a cold one and be on their way.

"My desk was over in this corner," he says, pointing to the right. "Oil heat. We had electricity, but that's about it. A lot of memories in here."

Like the first tubeless tire he changed; it belonged to an old Buick. Like the night he got robbed, after he had closed for the night and went home—a block east—to Doris.

"You want to stop people from robbing this joint?" his friend had said. "Hang up an old shotgun on the wall."

"The next time I got robbed, they stole the gun," says Norm.

He remembers slick guys who would come in and quick change him, acting like they wanted to purchase something for fifteen or twenty cents, handing Norm a $20 bill. As he counted out their change, they'd grab that money, along with the $20 and the fifteen- or twenty-cent item they were "buying" and make a run for it.

He pauses, looks around again. Smiles, and then puts his hand on the door. He wishes he hadn't sold it. Wishes it wasn't sitting here in the shadow of the metal grain bins.

After a few years, when the station finally started making some money, Norm told Doris that he wanted to buy some land so he could farm. She let out a big sigh. *Okay, Norm.* He'd close the station for the night and head out into the field, where his 320 acres of alfalfa, wheat, and oats were waiting. It was after midnight by the time he'd get home.

"For forty years, I kissed everyone's ass. 'Yes, sir,' 'No, sir,'" he says. "Out on my farm, I could sing, whistle, whatever. And I loved it."

The Morning Coffee: Wednesday

The donation box is held together by tape decorated with orange and red flames. It is nailed to a support post at the bar, and underneath is a red bin filled with Tootsie Pops. "HELP OUT THE GOOD OLD BOYS AND SUPPORT A NEW BIG SCREEN TV."

"I don't know how much money is in there, but it's not that much," says Betty.

It's well before dawn. Larry's the first one in this morning and has the red lid to his white travel mug shoved into his coat pocket.

"Was good it rained last night. Good it's raining this morning," he says. It's cold and gray outside. Wet. First time since September, really, that they've had a soaker. The gully washer they've been waiting for, the one to fill their ponds. "Can't plant anything, though," he says. "We'll plant when it dries up."

Which probably means that everyone will be planting late. And if farmers are planting late, they'll be harvesting late, too.

"I've had all the pickin' corn in snowstorms I've wanted to do," he says. "You know, I wonder when all that water they have allocated from Lovewell Lake will be reallocated to the cities. Pumped into water systems and out of the canals and laterals and irrigation pipes here in Courtland," he says. "Those cities, all those people needing water . . . ag's already regulated to death. And the water, I can kinda see that happening next. It's always somethin'. I heard on the radio this morning that the American farmer makes pennies on every food dollar spent."

This is a problem that is not new, keeps getting worse, and has been primarily responsible for squeezing the American farmer to death for almost a hundred years.

"Because the money goes to the middleman, the government, the traders, and God only knows who else. All anyone knows is it sure doesn't go to the farmer. We don't have built-in profit margins," Larry says. "All those middlemen do."

Middlemen are anyone standing in between the American farmer and the consumer. Steve and Larry Brown don't get to determine the selling price of each bushel of wheat, corn, or soybeans they produce; neither do Joerg, Kenny, Slug, Hootie, or Carlson. The American farmer is *told* what they will sell it for as per the Chicago Board of Trade. What happens to the price of something like wheat after it leaves the grain elevator has nothing to do with them.

If an elevator wants to pay a farmer $4.65/bushel of wheat and sell that same bushel to a miller for $5.65, no one's stopping them. After all, they need to cover transportation costs to where that wheat is going as well as the cost to store the wheat in the elevator, and good margins mean good business. This is why if the miller wants to raise the price another dollar and sell that same wheat to a food processor like Sara Lee for $6.65, there's no one stopping him, either. It's why the American farmer ends up getting a $3 cut from the forty-two loaves of bread that will generate a total of $125.58 in profit.

This is also why they're only going to reap a profit of fifteen cents for every American dollar that is spent on food this year. Never mind that it was the farmer who was out there babying his wheat for the past eight months. Never mind that he's still getting paid either the same amount of money, just slightly more, or even less per bushel of wheat than dad got in 1973 or great-grandpa got in 1920. Never mind that it takes $3 million in loans just to get an average Joe farm up and running these days.

Larry wishes the government would just stay out of it. Keep their policies to themselves. "I once paid $250 to attend a marketing conference in Salina. The first thing out of the guy's mouth from the Board of Trade was, 'If we don't make these markets move up and down, we don't make any money.' Who's the *we* that you think he was talking about?" Larry asks. "Not *us*. And let me tell you something about government subsidies. I don't want a damn handout. All I want is a fair, honest price and I don't get that. Why do I still farm? We was born into it. Raised in it. What about those other jobs? Why be a fireman? Why be a cop? It's open season on cops these days. Although, now everyone is talking about how we need to get rid of guns."

"We'll give up our guns one bullet at a time," Joerg says, grabbing a coffee pot from the Bunn.

"We'll give up our shells," Jim adds as his mug gets filled.

"The only thing locked up at my house is my gun safe," Larry says. "Two in the pickup that I have every day, though. I forgot the damn combination to the safe, but the wife knows it."

"It'd be a civil war all over," Steve says. "The streets will run red with blood." And he believes it. It's the same thing he told that reporter down in Kansas City, the one who had a cameraman, a microphone, and a question for him as he was buying another gun to add to his collection.

"The bottom line is that guns don't kill people, people kill people," Don says. "And it won't get the guns away from the bad people," Joerg adds.

"No way," Larry agrees. "It'll be like prohibition. You couldn't drink anywhere but there were two stills out here."

"There are still a few," Steve says. "That white corn," he whistles. "That'll tickle your tonsils."

"We have a white side and a dark side," Jim says.

"We're not racist!" Joerg says.

"Well, I didn't mean that!" Jim explains.

"We're *not* racist here. Just those damn Democrats that bother us out here," Larry laughs.

"Come on," Jim says.

"You're not really a Democrat," Joerg says. "You just like to try to get Kenny all riled up. It's a basket of deplorables out here. And no one minds if someone is on welfare, either. We don't mind giving it to someone who needs it."

"Not at all," Larry agrees. "But when you see someone walking out of Walmart with a huge bag of dog food, a huge bag of cat food, pop on one side of the cart, and a bunch of crap in it that they used food stamps to get, and then buy cigarettes with cash, that burns the *hell* outta me!"

If people were smart, everyone concedes, they would not be so damn dependent on everyone else. If people were smart, they would come *here*. People *should* come out here. Learn a thing or two about how to survive. "Do you know what alfalfa sprouts look like? Can you walk along the river and know which tree bark you can eat in salads? Can you butcher an animal? Cut up a chicken? We do," Larry says. "Out here, we have fish, turkey, rabbit, livestock. Out here, if you go hungry, it's because you're lazy."

"I guess I should say that we have a good side and a bad side, not a white side and a dark side," Jim says.

"Finished 5–2 against Milwaukee last night," Don says, checking the score on his phone while Carlson and Joerg discuss the strong possibility of heading over to Belleville for Hamburger Night at the country club.

"I can't believe you guys," Betty says, taking a break from the eggs she's frying on the griddle. "Why aren't you acting like yourselves? You're behaving so well."

"Turns out, I did have a hole in my fence, but they didn't get out," Joerg says. "Thank God. I once had a whole herd, about fifty, sixty get out. They lay down right in the middle of 36. A semi came along and since it was dark, didn't see the Black Angus until he was up on them. Took out five or six. The state had to clean it up. There were a few guts hanging."

It's getting close to 8 a.m. The conversation has been as schizophrenic as the weather. The rain that started last night hasn't stopped. No one can plant. Everyone will find something else to do.

Kenny will probably work on his truck and tractor.

Slug will take his sister-in-law to Salina.

Steve will probably go feed his cattle. "Make sure they're not out on the goddamn roads."

So will Larry. "Even when it's raining and nasty out, you still have to check on your livestock," he says. "You take care of your livestock and 99 percent of the time they'll take care of you. That's your livelihood out there."

SUMMER

Commodity Prices (per bushel)

	July 1920	July 1973	July 1984	July 2018
Corn	$1.50	$2.47	$3.08	$3.41
Wheat	$2.45	$3.05	$3.46	$4.97
Soybean	$2.68	$10.08	$6.33	$8.19

The Morning Coffee:
Wednesday

Steve is the first one into Pinky's this morning. Just a few minutes shy of 6 a.m. Gray T-shirt. Not looking forward to what he has to do today.

"So," Betty asks. "How bad is it?"

"It's bad," Steve says.

His cattle are somewhere out in the pasture. About 140 of them. Who knows where? Some might have gone in one direction. Some might have gone another. Last Saturday, one of the neighbors decided to set off some fireworks during the Fourth of July. Eleven of Steve's cattle heard the *boom, crack, hiss,* and took off running.

"They're like women," Joerg says when he arrives half an hour later. "A mind of their own."

"No one ever believes this story, but I'll tell it anyway," Larry says. "Fifteen years ago, I found two cows. Nice cows. Calves with them. I asked everyone, but no one claimed them. They were branded, but not in the Kansas book. Well, one day I'm up in Superior at the vet, thumbing through their branding book and damn if I found them."

So, Larry called the farmer. He lived in Franklin, Nebraska. Eighty miles from Courtland, Kansas.

"You're pullin' my leg. Where do you live?" the farmer asked.

"Courtland, Kansas," Larry repeated.

"How in the hell did they get down there?"

"They followed that damn river," Larry said. "That's what they done."

Two days later, the farmer drove down to Courtland. Saw that the cows were his. Cows that had been missing for the past four years and somewhere along the way, had managed to get bred.

"Let me pay you something for your trouble," the farmer said.

"Hell, they've only been on my pasture for two, three weeks. I don't want nothing," Larry told him.

So, the farmer took them back to Nebraska. Which was a shame. "Damn nice black cattle," Larry says. "I woulda kept 'em!"

People find cattle that don't belong to them in their pastures all the time. The only people who don't have cattle getting out are the people that don't have cattle. This is why no one really gets annoyed when they find your cattle in their pasture. Except when you're that *one guy* in town.

"He never fixes his fence," Don explains. "So, the cattle are always getting out and end up all over the place. They'll cross 36 and get into the cemetery. Then they rub up against the stones and knock them over. That cemetery is so old. I think it's from the 1800s. So, if a cow starts rubbing against a stone it just falls over."

Joerg's cattle got out last week. Through the gate or something. Crossed Highway 36 and went for a mile or two into Carlson's pasture. "Thank God they didn't get into anyone's damn corn. They get in there, you can't get 'em out. They are not dumb animals. They see you coming and turn around and go in further," he says.

When Joerg went to pick them up, nine of them went into the trailer without a problem. Two took off. They caught one and chased the other one. Never did get him. They ran him and ran him and ran him until he got tired and flopped down in the grass. "That was it," Joerg says.

The steer's still there, in almost the same spot that they left him. There's not much you can do when a twenty-four-hundred-pound animal decides it's not moving.

"I'll have to dart him and pull him into the trailer," Joerg says.

"You have to remember that these are steer, not women. You can't sweet-talk them," Larry explains.

So, probably sometime this week, Joerg will go out and dart his steer. Maybe. Today he's going golfing up at the country club in Belleville. Hamburger Night. Wednesday is also Golf Day; when Carlson, Joerg, and two of Joerg's old friends, Jerry and Bill, hit the green. The usual foursome. But Carlson has been fishing up in Canada and isn't sure he'll make it back in time for golf or hamburgers. And since Jerry has something to do today, it's looking like it'll be a twosome.

"They'll probably just go to the nineteenth hole," Steve says.

"Geez," Joerg says, shaking his head. "No, I will actually *play* golf."

"Is that what he calls it?" Steve asks Don.

"Well, he shows up," Don says.

"We play eighteen holes," Joerg insists. "Then we have three beers. Maybe four."

"Maybe six," Steve says.

"Well, we start at 1 p.m. and are done about four-thirty, quarter to five. But they don't serve food until six so we have to drink until six. Then we'll eat our burgers. Be home by seven," Joerg says.

"In the morning?"

"No!" Joerg insists. "Not in the morning."

"Boy Scout," Betty says, shaking her head.

"What?" Joerg asks innocently, holding up his hands.

While Joerg is out golfing and Steve is out rounding up his cattle, the sun is going to be blazing.

"Ninety-eight today," Steve says, checking his phone. "Cool day tomorrow. Ninety-seven."

"At 7 p.m. last night, the temperature on the bank said 100 degrees," Slug says.

"In 1954 it hit a high of 111 degrees today," Larry says. "I remember that. Four, five, and six, dad never picked an ear of corn. It all burned up."

It burned up because there was no irrigation in 1954, '55, or '56. No Lov'll Lake. No canals. No laterals. One guy in town decided to dig a well and put some pumps in, but otherwise, if you wanted rain in Courtland, you had to wait for God to give it to you.

Not like it matters right now.

"It's so ungodly hot and humid that corn can't take up moisture fast enough to sustain itself. Doesn't happen often but it does happen," Larry says. "I've seen corn burn up standing in water."

Eighty-eight degrees and a little bit of rain would be perfect for their corn right now. But they're in a hot spell. Which happens every year. Some years are just hotter than others.

"We get a lot of extremes," Larry says.

"Eighty-four next Wednesday. Hurry up and get here," Steve says to the radar on his phone. "It's a week out, though. Watch. It'll end up being 105 with no rain."

Despite the rain and the mud during the spring that threatened a late planting season for everyone, Steve got his corn under the ground by the first of May. Most of the other farmers did, too. And everything was fine until the storm rolled in a few weeks ago. Seven inches of rain in two hours. A green blob on the radar that stretched for four hundred miles; from Beatrice, Nebraska, back to Garden City, Kansas.

"Came in from the northeast, which almost *never* happens. The damn ground was so dry, and the rain came so hard and for so long that the water started running off of the soil pretty quickly," says Steve.

It wiped out fencing, caused flooding, and gave everyone a headache.

"Piles of corn about two feet deep pushed up against the fence," Steve says. "Or, what was left of the fence." By the time that green blob was done with Courtland, Kansas, the only thing that remained of Steve and Larry's fence was a post or two and a tangle of knotted wire.

"That corn washed down from about half a mile north," says Steve. "But you never hear about that on the news. If that had happened in Missouri or the three "I" states, it'd be all over the news."

The three "I" states are Iowa, Illinois, and Indiana.

"Big corn and bean country," Steve explains. "The Board of Trade in Chicago always talks about the three 'I' states. We're just peons out here."

The Lambs

There are 150 lambs that need to be wrangled. And there are three people and one dog trying to get them out of a pen and into a Wilson trailer that's headed six and a half hours east to Minnesota.

"Come on babies," Quinten Bergstrom urges. "Come on!"

Baaaaa!

"Is that fifty head?" the buyer asks.

Baa! Baaaaaaaa!

"I counted fifty-one," Quinten's wife, Melissa, replies.

Baaaaaaaaaa!

"When they say to count sheep, this is what they mean," Quinten laughs. Quinten is a fourth-generation livestock farmer, buys and sells all classes of sheep, and always looks like he's in a good mood. Always smiling. He is wearing jeans, a red and white polo shirt, and rubber boots, trying to shepherd his herd with what looks like a plastic oar for a canoe. "Sit, Buddy!"

His dog immediately drops his hindquarters, waiting patiently for permission to start helping again, which he does after a few minutes, bringing up the rear.

There's a lot of separating going on. Separating the lambs from one pen to another. Separating the mothers away from the lambs and into another pen. Separating the separated lambs into a separate group of about fifty. "It's like a puzzle you have to piece together," the buyer says.

Everyone is trying to convince the lambs to run up the ramp and into the trailer heading to Minnesota. Including Buddy, who's still faithfully bringing up the rear.

"Come on, babies!" Quinten urges again, tapping hindquarters lightly with his oar as the lambs just stand there.

"Tsssst. Tssst. Tsssst," Quinten urges again.

"Hup, hup, hup!" says the buyer.

"Tsssst. Tssst," says Melissa.

An hour and a half later, 150 lambs have been loaded, Quinten has his check, and the truck and trailer are heading toward Minnesota.

Selling 150 head of lamb in one clip is nothing. Back in the day, you'd see semi-trucks that were able to carry 350 lambs *each* lined up alongside the road, just waiting for the Bergstroms to hand them a check. Which they'd do. Buy the lambs, fatten them up, and sell them. Or, buy them as fat lambs on a commission basis, then turn around and sell them to a packer. The Bergstroms would be buying lambs all day long.

"Now it takes us a week to buy three hundred," Quinten says.

His dad, Marvin, was just a teenager when he got his first lamb. It came from the neighbor, this little woolly thing that was so sickly looking. But Marvin nursed it back to health. Afterward, anytime he got a little bit of extra money, he'd go over to the sale barn to buy more lambs. And eventually, he got so good at picking them out that the packing plants started calling him. *Hey, would you go look at some lambs for us?*

"My dad had a love of livestock," Quinten says.

Back then, the sheep market was good. *Really* good. Big flock farms would put their sheep out to pasture in Wyoming, North Dakota, and South Dakota to fatten them up, then bring them home to feed on cornstalks left over from the harvest. A lot of the meat would get shipped to Mexico where people considered it a delicacy and would sit around the dinner table and ask for seconds. And it didn't matter if you had ten head of lamb or ten thousand; sheep would get sheared every spring and everyone would take advantage of the wool and mohair subsidy.

The subsidy came into existence after the United States became concerned about its declining sheep and wool industry, and as a result, realized it was importing half the wool needed to uniform soldiers shipping off to fight in World War II and then Korea. *Let's reduce dependence on foreign fibers,* politicians said. *We can insulate our producers from foreign competition.*

Congress signed the dotted line on the National Wool Act of 1954. The USDA was put in charge of calculating the rate of the wool price support payments to stabilize the market. In 1988, that rate was 29 percent. The national average price for wool was $1.38. The wool price support level was pegged at $1.78. So, wool producers received a payment of twenty-nine cents for each $1.00 of wool they sold. "According to USDA, using this percentage method, rather than making a uniform flat payment per pound of wool sold, encourages producers to obtain higher market prices by improving the quality and marketing of their wool," stated a report from the General Accounting Office. There were also no payment limits placed on how much a producer could receive.

Between 1955 and 1988, nearly $2 billion in subsidy payments were made to producers in the United States. The Wool Act wasn't turning any sheep farmer into a millionaire, though. Most producers, the majority residing in the Midwest and Southwest, received annual payments of a hundred bucks or less. Around 10 percent of producers, mainly commercial, received over $1,000 with .5 percent receiving over $25,000. In many cases, especially for a small producer, the money received from the subsidy made the difference between finishing the year in the hole or not. "That little extra amount we'd get helped feed our ewes," Melissa says. But while there were 283 million pounds of sheared wool in 1955, by 1988, that number had tumbled to 89 million. The military had also begun opting for synthetic materials in the fabrication of their uniforms instead of wool and mohair, and those fibers were no longer deemed "strategic material."

"The wool program has outlived its usefulness, and its continued implementation only exacerbates inequities in levels of public support between wealthy and marginal producers. In addition, it has failed to stimulate domestic production and acts as a lightning rod for public criticism of government spending," declared the Department of Agriculture.

It wasn't the first time the subsidy had come under scrutiny. President Reagan had tried unsuccessfully to eliminate it in the Farm Bill of '85, and it took over a decade before it was finally phased out in the 1990s during the Clinton/Gore administration. Once removed, the United States found itself with an extra $500 million in its pockets. Which was about the same time that every sheep farmer's good years started to turn into not-so-good years.

"The numbers started to decline, and we weren't trading as much with Mexico anymore, where lamb is considered a delicacy. And it became a lot harder to get sheep across the border into pastures like Wyoming, North Dakota, and South Dakota because of all the government regulations on land they could run on," Quinten says.

Things did perk up a few years ago. The first bounce the Bergstroms had seen in a long time. "An increase in the population of Muslims, Somalians, Ethiopians, Mexicans, and Saudis in this country resulted in an increased demand for lamb meat, but they were often taken advantage of when they'd go to the packinghouse to buy it," he says.

"That was terrible," Melissa agrees.

But the same people that were being taken advantage of also figured out pretty quickly that by eliminating the middleman (the packinghouse), they could go directly to the source (the Bergstroms) to get their lamb for an honest price.

"They'd buy it and eat it the same day," Quinten says. "They also use every bit of that animal. There is nothing left when they're done with it."

It's a different kind of customer than Courtland has dealt with in its 150 years of existence, but Quinten and Melissa don't really see it as being that big of a deal. "I strive to treat my customers as I would hope to be treated. Trust is more important than color or individual preference," he says. "I respect most everyone's choice of religion, as I would wish them to respect mine. Any religion that promotes 'fruits of the spirit' type traits, I can appreciate. We may have differences in methods of how to obtain them or share them, but concur on foundation values."

But while the bounce was nice, it wasn't like suddenly, the Bergstroms found themselves living on Easy Street.

"For all the sheep we grow in the US, we only produce 48 percent of what's consumed," Quinten says. "The rest comes from New Zealand and Australia, where, because of the currency rates, you can basically buy two lambs for the price of one of ours. So, who *wouldn't* do that?"

He and Melissa are some of the youngest sheep farmers in the area. "And we're in our mid-fifties," he laughs. There aren't many sheep farmers left in Kansas. No dairy farms or hog farms or chicken farms left in Courtland, either.

"Margins got so small," the farmers say. "All corporate now."

"Can buy them cheaper than you can raise them."

Both Quinten and Melissa are college graduates. Quinten went to Kansas State and got a history degree. Melissa went to Oklahoma State and got a degree in physical education. She was also on the same track team as a guy that everybody now knows as "the Garth Brooks."

"If a reunion ever happened, I'd be on the market again," Quinten laughs. "And I would totally get it."

Quinten and Melissa each did the marriage thing before, took a breather, then exchanged vows eighteen years ago. They raised a blended family and live on the farm a few miles north of town, eighty quiet acres where the only thing that breaks the silence is the bleating of their sheep.

They deal the most in wool breeds and the number of lambs they have at any given moment varies from time to time. Last summer, they fed a thousand lambs. But between the health problems and the intense heat—"Try gaining weight with a wool coat on," Quinten says—it just wasn't that great of a deal. And then, things got a little worse.

"The older generation won't share the accounting books with the younger one," Melissa says.

"So, when my dad finally did, we were both like, 'Wow . . . so that's how things *really* are.' We all think we're going to live forever, which means that carrying on a financial legacy can be challenging," says Quinten. "You're trusting in the finances, and those conversations where you're being told,

'This will all be here for you one day.' Meanwhile, there's no 401(k), no savings . . . "

"Try explaining to an eighty-four-year-old that they aren't just going to hand you money anymore," Melissa adds. "They don't understand how much the banking industry has changed. Bankers just don't want to deal with it. We always said we'll take Walmart wages because we want to put as much as possible back into the operation."

When they realized that the financial legacy that was supposed to be there for them no longer existed, they had two options: stand or fall.

"Don't cry about it," he says. "But that's the scary part when it's all you've ever known. Because really, when you start thinking about it, what else are you going to do?"

Quinten also isn't crying over the trade war with China.

"Most of us feel that what's right is right. What's true is true. If we're not getting that from others, even if it hurts us initially, it's what's right and it'll make it better for us down the road," he says. "As farmers, we're willing to get beat up to make it right. And who knows? Maybe by getting beat up a little, that will help the steel and auto industries, too."

They're willing to take their lumps in the short term because they want the playing field to be even and would still support the tariffs with or without any of the subsidies, too. "Fair and equal trade must be in place to promote growth and sustainability," he says. "As in personal relationships, the less divide among giving and taking, the healthier/happier the pair. Inequalities lead to inefficient interaction and inhibit 'blue-sky' growth. Trade needs to be fixed for farmers to benefit in the long run."

But what does bother him is the Farm Bill.

The federal Farm Bill has been around since 1933, another bone that FDR threw to the American farmers during the height of the Great Depression and the Dust Bowl. His feeling was this: the government should provide help to a farmer by way of a subsidy payment to cushion the blow from low prices and low yields. By keeping a farmer in production, the Farm Bill would also ensure that people would be able to enjoy a dependable food supply, i.e., not go hungry.

It also does a pretty good job of stirring up conflict and controversy because of its massive budget that everyone thinks goes directly into a farmer's pocket.

The biggest piece in the Farm Bill pie? Food stamps. A whopping 76 percent, or $326 billion of the 2018 Agricultural Improvement Act's $428 billion budget, was allocated for food assistance programs. Most people hear "farm bill" and "$428 billion budget" and naturally get the wrong impression.

"You can see how people not involved in the industry would think that the government is funding the farm," Quinten says.

Around 23 percent, or $99 billion, is allocated for things like federal crop insurance and dairy support programs, which pay a dairy farmer for the difference between what they are getting paid for milk versus the cost of feed, although that money isn't always free. Sometimes, a farmer must pay a premium for that kind of protection, much like you do for homeowners or car insurance.

The Farm Bill is renewed every five years and it's the food stamp portion that usually has Congress in a stall. When it came time to renew the bill in 2018, one of the major points that House Republicans pushed for was to make eligibility stricter for those receiving food stamps via the Supplemental Nutrition Assistance Program (SNAP). *Enroll in job training. If you're between the ages of eighteen and fifty and aren't caring for a minor, work at least twenty hours a week. If not, you risk having your benefits cut.* The requirements were predicted to cut at least 1 million people from the SNAP program over the next ten years; a little nudge from the federal government promoting the idea that many of SNAP's 16 million able-bodied adult participants, both with and without children, could achieve self-sufficiency through work.

"Long-term dependency has never been part of the American Dream," Agriculture Secretary Perdue was quoted in the *Washington Post*. "Everyone who receives SNAP deserves an opportunity to become self-sufficient and build a productive, independent life."

Nah, Senate Democrats balked. *Not fair.*

A few days before Christmas, President Trump signed the 2018 Farm Bill's 807 pages into law. It did not include the work requirements for SNAP that House Republicans had lobbied for.

The Bank

"We're a young bank. One of the youngest in the state of Kansas."

Tanner Johnson is forty-two years old. Blue jeans. Blue polo. President and CEO of the Swedish-American State Bank and the Courtland Community Arts Council.

And when he says, "We're a young bank," he doesn't mean that they just opened for business, like, two years ago. What he means is that the Swedish-American is the employer of nine people who are all his age or younger. Six of his employees are graduates of Pike Valley High School. Brock Hanel, the chairman of the board, is thirty-two years old, runs the veterinary clinic out on Highway 36, and spent an hour this morning buzzing around at low altitude in his Ultra-Lite.

"It's a cot with wings," Tanner says.

The bank sits right on the corner of Liberty and Main. Outside is the digital clock and thermometer that flashes the time and reminders of the obvious: It. Is. Hot: 98°, 100°, 103°. It. Is. Cold: 10°, 2°, −5°.

The Swedish-American was established as a charter in 1913 when a handful of local businessmen got fed up with the shenanigans of the existing bank in town. *Look, if we're gonna make it we need a stable bank.*

In 1922, Tanner's great-grandfather, Chris Green, purchased a controlling interest in the bank. He then passed it along to his daughter, Dorothy, or "Dot," who gave it to her husband, Herb, who eventually gave it to their son, Mike, who was Tanner's father. Always family-owned. Always in Courtland. Tanner is a fourth-generation banker.

He was perfectly happy living in Oklahoma City with his wife, Cathy, after graduating from Oklahoma University. "You'll probably never hear of anyone else with a degree in percussion and finance," he says. Life was good. He started a web development business. Loved it. But things were changing generationally at the bank. His dad was getting older. So were

Tanner and Cathy's kids. And Tanner started thinking more and more about Courtland.

"What if we moved back to my hometown?" he asked her. He wanted their kids to have the same experience he did. Jump on your bike. Ride to a friend's house. Cannonball into the community swimming pool.

Let's go!

Then, they told their friends. *Are you crazy?*

"The key is that you talk to people in minutes, not miles. If you say to someone, 'The nearest store is fifteen miles away,' they think, 'Whoa!' But if you say, 'The nearest store is fifteen *minutes* away,' they say, 'Oh. That's not bad. So is mine,'" he says.

Tanner started working at the bank in 2011. In 2014, his grandfather, Herb, died. Then, a year later, his father died unexpectedly. Which is when Tanner took over. His office is tucked into the corner of the bank. Wood paneling. Framed family photo on the desk. Open door.

Most of the banking at the Swedish-American happens in the lobby, where a teller sits behind a counter, not ten inches of bulletproof glass. When you walk in, they know your name—*Hey Dan! Hey Beverly!*—and they always look forward to seeing Sherie Mahin and the day care kids, making sure the cookies and popcorn are ready.

The bank's primary services include deposit and savings accounts, certificates of deposit, traditional and Roth IRAs, agriculture, real estate, consumer, and commercial lending. Heavy on the agriculture.

The bank has been modernizing. They're trying to entice more of their customers to try online banking, launched their own app, and yes, can accept mobile check deposits. No drive-up window but they finally broke down and installed an ATM. When you call on the phone, an actual person will answer it, not an automated system. *Hey Jeff!*

Up until the early eighties, if you wanted a loan from your neighborhood banker, you just kind of waltzed into his office and asked for one. No tax returns. No projected income. I know you. You know me. I trust you. You trust me. Here's what we'll loan you. Here's when your payments are due. Sound good? Sign on the dotted line, friend.

"Loans were one-third of a page," he says.

Those days no longer exist. Blame the farm crisis of the 1980s, the economic slide in 2008, and all the new government regulations that came rolling out because of them. These days, if you want some money to get a new hay baler, you'll practically run out of ink filling out a very detailed loan application that's six pages long, because the bank wants to know more than just how your dad is doing these days. "Tax return, three years of balance sheet and income statements, a projected income statement, and some trended ratio analysis," he says. Nothing personal. The Swedish-American still trusts you.

"I have had farmers get angry with me, mostly because they think, 'Is Tanner asking me for all this because I'm in trouble? Am I doing something wrong?' They're not. But if we're gonna continue to have a bank in this town, this info has to be in our files."

It's a lot of info. After the farm crisis in the eighties, when you were having to foreclose on your lifelong friend because he hadn't been able to make a mortgage or loan payment in months, the Swedish-American had to get savvier if they wanted to survive the market *and* the government regulations.

"It's not fun anymore," he admits. "Kind of like medicine. But that's just the way it is. Things have changed." There's a heavy load of regulatory burden in agricultural lending. And when the banking industry says, "Oh, you're an ag-concentrated bank," they don't mean it as a compliment. No one has any romantic notions about the risk involved with lending very, very large amounts of money to someone who can do everything right, watch an amazing crop sprout out of the ground, and then find themselves standing by helplessly while without warning, the sky spits out a hailstorm that in five minutes can wipe out their entire income for the year.

"You just deal with it," Tanner says. "The only thing that keeps me up in a cold sweat is the regulations, not necessarily downward commodities. Farmers are very resilient and will adjust their spending, which is why it's hard to look at agricultural banking from a strictly analytical point of view. It's hard to look at a farmer's income and quantify their ability to adjust their spending levels. Because we're talking about row crops. And you can't control the pricing; whether it's up or down."

One thing the bank has learned over the past hundred years is that bad things usually don't just happen overnight. Tanner's grandfather, Herb, used to have a saying: "When the borrower stops talkin' to you, that's when things are goin' south."

"As long as you're talking to me and I'm talking to you, things can be worked out," Tanner says. It's when you don't mention that you were diagnosed with something serious, just lost all your corn to a green snap, had your beans decimated by hail, are going through a divorce that's getting nasty, and can barely keep your head above water that causes a problem. This is why he always keeps a box of Kleenex in his office. "People tell me everything. More than I want to know." Tanner is your banker, your psychologist, your counselor. "Your life coach," he says. "If something is happening in your personal life, it's affecting your finances."

But if you're just an average Joe looking to buy an average Joe farm, don't expect to walk in the door with a John Deere dream and out with your $3 million loan from the Swedish-American to make it all happen. "It's almost impossible to get that kind of loan unless you come in with outside financial backing," he says. "You'll spend $1 million on the equipment alone. And if you rent ground, it'll be less profitable, but if you buy it, you can expect to spend about $2 million on that alone. You could probably get a few acres and concentrate on a specialty crop, but you're not going to operate something on the level that these guys do out here."

This is why there are fewer family-owned farms than ever before. Kind of like a family-owned bank.

But there's a reason why the Swedish-American still places a weekly ad in the *Courtland Journal*, why there's a sticker on the front door that reads, "Kansas Bankers say 'Thanks!' for shopping your hometown *first!*" It's the same reason why they've been the banker for other family-owned businesses in town, like Pinky's, the *Courtland Journal*, Tebow's Plumbing, the Depot Market, C&W Farm Supply, as well as the Kansas Bostwick Irrigation District, and family farms for decades, and why they wanted to support Shanna and Michelle so they could open Soul Sister Ceramics right across the street.

"I'm a Kool-Aid drinker. I'm pouring it and drinking it," he says. "When I'm old, I don't want to drive through Courtland and see a bunch of windows boarded up. Which is one of the reasons why we're here."

The City Council Meeting

The Mayor's got a city council meeting in an hour. He just poured a margarita, is wearing a Hawaiian shirt, and has a kite in his hand.

"It's not a kite, it's a sled," he says. He got the sled from ProKites. It's a nice kite. Not like those box kites you got as a kid and paid like, five bucks for; the kind that forced you to huff it into a cardio burn before it gave any thought to going airborne.

This is a *sled*. He likes to attach an antenna to it. So, "wolf, zero, fox" can get on the airwaves and talk to someone in Australia.

The kite is very big and very colorful, and the only one he has left.

"*Sled*," he corrects. "The other one was a little smaller. It blew half a mile that way."

It blew away on the Fourth of July. He was out there in the yard and the kite was catching a good breeze, flying at a nice altitude. Smooth. So, instead of reeling it in when he had to go inside, he tied it to his golf cart, and totally forgot about it until some time had passed.

I gotta go check on that kite.

He went back outside. Saw his golf cart sitting there. Did not see the kite.

Where the hell did it go?

Which is when he saw it. Half a mile that way and going down fast, right toward Quinten and Melissa Bergstrom's lamb farm.

"It had about five hundred feet of string trailing behind of it. I tried to look for it," he said. "But it's kind of hard to spot, this little thing in a huge field. They'll find it when the combine chews it up during harvest. I wonder if I should tell them about that . . . at least it didn't get caught in the power lines. That would have been electrifying. But it was a hundred dollars down the drain."

A few people saw the kite while it was still airborne. Two of them called the police.

Aliens!

He's pulling the kite he does have left out of the garage, inside of which sits his red Mustang convertible. It's his third Mustang and his third convertible. "Six-cylinder so I don't get into trouble," he says.

It's 100 degrees outside. The sun is beating down. A small breeze is rustling the fields and the leaves in the trees, but not the Mayor's black and white kite with the pink, purple, yellow, and green accents.

"Sled," he says as it tries and fails to catch air.

He slowly walks through the yard, dragging the kite. "I'm not running," he says. "It's gotta feel it."

For a moment, the kite lifts. Catches the breeze. Gets about five feet off the ground. Then it drops. Unceremoniously.

"There's no wind," he says.

He moves a little further across the yard as the kite continues to drag. "There's no wind in Kansas," he says again as it sits in the grass, an occasional rustle in the breeze but not moving. "No wind."

But there is the monthly city council meeting in thirty minutes. Might be one of his last. "I told you what my campaign slogan is for next year: Vote for Someone Else."

No one believes him.

He finishes off his margarita. "The only thing that keeps my blood pressure down," he says. "I hear there's a mob coming tonight." Within minutes, the kite is back in the garage and the Mayor is on his golf cart, heading down Courtland Avenue and onto Main Street toward city hall. Still wearing the Hawaiian shirt; a vibrant button-down of orange, yellow, green, and blue with images of palm trees printed on it, along with cargo shorts and white Nikes.

When he takes his seat at the three white plastic tables pushed together to form an "L" shape, he joins his five city council members and the city clerk. Jenny Russell is there. The rumored mob is there, too; which turns out to be a married couple who signed up to participate in the "citizens comments" portion of the meeting, during which they'll get as much time as they'd like to speak, now or forever hold their peace.

"But when they're done talking," the Mayor says, "that's it. We don't like for these meetings to go two minutes over eight o'clock."

The two-person mob is here to discuss the sidewalk situation on Grant Street. Thanks to a grant written by JenRus Freelance, the Healthy Republic County Coalition just awarded Courtland $19,000 to get some new sidewalks put in. The couple is congratulatory about the grant but worried that the sidewalks are going to disrupt their new landscaping.

Twenty minutes later, they have conceded that the sidewalks on Grant

Street are happening whether they're on board or not, although Jenny has promised that whoever puts them in will *not* mess up their shrubs.

"It's not something we want," says the husband as they get up to leave. "But we understand. Thank you all for your good work and congratulations on the grant."

The council spends six minutes talking about the new signs that are going to be erected around town that will tell visitors which direction to go in for food, fuel, the ballfield. The signs are happening because a few months ago, a group from the nearby towns of Clifton and Vining took a field trip to Courtland as part of the First Impression Program, a joint effort between K-State's Research and Extension and the Dane G. Hansen Foundation.

The idea of the program is for one rural town to buddy up with another rural town. We tour yours. You tour ours. Then, everyone who has toured jots down everything they liked (*Very friendly place!*) and didn't like (*Where's the grocery store?*) in the town they visited. Kind of like an official suggestion box.

Courtland read the report and decided to start with some signage. So, with the help of JenRus, the city applied for a grant, won, and now the design for the signs is ready for approval.

"All steel construction. Double-sided. Navy blue with white lettering. Life span of twenty years."

"That'll outlive me," the Mayor says. "Do we need a vote or a pair of blessings?" he asks.

It gets a pair of blessings and the Mayor checks it off the agenda, which has twelve items on it. Like the decision to replace the missing shingles on the community pool shelter.

Check!

Like how much they should charge Dan Kuhn for the old shredder that the city never uses anymore.

"Hundred bucks and a watermelon," says the Mayor.

Check!

They move on to the hose report from the volunteer fire department. "It's $6,300 just for the new hose, which is thirteen hundred feet long. Or, we could just put a new hydrant in on the corner, which seems to make sense. Try dragging thirteen hundred feet of hose and rolling it back up again."

"Look into the hydrant," says the Mayor.

Check!

Then it's time to talk about whether they should tow the white Continental that *you know who* just left abandoned at the curb, right on Main Street, like, three weeks ago.

"All it needs is a fuel pump? Are you serious?"

"So, are we having it towed?"

"Maybe we should keep it . . . "

"For what?"

"Maybe we could sell it? At least we could get the six hundred bucks out of him that he owes us for rent."

"Just tow it."

"Two blessings," says the Mayor. *Check!*

By the time the Mayor checks off the last item on the agenda, it's 8:01 p.m.

"I make a motion to adjourn."

"I second that."

It is about an hour before sunset, and still 100 degrees outside. The Mayor steps onto the sidewalk outside of city hall, lights his pipe, gets back into his golf cart, and glances down at his phone. "We went a minute over," he says. "Not bad."

The Morning Coffee: Thursday

WIBW-AM 580 *News Now* in Topeka is saying that the high heat index has been extended to Saturday. Forty percent chance of rain on Friday, 60 percent Friday night. It's 6 a.m. and already 79 degrees outside.

"Heat goes up, grain goes down," Steve says.

He finally got his cattle back together. All but two. Took ten minutes just to get them into the catch pen. "Then they stood there like, 'What the devil are we doin' in here?'" Larry laughs.

The weatherman is preparing everyone for a spike to 103 today, which is what July usually feels like in Courtland.

"Gonna be hot for Fun Day."

"Not if you plant yourself in the beer garden."

Courtland Fun Day is about two weeks away. It has been held for more than fifty years, has morphed into three days of fun, is always held the last weekend in July, and has been known to draw a thousand people out of the surrounding area and onto Main Street. People who left Courtland fly back just for Fun Day. Kids come home. Vacation plans are altered. You do not miss Fun Day. Fun Day is a *thing*. There are activities all day, bands all night. Most everyone in town is on a committee, like the BBQ Pit Committee, Sand Volleyball Committee, Band/Music Committee, Children's Parade Committee, and everyone is always very excited about the beer garden that is usually set up in the empty lot next to Pinky's. This is why Betty is worried.

"People from out of town get drunk and trash the bathrooms! And it's not the men. It's the women!" she says. "I'm going to hire Steve as my security guy."

Steve's about to go check on his pivot, which he thinks is stuck. "Could be a gearbox out, electrical motor out, an electrical motor at the box . . . who knows?" If he can't figure it out, he'll call his service guy, who will charge Steve two hundred bucks just for saying hello. The last time the service guy came out to see what was wrong with the pivot, he took one look, handed Steve a wrench, and told him to tighten up the bolts.

"Two hundred bucks," Steve says.

And there's still no rain, except for what WIBW-AM 580 Topeka is predicting for Friday. Which the corn needs. Badly.

"As soon as it starts silking and producing an ear is when it's using the most moisture. Which is where the corn is right now. Rain is so much easier and cheaper than the pivot," Larry says.

The Browns have nine pivots. If it's not raining, those pivots are spraying water, thanks to a surge of electricity, propane, or diesel. "It costs us three thousand a day to run 'em. Three thousand *a day*."

Don doesn't trust the Topeka forecast. "I'd rather hear what Hastings has to say about it."

This is because Courtland's in a weird spot. Topeka can usually predict the weather for northeastern Kansas. Hastings usually nails it for southwest Nebraska and southern Kansas. And Courtland sits somewhere on the fringe of the weather patterns affecting both, which usually means you can look at the radar and then take a wild guess as to what you're going to get.

"That's because we have three fronts to worry about," Don says. "It's not like California, where all they have to worry about is the western front. Here, we've got fronts rolling in from the north, west, and south since storms generally don't come in from the east. One small change to any of them and what was supposed to be a 60 percent chance of rain on Friday night suddenly goes down to zero."

Which would be a damn shame because they really could use some rain. Just an inch would be nice. *Something.* If they don't, they'll see the potential of growing 130 bushel of corn per acre drop down to below 100 bushel.

"That thirty bushel is at $3, so figure, that's $90 an acre and if you have a hundred acres, you're losing $9,000," Joerg says.

If a farmer can manage to get 130 bushel of corn, then most likely they'll break even. Maybe. Which is better than they'll probably do on wheat.

"God knows the wheat prices are not good," Steve says.

And the soybeans? It'd be nice to see soy at $10 to $12/bushel. It got as high as $18/bushel in 2012 when a drought burned up beans across the Midwest and demolished the supply. But now? When the United States and Brazil have both been harvesting a bumper crop?

"I didn't even bother to look," Steve says.

"We overproduce," Joerg says.

"You go to the grocery store, you want cheap food, right?" Don says.

"The Board of Trade sets the prices. They say, 'This is what we're offering today. Take it or leave it,'" Joerg says.

"And you're paying property taxes whether you produce or not," Don adds.

"What we need is a union," says Joerg.

"We tried a couple of times," says Kenny.

"Oh, I know. We tried but it didn't really catch on the way we wanted it to," says Joerg.

Given that the farmer is responsible for feeding the world, it seems logical that they should be the ones holding all the cards. Manipulate the market, cut down on supply, increase demand, increase prices.

"Oh, if we hold back, someone else somewhere else will just double plant to make up for it," says Joerg.

So, everyone's just waiting it out. Because always, the market, the weather. What else can you do? Hold off on buying that new hay baler and pray to God for an inch of rain. And because they're not buying much of anything, they're fixing a lot of everything. Something *always* needs to be fixed.

"On my 275, you punch a button to lock a gear . . . it don't do it," Larry says.

"You got anything that's workin'?" Joerg asks.

"At least it's an excuse to go to Harbor Freight," Steve says. "Slug . . . you wanna go? We can take a detour."

"Oh," Joerg laughs. "Oh my. What was the name of that place . . . the 'www' something?"

"Something," Slug agrees.

"What was the name of that place?" Joerg asks again, shaking his head. "Oh! The Shady Lady. Yeah, that's it. It used to be the Wild, Wild, West."

"Brass pole," Steve explains. "Right next to Harbor Freight in Salina."

"If you're doin' that, I'm not gonna irrigate for you," Larry says. "And that's something else; they drive like they're doggone crazy on the interstates. You get on Highway 81, if you're goin' eighty, eighty-five miles an hour, you're not passing anyone, everyone is passing *you*. But they're not as crazy as those motorcycles."

"Don just took a four-thousand-mile ride on his motorcycle," Joerg says. "He didn't have one of those things on the back, though."

"What? A trailer?"

"No, a biker bitch," Joerg replies.

"What?" Betty asks sharply.

"What?" Joerg replies innocently, throwing up his hands. "It's what they call them!"

"You mean a woman?" she says.

"Yeah, well, that's what *they* call them. I don't know," Joerg laughs, shaking his head. "Oh Lord, foot in my mouth again."

Joerg's golf game didn't go too well yesterday. "It sucked," he says. But Carlson made it back from fishing in Canada, just in time to tee off.

"Winnipeg was great. The lodge was amazing. We came in at 9 p.m. and they had prime rib waiting for us," he says.

The lodge sits on Lake Reed. Fourteen miles long and ten wide, about as far north as you can get. Two hundred and fifty kilometers between gas stations. Islands everywhere. Every day at noon, they'd meet on one of them, wait for the guy to clean the fish, and eat lunch.

"Did you catch anything?"

"Yeah he did; a snaggletooth squaw!"

"Nothing penicillin won't take care of!"

"What was that saying? If she ain't two-eighty, she ain't a lady?"

"More to love."

"Yeah. Warm in the winter. And shade in the summer."

"What are you guys talking about?" Betty asks accusingly, two plates filled with biscuits and gravy in her hands.

"Betty's going to be a lot happier with you," Carlson says to Joerg as she rolls her eyes. "You're finally acting like your normal self."

The Ditch Rider

"Truck 2 to Truck 6."

"Go ahead."

"Yeah, Dave. I need a minus seven."

"Okay."

"Okay. Thank you."

There are seven feet of water that Dan Reynolds needs to take out of the canal. The White Rock Extension Canal. One of several canals that deliver water from Lovewell Lake to the forty-three thousand acres of irrigated land in the Kansas Bostwick Irrigation District, which stretches across Jewell and Republic Counties.

Dan's responsible for watering four thousand of them. His run is thirteen miles long. "Dan's got the prettiest route," they all say. He's one of six ditch riders working for Kansas Bostwick, who deliver water to farmers in Courtland like Dan, Slug, Kenny, and Steve and Larry Brown.

Most of the ditch riders have been at it for years. Dave started in 1972. Phillip came on in '74.

"I've been doing this for over forty years," says Dan.

In 1973, Dan Reynolds was fresh out of high school. Went on to graduate from the vo-tech in nearby Beloit and needed a job. "I grew up in Lovewell, helpin' my dad," he says, maneuvering the truck along his canal as a great blue heron skims the water. "He was a farmer. And farmin' gets in your blood and it's hard to get out."

Farming was pretty good in the early seventies. But by the time Dan was married with kids, farming had gotten pretty bad. But the irrigation office was hiring. So, in 1979, he applied.

The CB in his red Ford F150 has been squawking ever since he started his run today at 6:30 a.m. with calls between the irrigation office, Dave the water master, and all six of the ditch riders.

"Truck 4 to Truck 6."

"Go ahead . . . "

Dan's in Truck 2. He and the Ford are eleven miles northeast of Courtland on a dirt and gravel road winding its way through a cornfield and a soybean field and one more of each. The sky is blue. The air is sweet. The breeze is hot. And all you can hear are God sounds; birds chirping, crickets, and the water rushing by as he pulls out a 2x2 that they call a log using what looks like a pitchfork with a blade that curves out at a 90-degree angle.

"Weed hook," he says. "Basically, it's an old-fashioned corn rake."

The weed hook is in the bed of his Ford. And every few minutes, he'll stop the truck, get out, grab the weed hook, walk through some grass or the gate of a barbed wire fence or over a steel ladder standing over a string of electrical fence. He'll do this so he can stand on a concrete plank that straddles the weir, which was built across the canals so the water levels could be diverted or raised by inserting or removing the logs.

Dan's got twenty-six checks to check. "We need to log for three feet of water at every check."

Right now, he's doing a check at Tater's weir. "Tater's like, five hundred pounds," he says. "Tater's a good guy." Tater needs 1.8 cubic feet of irrigated water for his crops today. Which Dan will release by sticking the weed hook into the log slot and pulling out a 2x3 log, and then a 2x4, adding a 2x2 and then the 2x3 again, pushing both snugly into the log slot with the weed hook so that all the logs are submerged under the water, thus controlling how much is being distributed into the pipes that will irrigate Tater's crops.

"That's what's controlling the flow out of the weirs," he says. "And what I just did will give Tater the water he needs."

Monday through Friday from 6:30 a.m. to 2:30 p.m. and Saturday until noon during irrigation season, Dan is in the Ford, checking his twenty-six checks. Drive. Stop. Get weed hook. Get to weir. Pull out logs. Push in logs. Repeat. Giving the farmer more water. Reducing the flow of water. However much or little irrigated water his farmers need for the day, guys like Howley, Sandell, Morris, Tater, and Bard. He keeps track of who needs what and how much of it by marking it down with a pencil in a spiral notebook he keeps open on the center console.

"You have to use your mind," he says. "If you over log all the checks, it'll dry a farmer up. You just have to keep track of the water and think about what you're doin'. You know when you've made a mistake, and then you can catch it and cover it."

And while the farmer is paying for the irrigated water, he's not the one tasked with regulating its flow. "You need to have control," he says. "We answer to the Bureau of Reclamation. Everything is accounted for."

This means that a farmer can't just open his irrigation pipes and use them like a garden hose. "They're supposed to give us forty-eight hours' notice, but twenty-four will do just fine," he says. You also can't help yourself to the water flowing through the Republican River even if it runs through your pasture or be what they call "gettin' happy with the turnout wheel" to increase the flow of water to your pipes without ordering it. Every drop of water in the irrigated district is metered. "If you let the farmer log the water, you'd have people shootin' each other," he says.

Someone once asked Dan, *So, what do you do for a living?*

"I told them I was a ditch rider and they looked at me kinda funny," he says. So, he started telling people he was a water technician. "Because I guess you could say we deliver and measure the water."

Which Dan continues to do for the next three and a half hours. Drive. Stop. Get weed hook. Get to weir. Pull out logs. Push in logs. Check the check. Repeat. Country music on the radio. AC on full blast. CB always squawking with calls.

"Hey, Larry!"

"Yeah?"

"You forgot your check at the office. Want me to distribute it to everyone equally?"

"Wouldn't be that much to distribute."

"Irrigating is something you do while you're waiting for it to rain," Dan says, heading north. "It's guaranteeing you're gonna raise a crop, barring a hailstorm." He likes to do his checks backward, starting low and ending high. The location of the checks is determined by elevation, each situated on a grade that drops about two-tenths and so many feet. "You keep the logs in the bottom to make the top water move. Basically, we're moving water over water."

When he turns in his paperwork at the KBID office on Main Street and clocks out at 2:30 p.m., he'll stop at the Depot Market for a diet root beer and to see his wife, Mary, who works there, and is also the love of his life. Then, he'll head home to start farming the 360 acres he owns and the 320 acres he rents. Farming things like cattle ("all raised from babies") and Sudan Grass ("it's a hybrid foliage that doesn't produce grain").

"My Ponderosa," he says as he pulls up to a tidy ranch that sits nestled in the country a few miles north of Courtland. He and Mary built it in 1979. Mary was a teacher for a total of thirty-five years, thirty-three of which were for Pike Valley. By the time she left, she was teaching the grandkids of her original students. She and Dan just celebrated their forty-second wedding anniversary. They have four kids. Twelve grandkids. They've survived her breast cancer, and his skin cancer, and diabetes.

"What's the secret?" she says. "I'd say communication."

"We really never fight," he says.

"Well, there was that *one* time we didn't talk for a week and a half," she says, preparing lunch in the kitchen. Breaded fish. Fresh cucumbers from the garden. Sweet corn on the cob. Macaroni and cheese. Cantaloupe. Watermelon. Banana nut muffins.

"After that," she adds, handing him an ear of corn, "I thought, 'We just need to communicate better.'"

"The secret is simple," he says. "It's 'Yes, dear.'"

"Oh, really?" she laughs. "Is that it?"

Mary adores Dan just as much as he adores her. They celebrated their anniversary with their first flight, which took them on their first cruise to Alaska. She wants to see the East Coast next, maybe take a bus tour, stop in some small towns along the way. "New England in the fall, with all the colors," she says.

When Dan retires, the first thing he wants to do is take a baseball bat and smash the alarm clock. "I'm not going to sit on the porch and drink coffee all day," he says. "I have to be doing something. But it's more about doing what I want when I want."

When Dan was younger, he watched his mom and dad retire from farming and buy a shiny, silver Airstream, heard them say they were going to travel, enjoy life, see things.

"They pulled that Airstream into Colorado maybe twice," he says. "It's one of the reasons I decided to retire when I still had some life in me. I once told my son, 'Don't go through life, become forty or fifty and think, 'Why didn't I do that?' You gotta try it. Sure, it might be hard at first. But you gotta at least *try* it."

The Family Business: C&W Farm Supply

It's quiet this morning. *Eerily* quiet for a Monday, that's for sure.

"The calm before the storm," says Jeff Sothers.

It's usually crazy on a Monday morning at C&W Farm Supply. And Jeff usually has the office phone on one ear and his cell phone on the other ear. People needing parts for their machinery, placing orders for new machinery. This broke. That broke. Minor fixes like, "I need an oil filter for my TC30." Major emergencies like, "My damn pivot is down!"

There are two puppies under his desk. Jazi and Huck. Both are Jack Russells. Both are currently sprawled out on their backs, paws in the air, half-asleep at 9 a.m. as two giant white fans blow in Jeff's corner office where lots of things hang on the wood-paneled walls. Things like the mousetrap glued to a block of wood that says "Complaint Department—Press button for Service" and another that reads "A CLEAN DESK IS A SIGN OF A BLANK MIND." On top of his desk are piles of paper, a calculator, and brochures for New Holland's Workmaster 55, 65, and 75.

Jeff's family has been selling New Holland farm machinery since 1959. His mom, Beverly, and his dad, Ralph, opened the place when Jeff was five years old.

"When did we open?" he asks her.

"1959."

"I know 1959. What *day* did we open?"

"December 1."

Since December 1, 1959, the Sothers have been supporting the FFA and 4H, banking with the Swedish-American down the street, and running blue. Well, kind of. They started out running gray and red—the original colors of Ford farm machinery—but then Ford sold off their agriculture division to

New Holland, which is blue. In Courtland, you're running blue (New Holland), green (John Deere), or red (Case IH). And if your granddad and daddy ran blue, then you run blue. If your granddad and daddy ran red, you run red.

"It's like Republican and Democrat out here," he says. "But they do switch from time to time. I've sold blue to farmers that have run green or red."

When the Sothers had their grand opening celebration for C&W—"Stands for Courtland and Washington, where we used to have a store," Jeff says— the building was located a few steps away from the one they're currently in. Even back then, their shop was hard to miss, thanks to all the tractors parked outside.

"I can remember havin' a load of 8Ns," Beverly says.

"That wasn't 8Ns," Jeff says. "They were 600s and 800s."

"They were 8Ns," Beverly insists. "But they were used ones."

"They were brand new," Jeff says. "But they weren't 8Ns. They weren't building 8Ns in 1959."

"Well, they looked like 8Ns," Beverly concedes.

"We don't have any disagreements here," Jeff says.

"All the time," Beverly replies.

And business was good but for the fact that the city council wasn't too happy about the tractors taking up all the parking spaces outside. So, the Sothers moved a block south into the old Ford building. You can look down on the ground and still see where steel wheel tractors used to chew up the concrete.

Beverly is the matriarch. "I'm just here," she says. After his dad died, Jeff took over the business in 1980 when he was still in his twenties. He grew up here. Worked in every department throughout junior high and high school. Now he runs the place. And the building that they are standing in has been added onto five times, plus there's another building across the street. Combined, they're holding about $3 to $4 million dollars' worth of parts; tires and rims and rear axles and complete engines and every part of the engine, spindles, and rods and disc bearings—*tons* of disc bearings—and shredders . . .

"Farming is a complicated business," he says. "I think farmers are one of the most complicated businessmen in the world. They know *exactly* how much they need to break even on their yields. They just calculate *everything*. Their minds are clicking *all the time*. Even when it comes to equipment."

When corn is selling for $7 a bushel, Jeff is selling a lot of equipment. When it's selling at $3 a bushel like it has been lately, Jeff is doing a lot of repairs on old equipment. He's weathered more storms with the farmers than he can count and really doesn't want to anyway.

"The eighties were a bad time," he says. "I lived through that one."

It was bad. If you wanted to survive the farming industry in the eighties,

you had to adjust. So, Jeff expanded the business. "We were gonna go from selling equipment to repairing it. And that's exactly what we did. They'd bring one in here and here and here," he says, pointing around. "We were running out of space."

This is why he built another 120 by 70 building, inside of which are four mammoth tractors in various states of repair, and an ATV that Randy is wrenching under. Taking a nap, he jokes, waving his hand.

The ATV came from a farm out in Hill City, about a hundred miles southwest of Courtland. Back in the day, there was a farm machinery dealer in every town. But now? "You'll go at least thirty miles," Jeff says. "And for my own brand? It's more like seventy."

And what they were selling back then was a lot cheaper, too. "In the 1970s, a 130-horsepower tractor listed around $20,000. Today, a similar tractor lists at $67,588. So, three times as much. Our expenses have tripled, but during that same time, the prices that we get for commodities like wheat, corn, and soy, have barely increased, if at all." He also still remembers the day he looked at his first invoice over $100,000. "I called my rep and said, 'How am I supposed to sell this?' I was in sticker shock."

But pretty soon, Jeff sold it. And then another one. And another. And then it was no big deal. Nowadays, it's not unheard of for a piece of farm machinery to set you back $200,000. The most expensive one Jeff ever sold was about $300,000.

Everything is more expensive now. "Even seed. Seed used to be thirty bucks a bag. Now, it's a hundred. Those were the days; when a new tractor only cost $20,000," he says. "When you could raise 130-bushel corn and be smokin', instead of raising 200-bushel corn and be slippin'."

Back in the day, there was a farmhouse on every quarter section in Courtland, and the Atchison, Topeka & Santa Fe would come screaming down the tracks with their shiny silver engines. Saturdays were the best days. "On Saturdays, all the kids would come out to watch the train come by and snatch the mail off the mail hook. If they missed, they'd pay us a penny apiece to pick up the scattered letters," he says.

Courtland has been home to the Sothers since his dad's family homesteaded here in 1870 before Courtland was even on the map. Jeff still owns the original property and was born in a Sears & Roebuck house east of town. The business has always been a family one; out of his fifteen employees, about half are related to Jeff and Beverly. Jeff's wife, Brenda, works here, too. And just like Pinky's and AnTeaQues and the Depot Market, finding someone who will be motivated enough to clock in for the day has not been easy.

"It's hard to find young guys who want to work. No one wants to do any manual labor."

And not many people want to be woken up at 3 a.m. to go fix a baler either. "I've left at three, four, five o'clock in the morning. Balers never break down during the day. They *always* break down at night because farmers want a little bit of dew to make the hay stick. And you don't get dew during the day."

Jeff's basically on call 24/7, 365 days a year because if it's not a broken valve on your pivot during irrigation season it's your baler during hay season. It's always something.

Jeff pulls out a big blue album from behind his desk. Inside are things like photos from the day C&W opened their doors, a copy of "The Customer Ten Commandments" from McDonald's Corporation ("Rule No. 1: The Customer is the most important person in our business"), and a handwritten letter he received from one of the kids in town. "Dear C&W Farm Supply, Thank you for donating to my goat sale premium and heardsmanship award. . . . I had a great first year."

There's a reason why Jeff's coming out in the middle of the night to fix your baler. "We all understand what's goin' on. We all try to help each other. It's what I'm most proud of. If someone falls on hard times, *everyone* is there to help. Even if they're rivals, they are there. Even if they don't like each other or are both bidding on the same property, they put it aside and come out to help."

Like the time a tornado barreled through town, taking a few houses and half of the feedlot before it left. "Within an hour, you couldn't even find a place to park, there were so many people who immediately came out to help. Whatever they could do. Whatever needed done. I donated loaders and backhoes."

He stands side by side with the farmer. The good years. The ugly years. The 3 a.m. emergency calls in the middle of the night when he'd rather be sleeping. Surviving the market. The weather. Whatever.

"Farmers are very optimistic people. They're always willing to try a change. I guess I am optimistic, too. I know things will come back. It's inevitable. It can't stay down forever. But there are times I look at my inventory," he laughs, "and want to choke."

LATE FALL

Commodity Prices (per bushel)

	October 1920	October 1973	October 1984	October 2018
Corn	$1.50	$2.54	$3.53	$3.74
Wheat	$2.45	$4.62	$4.27	$5.17
Soybean	$2.68	$5.29	$6.25	$8.57

The Morning Coffee: Thursday

The coffee is brewing on the Bunn, but the white plastic cup is gone from the white Formica table.

"Well, we had to get rid of that," says Kenny.

"Some people would forget to pay," says Joerg. "I've done that a few times and then I'll call Betty up and say, 'I forgot to pay my coffee,' write it down on your list. Not everyone called to tell her that, though."

"Or people would not forget to pay and just walk out," says Kenny.

So, Betty got rid of the cup, raised the all-you-can-drink coffee from a buck to a buck fifty, and started keeping tabs on who was filling their mugs.

"Who can blame her?" says Joerg.

"Probably shoulda done that a long time ago," says Kenny.

It started raining last night around 7 p.m., which shut the combines down, and now the corn is sitting. The beans are sitting, too. And there's probably no way they're going to get the wheat into the ground by November 1st, which is the bullseye if you want crop insurance to keep you covered when a gray cloud spits out hail the size of golf balls in the middle of June.

What the farmers need right now is to be able to plant wheat and harvest corn and beans. What they don't need is to be worrying about hailstorms, and winds that blow so hard, they leave what was going to be your tallest, best corn looking like bent sticks poking out of the earth.

"We call that a green snap," says Joerg.

But nothing is being harvested right now. Or planted.

"At this rate, it'll be the end of November before everyone gets their semi-trucks to the elevator," Joerg says.

"We already sat around for two weeks and didn't spin one tire because the ground was too wet to harvest," says Steve. Too much rain for too many days and don't forget the snow they woke up to in the middle of October.

"It leaned the beans but didn't lay them down," says Hootie.

Right now, everyone's worried. Everyone's thinking that at this point, it'll basically be a waste of time to even plant the damn wheat, they say. Because not only will it cost them about four bucks to get it into the ground, it'll be another two bucks to treat so that the bugs don't devour it. And losing an extra two bucks doesn't sound like much until you start to multiply all those two lost bucks by a thousand or fifteen hundred or twenty-five hundred acres.

Don't even get them started on corn. By the time they get that harvested and out of the ground, the quality will probably have gone down, which means that the test weight will have gone down, too.

"We don't want to figure out how much we'll be losing there," says Larry.

"One night of rain sets us back three to four days," says Steve, wearing a gray T-shirt layered under a plaid shirt-jacket that he's in the process of peeling off. Because always, a T-shirt. "With beans, the headers have to be able to slide on the ground, or else we can't get 'em out."

"Didn't set me back," Joerg says. "I just wrote out checks."

"Yeah, because you're retired," Steve says.

"Or retarded," Joerg replies.

Joerg played golf at the country club yesterday. Then went to the bar.

"Probably just sat in the bar," says Steve.

"Oh, come on now. I *played* golf," says Joerg. "*Then* I went to the bar."

This is about when the rain started, and while Joerg was at the bar at the country club, Steve was walking into Pinky's for the poker game, which is why he's ordering breakfast this morning.

"You're actually having breakfast?" asks Betty.

"Yeah," says Steve. "Biscuits."

"How many?"

"Two."

"Two?" says Betty. "Wow, you really did have a rough night."

The rough night lasted until two in the morning, which is fine because no one's going to be doing any harvesting today anyway thanks to the rain that didn't come over the summer and now won't stop.

"How much did you get at your place?" asks Larry.

"I got fifty-five hundredths," says Joerg.

Enough to shut the combines down in the fields, which is where they'll sit for probably three to four days unless it gets windy tomorrow and dries the soil out, and then *maybe* they can run on Saturday. But for now, no one is doing anything. Maybe they'll fix things. Or pay some bills. What else can you do?

"In '72," Kenny says, "Harvest started in the fall and ended in spring of '73."

The market was good in '73. "I got more per bushel for wheat in '73 than I can get now but our expenses are ten times what they were back then," he says.

"Wheat Tops $4 a Bushel to Reach a Price Record" screamed the front page of the *New York Times* in July of 1973 when global demand for grain exports spiked after the Soviet Union surprised everyone with a massive order for wheat. "For the first time in the nation's history, the price of a 60-pound bushel of wheat crossed the $4 level," the article excitedly proclaimed. "The once impossible dream of the farmer became a reality yesterday on Midwest grain exchanges."

When the world needs grain, the American farmer is ready and willing to produce it, but that's not always a good thing. "We raise more than we should," says Joerg. "We just *have* to do the max. We're able to raise a lot more bushels now because of technology being what it is, but it cuts our throat."

"We try to grow our way out of poverty, but it never works," says Steve. "There's too much product on the market because genetics have made it so much easier to grow bigger, but that's worked against us. We raise so many more bushels than we did before that it drives the price down."

"It's the same with cattle," says Kenny, "Back then, if you raised a twelve-hundred-pound cow you were really doing well. Now, with genetics, you need a sixteen-hundred-pound cow to make your money. Every year it gets goofy. There are so many regulations. So much pressure and stress. Farming was fun thirty or forty years ago. It's not fun anymore. There's so much money involved."

"It's a competitive business," says Carlson.

"And it can be cutthroat," says Joerg.

And, yes, most of them will say, through it all, we still support President Trump. "Make America Great Again!" Which CNN and Twitter and millennials podcasting out of flexible workspaces with a community Keurig think is nuts, especially because of the trade war and retaliatory tariffs. Like the 25 percent tariff that China slapped on all imports of US soybeans. Which is taking money out of the American farmer's pocket. A lot of money.

Before the boxing match started, China was our biggest customer. Between January and October 2017 alone, they imported 21.4 million metric tons of soybeans from American farmers; representing 60 percent of our total soybean export and a $12 billion chunk of change. Once China and the US started duking it out, the number of our soybeans imported into China just one year later, between January and October 2018, tanked to 8.2 million metric tons. Never mind that prices going into November were already down two bucks a bushel from what they were in July, a number that wasn't too hot to begin with anyway.

But at least Trump is doing *something*, they still say. At least he's *trying* to help the American farmer.

"We love Trump," says Carlson. "He's evening the playing field for us."

"He does things that need done," says Kenny. "What comes into this country is not taxed the same as what goes out. Go into your local Walmart; 90 percent of everything is "Made in China." Trump came to Topeka about two weeks ago and people waited in line for three hours to get in. He says he loves them farmers. And we believe him, yeah."

"We need people to care about the United States," says Carlson. "Who is listening? Who gives a damn? I'll tell ya; it really burns me up. These politicians, Republican *and* Democrat, there's no bipartisanship *at all* anymore."

"Trump is the first guy who ever offered to help us out here," says Joerg. "We need an even playing field."

America has a notorious track record when it comes to its relationships with industries, behaving kinda like a bad boyfriend. It falls in love with whatever is contributing the most to its economic backbone—railroads, textiles, apparel, mining, automobiles, steel, framing—then goes out of its way to court it, woo it, and bend over backward for it. There is as much giving as there is taking. But as time goes on, the seduction of competitive advantage takes over. There's an overabundance of supply, created with the cheapest labor possible. It's about quantity, not quality. The bottom line becomes the most important part of the equation. Not fair labor or giving consumers something that will actually last. There is less giving, more take, take, taking. Poorer wages. Fewer jobs. A demand for more at a much lower cost. The relationship begins to sour. The honeymoon is over.

When America has decided it is done romancing an industry, the breakup can be swift or feel like a slow, painful death, but either way, it is inhumanely cold, always brutal, and leaves a devastating trail of destruction—economically and emotionally—in its wake.

"It's not a question of whether it's going to happen to the American family farm," Larry says. "It's already happening. We are starting to disappear."

The Broker

The boys at the Chicago Board of Trade are represented by one boy here in Courtland and that is commodities broker Troy Newman. Ag Marketing Partners shares office space with JenRus Freelance at 301 Main, and when Troy sends out an email, it comes with the standard industry disclaimer: "Trading advice reflects our good faith judgment at a specific time and is subject to change without notice. There is no guarantee that the advice we give will result in profitable trades."

Troy is very laid back. He coaches Little League, has three kids and is married to Christy, one of the country's top-selling distributors of Mary Kay Cosmetics.

Troy grew up here in the eighties when things were *really* bad. Which was enough of a cautionary tale for him to say, "Um, thanks, but no thanks," to a lifetime of planting, harvesting, and praying.

"Would I like to farm? Yeah. But I'd also like to eat," he says.

So, he went to K-State and got a master's degree in agricultural economics instead. Troy gets why the farmer has a migraine. He gets that he's probably not the most popular guy in town sometimes, too.

"Well," he laughs. "I don't cause the markets, but I guess it's like cussin' out the weatherman. What they're really cussin' is a slow harvest, the rising costs of machinery and supplies, and the mud and the rain which all eat into profits."

Which weren't going to be very high in the first place. Not this year. Certainly not the last few years. And probably not next year, either. Although he's seen worse.

"Commodities were about half this price when I started in 1998. Costs were much lower, however. Profits or lack of them was about the same. Land values have increased a lot since then, which gives those who own it equity, but that doesn't always create a lot of cash flow," he says.

Headlines and podcasts and tweets about subsidies and handouts and farmer's welfare that'll only make them rich farmers even richer? Please. It's enough to make Steve, Larry, Slug, Kenny, Joerg, Carlson, and Hootie howl.

"Asset rich, cash poor!"

"The only rich farmer is a dead farmer!"

There's always something eating into your profits: Hail the size of golf balls in June. Too much rain when you don't want it. A drought when you desperately need it. Insects. Politics. Taxes. Costs. The market. The weather. Roll the dice. Press your luck. Sorry, try again. Thanks for playing!

Beans slipped a bit because of the trade war with China. But also adding to the unpleasantness is the record soybean production in the United States and Brazil over the past few years, resulting in too many beans and not enough buyers.

"Usually, demand is growing year after year but because we have a surplus, we have a decrease in demand."

This also means that beans are trading for low prices. And when you've got too many beans in the field and not enough interest in buying them, beans pile up.

Things had been looking up thanks to a drought in Argentina, which raised the prices to around nine bucks a bushel. So, American farmers got excited and planted more beans. This is about the same time they realized that Brazil had a similar epiphany, just in time for everyone who was planting beans to watch the price of beans start to slip.

"Add the tariff, which no one expected, and now you've got a perfect storm," he says.

That perfect storm resulted in the price of beans dropping $2 per bushel. Which doesn't sound too terrible, until you start to count. There are around 85 million acres of soybeans in the United States. If the average farmer has a thousand acres of soybeans, he's raising about 50 bushel per acre. And at $2 less per bushel of beans, that's $100 less he's making per acre. Which is $100,000 less in total profit.

"Which is a lot of cash to lose," Troy says. "And that really impacts everyone. Take a hundred dollars an acre away from every acre in the county and you're taking away all that money from the county, too. It's boom or bust. You have to be an optimist and just hope it will get better."

You have to keep hoping. That the gully washer will come. That the gully washer will stop. It's the faith that Larry and Steve talk about. The risk that Hootie is willing to take for the freedom of doing what he loves. The reason Tanner doesn't hit the panic button at the Swedish-American every time the market dips.

"What we do here is help the farmer market their crops," says Troy. "We use futures contracts and options from the Chicago Board of Trade to lock prices in for the farmers. For example, a lot of them tried to contract to sell as many beans as possible in the spring when prices were high, but then there's always that fear that you're going to overshoot what you actually produce. When that happens, you have to make up the difference in price."

If you can't deliver what you've contracted to sell, you can't just shrug it off and say, "Oops. Sorry." The person you're contracted to deliver to is under contract to deliver to someone else, too. And if you can't deliver to them, they can't deliver to anyone, either. Which is where crop insurance can help. But it's still only going to pay out a percentage of what you would have made had you been able to deliver all two thousand bushel of beans you were contracted to sell at $9/bushel. Someone has to pony up to cover the difference, and that someone is you.

You're also hedging your bets that when you lock in your contract, the price of beans is going to be a lot better at that very moment than it will be when it's time to harvest them. But because you don't have a crystal ball, if you guess wrong and contract your beans at say, $9/bushel, and by the time you get to harvest them, the market spikes to $12/bushel, well, that's too bad for you.

"There is always something to worry about if you're a farmer," says Troy. "It's everything; if the price is good, then the weather is bad. If they have a record year of production, then so does a competing country." This is kinda why you might not feel too bad that your neighbors south of the equator get smacked with a drought. Nothing personal. But when catastrophe strikes, market prices will rise to adjust for the lack of supply and increase in demand.

The biggest influence on the price of a commodity by far is the weather, either here or somewhere else. So, just because Mother Nature is being nice to you doesn't mean you're going to be rolling in the dough. She might have been nice to everyone else, too. And when she's being nice to everyone, the market doesn't like it, because too much supply means too little demand.

"There are a lot of people buying and selling and right now, we're seeing low prices because more people are wanting to sell than buy," he says. "All it would take is for everyone to plant 5 percent less and it'd be fine. But there are too many producers and they can't get on the same page. They tried a union once and that didn't work. Also, most farmers are friends, but the reality is that they're also competitors, too."

So, everyone having a good year of production sounds lovely but really isn't a good thing. Having catastrophic flooding is a darn shame but usually *is* a good thing. This is probably why a farmer's drug of choice tends to be ibuprofen.

"Ten things are going on all at once all the time that tend to weigh on a person," he says. "But there is no villain against farming and people overestimate how much money someone who trades makes."

Most people also overestimate how much a farmer makes, too. "I heard someone on the radio talking about how a farmer makes a 50 percent return on his investment and I about fell over. If they make 1 to 2 percent, then they're doing really good and the reality is that a lot of times, that number is zero."

Farming isn't like owning an apartment building, where you expect to receive enough rent to cover the mortgage and then some to cash flow. In farming, the money is in the land, and land can't always generate a nice cash flow because of how expensive it is to get anything to grow out of it. So, if you are selling your land, it's because you have reached the end of your rope, you're way behind on payments for everything, the market won't cooperate, the weather won't cooperate, and the only way to stop the bleeding is to auction off your most valuable asset.

"It's why they say that no one lives poorer or dies richer than a farmer," he says. "To make it work you just have to not go broke and stay at it. No one gets into farming because they want to get rich, like someone who says they want to grow up to be a doctor or a lawyer might have in mind. People farm because they love to farm and they want to farm. It's a lifestyle as much as it is an occupation."

The Morning Coffee: Friday

It's 6:50 a.m. There are two pots of freshly brewed coffee on the Bunn and the griddle is empty. No eggs, no toast, no sausage patties, no biscuits. Nothing sizzling. Because no one is here. Not Slug or Steve or Kenny or Joerg or Larry. Just Don.

"Well, Larry has a doctor's appointment this morning so at least we know where he is," Betty says. The doctor's appointment is to follow up on the brown spots on his skin, just like Don and Carlson and Kenny, whose doctor removed thirteen brown spots and only charged him for nine. "But where is everyone else?"

"Sleeping in probably," Don says.

When his alarm went off this morning, Don hit the snooze button. The ground is still too wet to help out with the harvest so what's the point of getting up at that hour, anyway? He'd rather be on his Harley, heading toward Portland or Mount Rushmore, enjoying retirement, doing whatever he wants, which is why he's already got ten thousand miles on a bike he bought three years ago.

Don can still remember growing up in Southern California. In 1955, the state knocked on the door of his father's dairy farm, informed everyone that they were building a new, six-lane interstate highway right smack dab through their house, and gave the Lieb family the option of leaving now or leaving later, but either way, they had to leave. Which they did. After high school, Don joined the Peace Corps and headed off to Iran, which is where he met Carlson and Mrs. C.

"In 1974 I made the best decision I ever made by coming here to Courtland," Don says. "I don't lock my house at night. I keep my keys in my truck. I never liked lots of people and I never liked traffic."

He knows that a lot of people back in his hometown spend two hours commuting to work and two hours commuting home and thanks, but no thanks. "You couldn't pay me to move back to Southern California and not be able to leave the house between 6 and 9 a.m. and 3 and 7 p.m. because all six lanes of traffic aren't moving," he says. Every time he goes to visit his parents back home, he gets a headache.

You also couldn't pay him enough to keep working as an EMT. For the past forty years, he's seen enough carnage to the body to last him two lifetimes and it was time to give it a break.

"I'm starting to get worried," Betty says, glancing at the door again. It's past 7 a.m., the chairs are still empty, and where in the world is Joerg?

"Everyone probably woke up and went back to sleep," Don says reassuringly. He was supposed to be helping with the harvesting. But no one is harvesting and probably won't be until Monday. The ground is still too wet. The fields look like mud bogs.

"There he is!" Don says as the door swings open.

"Where were you?" Betty asks. "You're never this late."

"Oh hell, I don't know," Joerg says.

"Are your glasses foggy?" Don asks.

"Do you want breakfast?" Betty asks.

"Yes," Joerg says.

"So, you *were* at the club last night," Betty says.

"Did you make it into the house or only as far as the man cave?" Don asks.

"The house! I made it into my own bed," Joerg says. "Goddamn, I wasn't *that* bad."

By the time he gets his two eggs over easy with toast, Carlson, Jim, Norm, Kenny, and Hootie all have coffee in their mugs and conversation shifts from the weather to AOC and the Green New Deal.

"She wants to get rid of cows. Says all the methane gas they produce is polluting the air."

"*What* is she even talking about?"

"Oh, who knows."

"Has she ever even *been* on a farm?"

"Out of all the things polluting the world, the Green New Deal is worried about cow farts?"

"The gas that she's talking about comes out the front end anyway, not the back end."

"You know, they say that by 2040 most meat products will be meatless."

"Yeah, 'cuz of Meatless Monday."

"Maybe we should start buying stock in veggie burgers."

"Eh. It's just a fad."

There's talk about skin cancer and all the ads online and in the *Courtland Journal* from big-city lawyers who want to know if you think the Round-Up you used to kill all your weeds caused your non-Hodgkin lymphoma.

"One guy in the city sprays his driveway for weeds, gets cancer, and every lawyer in the country starts salivating."

"Been using it for years and we don't have any issues."

There's talk about the bobcats and mountain lions and coyotes that are prone to make the occasional appearance, any of which might have been responsible for the three calves that disappeared from Joerg's field about twenty years ago, but who's to say?

Since it's too wet for anyone to harvest, Kenny will probably help his wife wrangle all their cats into a new shed that he has been building for them.

"The cat house," Joerg says.

Joerg is going to the sale barn in Mankato around 1 p.m., not to buy any cattle, but just because. Carlson is going to play with the new toy that he took a picture of and saved to his phone; a shiny little skid steer from Case that Mrs. C kinda rolled her eyes about.

"We're supposed to be retiring, not buying things. But it makes him happy, so . . . "

But what everyone really wants to know is if it really is true that Joerg got a lap dance at the country club last night.

"I did *not*," he says.

"Was it as good as that time you kissed that guy?" Hootie laughs from another table.

"Will you pipe down back there?" Joerg says. "It wasn't like *that*."

"Are you sure?" Hootie prods.

"Oh, come on now, goddamnit," Joerg says, digging into his eggs, just as the door flies open and Steve storms in. He takes about six steps, huffs about something, spins around on one heel, and starts to walk out again.

"What's wrong with you?" Hootie asks.

"Fuck you, you big stupid fuck," Steve yells.

"Oooh, you're cranky," Hootie laughs.

"Damn right I am! After the morning I had you'd be in a fucking bad mood, too."

"And there goes the f-bomb," Carlson says.

"Fucking right!" Steve yells, his voice rising a few decibels.

"Brownie," Joerg suddenly calls out, slamming down his fork. "You need laid!"

"Damn right I do!" Steve hollers. But no one can hear what he's hollering about because everyone is howling. *You need laid, Brownie. Ha. Ha. Ha.* And everyone keeps howling while Steve is at the door barking about the fucking bad day he's having and how yes, *he would very much like to get fucking laid right now so you all can just go fuck yourselves!*

He finishes whatever he was barking about and storms out the door, slamming it shut behind him. Betty watches as the Ford speeds off, a plate of biscuits and gravy in her hand, looking like she wants to say something, but she doesn't.

"Damn is he cranky," Joerg says, shaking his head.

"Doesn't take much to get him wound up lately," Kenny adds.

"There are some issues going on there," Carlson says.

"Oh, I know," Joerg says, taking a sip of his coffee. "But he definitely needs laid."

The Veterinarian

It's Friday, around 8:30 in the morning at the sale barn in Mankato. About four hundred cows are waiting, and Brock Hanel is squeezing an old bottle of Dawn that's been filled with non-spermicidal lube into the palm of his hand.

"This is what poor vets use," he jokes as he rubs it around, coating the long, plastic glove he's wearing. It stretches up to his shoulder, clipped to his gray sweatshirt with a pair of surgical clamps. "We do the dishes with the Dawn, wash out the bottle, and fill it with lube."

The $22,000 squeeze chute opens, a cow walks in, and hydraulic gates keep it from going anywhere as Brock opens a door near its hindquarters and leans in. In a second, his entire arm disappears into the cow, checking to see how far along she is in her 285 or so days of pregnancy.

"Five!" he says as he pulls out his arm, which is now completely covered in manure. The squeeze chute opens, releases the cow, and another one comes in. He grabs the bottle of Dawn, squirts more lube into his hand, opens the rear gate, and leans in, his arm disappearing up to his shoulder again.

"Four months!" he calls out.

"Four?" Lacey replies from behind a laptop that's been set up inside of a bare-bones wooden shack with tin nailed to the side. The shack doesn't have air conditioning, although it does have two little heaters to keep it at like, 40 degrees when it's −5 outside. It's also home to a black field mouse that just darted across the floor.

"Four," Brock confirms.

Lacey is tall and thin and naturally blonde, with a head full of very thick, shiny hair pulled into a low ponytail that smells like something very fresh and clean.

She has been helping Brock out forever. "His dad was kind enough to bring me on and Brock was kind enough not to get rid of me. I'm not sure what my title is. . . . I like to say I'm his peon."

Lacey lives an hour west, smokes Marlboro Ultra Lights, is one of the few women you'll ever see on this side of the sale barn, knew exactly what she was getting into when she started this job, and has very little patience for the whole sexual-harassment-hashtag-me-too thing.

"One day, I was wearing a pearl button shirt and one of the old-timers came up to me and said, 'Blondie, you know what the speed limit in Texas is? Wide-open!' and he yanked my shirt right open. And there I was, everything hanging out. You have to be able to just laugh and not take things too seriously."

Brock and Lacey and the rest of his crew will be doing this until three or four o'clock in the afternoon. Open gate, herd cattle in, close gate, wrangle heifers and bulls and calves single file into the alley and then one by one into the squeeze chute. Tag. Record. Arm into the rectum for a preg check, if needed. Hands into mouth for mouth check to determine age, if needed. "The better the teeth, the younger the cow," he says. Release. Repeat. Arm. Rectum. Mouth. Arm. Rectum. Mouth.

Getting done at three or four o'clock in the afternoon at the sale barn on Friday is not a normal day. Normally, there are six to seven hundred cows that need to be tagged, mouthed, and preg checked, not just four hundred. On a really busy Friday at the Mankato Sale Barn, which is about twenty miles west of Courtland, he'll be here until two o'clock in the morning with his lube and his plastic glove and three thousand cows to put through the chute, stopping only long enough to grab lunch at the Buffalo Roam up on Highway 36. Pouring rain, blazing sun, freezing snow. It practically takes a blizzard to shut the sale barn down on Fridays, which means that whatever Mother Nature is dishing out, Brock and Lacey and the rest of his crew are usually taking for ten, twelve, or eighteen hours a day.

Brock knew he wanted to be a veterinarian when he was four years old. He watched his dad do the same thing he's doing now. And Brock has brought his six-year-old daughter Maddy along so often that she can sit quietly on a stool and munch on cookies while her daddy performs a C-section on a birthing cow. And when she gets dropped off at the Carlson's house to be babysat, she'll tell Mrs. C more than she ever wanted to know about things like prolapses.

"With stunning accuracy," says Mrs. C.

Brock's office is always open even when it's technically closed, he has been on the board of the Swedish-American for five years and chairman for two, and when he gets stressed out and can find a minute to get away, he'll grab his bow and arrow or his fishing pole or head twenty miles east to the Belleville Municipal Airport and fly at low altitude in his glider.

"Tanner says it's a cot. It's not a cot. It's an Ultra-Lite," he says.

Brock's wife, Angie, is a nurse. They have three kids, who Mrs. C often babysits, and they just renovated their house, which sits next to the veterinary clinic on 36.

Brock believes in a diversified portfolio to minimize monetary risk and maximize monetary gain, and has his hands in many different investments that he'll rattle off while he's opening this gate to open that pen to get the cows single file into the caged alley and then, one by one into the squeeze chute. He doesn't get the kind of people in town who were born here, raised here, and never left here . . . even to go out to dinner.

"It's absurd. Forty-eight, boy, victor, queen, fifty-four, fifty-five," he calls out to Lacey, who is in the wooden shack typing each of the cow's IDs into an Excel spreadsheet.

"This is a US Veterinary Service clip. So, this is an *official*, official ID. They could travel to another country and it's all traceable. They're gettin' so that they have it where it's all radiofrequency. There's our scanner," he points to a piece of plastic mounted on a beam above the head of the squeeze chute. "We're in beta but as the cattle run through with their EID tags, they'll be able to hit them like that. It's just like a K-Tag or EZPass," he says as the chute opens. Each group of cattle that comes in also requires a paper ticket that's filled out with the date, the sale owner's name and address, the number of cows, and what type of cows they are bringing to auction.

"The owner signs off on it because that's his legal way of saying 'I unloaded four cows' whereas if the sale barn accidentally marked it down as three cows, he might not get paid for a cow."

The traceability is important because if someone gets sick eating their Salisbury steak, the USDA can find out exactly where that beef came from. "It's why our meat is the safest meat in the world," he says. Whether you're moving your cattle across the street or across state lines, it's got to be tagged and accounted for.

Up for grabs today at the auction are calves, kill cows (going to the slaughterhouse), bred cows (pregnant), bulls, and steer. Brock will be seeing every one of them before the sale starts at 10 a.m. over in the new state-of-the-art auction barn, which is beginning to smell like hamburgers as the kitchen gets ready for the lunch rush and no, they didn't just whack one of the incoming cows and throw it on the grill.

"Beef needs to age before it tastes any good," he says.

"Come on girls!" he urges. "Blue tag! Forty-seven, Tom, entrée, Victor, eighty-six, forty-nine," he calls out. The kill cows will go straight to the feedlot to fatten up before they're sent to the slaughterhouse. Once they get there, they'll get a captive bullet to the head ("That captive bullet to the head is absolutely the most humane way to euthanize an animal," he says), have their throats slit to bleed out, get skinned, and then cut at the thirteenth rib with the efficiency of an assembly line so that a USDA licensed vet can take a look at the marble and grade the meat so that consumers can have an idea of what they're buying at the grocery store. Packages labeled Certified Angus Beef are the best. Choice is okay. Select sounds impressive but is basically the reason why McDonald's can get away with charging you only eighty-nine cents for a cheeseburger. "Select is basically crap," he says.

The bred cows are worth more money than a cow that isn't pregnant because you're basically getting a two for one. The bulls that are here, the ones that weigh eighteen hundred pounds, are about 65 to 70 percent edible, which means that one bull has about fourteen hundred pounds of meat on him; a nice paycheck for the farmer who sells him. When the auction starts in a few hours, the auctioneer will start his rapid-fire, incoherent chattering into the microphone. And men with cowboy hats will talk into phones and covertly cover their mouths with their hands while they make seemingly undetectable signals to bid on young calves and adolescent cows and bulls and steer and even the old family dairy cows they call gummies because they are twelve-years-old and don't have any teeth left.

The cattle will be bought at a price based on their weight at the auction, which is why it's a big no-no to lean on the gray railing that surrounds the pen.

"That whole area is basically a free-floating scale," Brock says. "So, when the sale is going, and you put pressure on this gray railing, it adds to the weight on the cattle. Which isn't fair to the buyer or the seller. But anyway, if the calf weighs five hundred pounds and it brings $1.50 per pound, you pay $750 for the calf."

The pen is a patch of dirt surrounded by a small auditorium with stadium seating, seats that are usually filled with a lot of spectators, and only a handful of buyers because people love to come to the sale barn to watch the sale, not necessarily to buy. The ones that do buy can bid in such subtle ways that it becomes nearly impossible to tell who's bidding, and if you really want to get back at someone who's been pissing you off royally lately, you bid on what they are bidding on, thus driving up the prices, and who gives a damn if you end up overpaying a few bucks per pound as long as your message gets heard loud and clear. Sellers love that.

Bid away, boys!

Maybe one out of two thousand cows that are brought to the auction won't be sold at the auction and Brock might buy six to seven hundred of them himself to take to the feedlot over in Scandia that he owns a 33 percent share of. Technically, a farmer could just skip the auction and take his cows straight to the feedlot, but no one wants the risk because the price of cattle per pound goes up and down as frequently as the wind blows. "Sometimes fat cattle are worth $1.30 and sometimes they're worth $1.00," he says. "The farmers work hard, they bring their stock in here, and they sell them so they can be done with it. It's hedging; just like you'd do in the stock market."

"The black cow's a bitch!" he warns as the animal begins pushing and pulling and making a lot of racket inside of the pen. "If she turns around when she comes out of the chute instead of walking into the pen, you've got about two seconds to jump onto the nearest fence," he says, which is why he has the Springer Magrath in his hand and four more cattle prods juiced up and ready to go.

"They create electricity, and it helps get the cattle in," he explains. "A lot of PETA people believe it's inhumane treatment because they will see a video that shows six guys on a down cow just going for her, but that's not what these are made for. Instead of beating on them with a stick, it's used to just tell them where to go and the proper placement and the way you stand keeps you in control so you can move them way better. You ask them to do something, and they understand," he says, opening the gate. "Go! Get in there! Go! Go! Go! Go! Go! Go!" he urges, giving a reluctant one a quick zap. "And see, that time I used the prod once, but if you didn't have that you would have had to stand here and beat on them and yell at them to get them to do what you need them to do. Cows are not stupid animals. They're actually pretty smart."

So smart that a cow knows to tilt its head so that it can maneuver its horns through the gates leading to the squeeze chute and another can stand there in the alley and make a racket because it knows what the squeeze chute means and it's not happy about having to go through it.

"Come on girl!" he urges, giving her a quick zap.

Each of the cows weighs about twelve to thirteen hundred pounds and the State of Kansas pays Brock fifteen cents per cow to put a back tag on each of them, which is another form of identification and traceability. Then Brock charges the owner of the cattle $3 to run them through the chute and do all his checks. "I basically say they're healthy enough to sell," he says. He also gets twenty cents for every head that sells. So, at the very least he'll get $3.35 per cow. If he adds a few more services, like a preg check for $4 and mouth check for $2, he'll get $9.35 per cow.

For bulls, he gets $5 instead of $3. "They're more work and tougher on all of the equipment," he says. "I can do six heifers a minute so I can make $18 a minute just on pregging. There will be days there's three thousand head in there. . . . So, we'll make a couple of grand, but we earn it. It's not an old man's game."

The Morning Coffee: Saturday

The regular crew was back to their routine this morning, which meant that by six o'clock in the morning, the Bunn was brewing, and the griddles were sizzling, and no one was telling anyone to go fuck themselves.

Instead, everyone is talking about the 74 degrees they're going to get today, how they'd love to see a nice breeze whip the moisture out of the ground. Because the forecast is calling for rain again on Tuesday. This means that even if they can get the combines running this weekend, there will probably be a lot of sitting around and waiting again in a few days. It'll be too wet and muddy to get the wheels on the ground when there could be corn and beans and milo being cut, and wheat being planted, and money being made. So, while technically God *did* answer their prayers for the gully washer they were asking for back in July, they just wished he hadn't decided to send it during the middle of harvest.

A lot of the beans are useless because they've been sitting in the fields for so long. All short and thin. Which no one wants. "We don't like 'em like we like our women," Joerg says.

"Since the combine isn't ready, I'll probably clean the auger wagon out and maybe I'll go down to Tallgrass to chase some bulls today . . . or maybe the vets," Steve says.

"You ain't man enough to chase them vets around," Larry laughs.

"The hell I ain't!" Steve says

"Brownie," Joerg interjects, "you need to get laid. That is no shit."

"Yeah," Steve agrees, sipping his coffee. "I do."

"You know, one of those boys already got to one of them vets," Larry said. "One of them is pregnant."

"Is she?" Steve asks.

"You know, when he was born," Larry says, pointing to Steve, "I called my father-in-law and he said, 'What'd you get?' and I said, 'I got a bull calf.' Boy, I could hear my mother-in-law cursin' her head off in the background . . . "

"You coulda said you got an adding machine," Steve says.

"Yeah," Larry agrees.

"Did you watch the whole thing last night?" Joerg asks.

"Sure did. Eighteen innings. Longest World Series in history," Jim says, reaching for a coffee pot.

"Who won?" Joerg asks.

"Boston," Jim replies.

"Hell, you didn't watch that game!" Joerg says. "I knew you didn't watch the whole thing."

"I did. Dodgers won 3–2," Jim says, topping everybody's mug off. "Damn game went seven hours."

"Oh, come on now, goddamnit!" Joerg says as Jim pours more than Joerg's mug can hold.

"Didn't end until two-thirty in the mornin'," Jim adds, ignoring him. "Longest World Series game ever played."

"I made it until quarter after eleven," Joerg says.

"I made it to ten," Slug says.

"I watched the whole thing," Jim says. "Longest in history."

"Well," Kenny says, "I'll probably help my wife out with her cat project again today. She wants to get them into the barn so that a bobcat or coyote doesn't get 'em."

"How is the cat house coming?" Joerg asks, a question that Kenny ignores.

"I had three cats once that went into the cornfields and only two came out. Don't know what happened, but the other two won't go in there no more," Slug says.

"I'm going to watch football," Joerg says. "Whoever is playing."

Carlson is probably going to play with his new skid steer that Mrs. C rolled her eyes over because really, did he *really* need to buy that?

"I told her that if I don't get that new skid steer, I'm buying her a new snow shovel," he says. "She didn't like that too much."

"He bought it just because he wanted a new toy to play with," Joerg says. "Goddamnit!" he exclaims as Carlson nearly overflows his coffee mug again with another refill. "You're just pissed that my beans got cut and yours haven't yet."

"You know," Larry says, "we might be able to cut corn this afternoon. It's hanging down and the shucks will shed the moisture off. Not the beans, though. Or the milo. Too much moisture in 'em. But there'll be someone out there who is dumb enough to try."

The Harvest

Someone *was* dumb enough to try to harvest yesterday and that someone was Larry.

"I'm going to show you why we quit," Steve says. "We'll run tomorrow."

The Browns can't run because their combine got stuck in seven inches of mud, started leaning, and was *thisclose* to rolling into the Republican River with Larry still inside.

"This is what dad did and he's fine," Steve's text read, along with a photo.

So, the Browns took a break but got out the next day, as did Jim File, who was driving the grain cart while his son-in-law, Al Reisenweber, ran the combine.

A farmer's grain cart sounds like some cute little Red Ryder type of thing but really, it's a massive, green metal bin on wheels that stands about twelve feet off the ground and is pulled along by a tractor with tires that are taller than your four-door sedan.

The telltale sign that the earth is finally dry enough to get whatever needs harvesting out of the ground are the plumes of what looks like smoke rising off the horizon; a tailwind of dirt and dust and residue kicking up from combines that are so massive, you need a ladder to get into the cab. When they're chugging along at five miles per hour, they're chewing their way through rows and rows and rows and rows of corn, soybean, milo, or wheat with headers that can be anywhere from twenty to fifty feet wide. Within eyeshot of the combine is the 18-wheeler that will be filled by an auger spitting out whatever has been harvested, which will then be driven to the grain elevator for it to be weighed. When they're done weighing what you've harvested, they'll hand you a check that'll have you praising God or cursing someone.

Right now, it's the corn and the beans that are giving everyone a migraine. They should have been harvested three weeks ago. But thanks to all the rain, everything is still sitting on the ground.

"So, now the beans are shellin' which means the pods are open and beans are falling onto the ground and so is a farmer's money," says Al. "And the days that the ground has been dry enough for the combine wheels not to sink into the dirt have been few and far between. But, that's life. You just do the best with what God gives you."

The spring-loaded seat of the combine he's driving absorbs every topographical dip or divot he's riding over. "I got twenty-two hundred bushel of beans out of my own thirty-five acres. In the spring, I pre-sold half of them for $9.71 a bushel. Which is really, really good. But I only got $7.16 for the beans I just harvested. So, I basically lost about twenty-five hundred bucks because no one has a crystal ball, which is why you don't sell more than half of what you're growing at a time. Because what if something happens? I can't show up to the elevator with half my beans when I've got a contract to fulfill for all of them."

The thirty acres he's currently harvesting in the combine belong to his father-in-law, Jim, who owns twenty-five hundred acres in total and is the one driving the John Deere tractor with the Grain Storm 1000 grain cart. When Al swings out his auger, it will signal to Jim that he's ready to unload about a thousand pounds of soybeans. Jim will take them to the semi and dump them into the trailer, then go back into the field and wait for Al's signal so they can repeat the process over and over until the trailer is filled and can be driven to the elevator. When the farmers are harvesting, it is an endless line of 18-wheelers on the road, lined up at the elevator, then heading back into the fields. Progress.

The head that's attached to the front of Al's combine is thirty feet wide and functions like a giant pair of scissors and a vacuum cleaner rolled into one, chewing through the beanstalks, cutting them, and sifting everything into a feeder hose. The feeder hose then shells, sorts, and spits things out; either beans into the back of the combine or residue back onto the ground, which is what creates the plume of dirt and dust that looks like smoke signals rising from the prairie.

Farm machinery isn't what it used to be with nothing but open cabs and rough, back-breaking rides. These days, your $300,000 New Holland CR8.90 combine has an interior with enough technology to launch a spaceship. Most of the cab is enclosed by windows that run from the floor to the ceiling. And inside the cab are monitors spitting out all sorts of information; your location according to the GPS you're locked into for autopilot, a digital map of the acreage that's being harvested, a live video from outside, the moisture levels of the crops you are harvesting. It is efficient, precise, and is constantly talking to you. *Bleep. Bleep. Bloop.*

The magic number for soybean moisture is 13 percent. The beans that Al

is cutting are registering at 13.6 percent moisture, which is just about perfect. Beans at 15 to 16 percent moisture mean they're too wet and the elevator will say thanks, but no thanks. If the moisture is at 9 percent, it's too low, and that will eat into your profits since your beans are measured by weight.

There are also a lot of buttons on the console that control how fast you're going, the speed of the fan, the rotor speed, the threshing clearance . . .

"I don't feel good about this," he says suddenly, throwing the combine into reverse. "The ground here is pretty soft."

When Al's in the combine, with its coordinates set and a GPS talking to nine satellites somewhere in space to help it run one perfectly straight line after another on autopilot, he sometimes writes songs in his head that may or may not be turned into something that he and his wife, Amanda, will sing on stage as the duo Deliberate Kin. "Bluegrass with a little bit of country thrown in," he says. They travel all over for gigs: Oklahoma, Missouri, Wyoming, Nebraska, Colorado, Kansas.

Al plays the mandolin and guitar, Amanda's got the percussion covered, and they both sing. They just released their first album, *Things Happen*, and people can buy it for fifteen bucks at their shows. Or, you can order it from their website, pay $5 for shipping, and wait for it to show up at your front door. Most of the songs are more of the uplifting sort and no, he really doesn't feel the need to get political with them. Al doesn't like talking politics at all and would rather just keep his mouth shut about all of it, but he will say that he hates Trump.

"As a person," he explains. "I just don't think that's the type of person that we should have as the president. I think he's a terrible human being and a bad example. But I want our songs to be positive, not political. I want people to listen to them and just feel good for a couple of minutes."

Al grew up in Sioux Falls, got his degree in horticulture, and owns his own construction company. He and Amanda have two girls that they home-school, and the whole family makes the most out of Amazon Prime since the closest big box store is Walmart, an hour and a half away.

"It's worth it," he says. "The cost of living here is next to nothing. It doesn't bother me that I can go days and not see anyone." He kinda likes it; doing whatever he wants and not having a neighbor to complain about it.

"I love it here," he says, detaching the thirty-foot-wide bean header onto a trailer that's hooked to Jim's Chevy Silverado. He's done with these beans for now. The ground that's left to harvest is still too wet and he doesn't want to get stuck like Larry did. So, the header will be moved ten miles east, to a much drier field. Which Jim will do with the Silverado, getting there in about five minutes while Al drives the combine over to meet him, taking three times as long, nimbly meandering along one dirt and gravel road then another, never passing anyone in the fifteen minutes it takes him to get to where Jim is already waiting.

He doesn't say a lot as he drives, often looking out onto the horizon. Al and Amanda have a dream. They want to pack up the kids. Go on tour. Write songs and perform shows. Maybe they'll come back in the spring and help Jim with the planting. Or maybe they'll put the house up for sale and just . . . go. His brown hair is pulled back into a ponytail, his face a few days removed from a razor, arms draped over the wheel of the combine. It is quiet in the country. The sun is shining. A brilliant blue sky that stretches ever onward. Surrounded by nothing except what God and the farmer put into the ground.

The Family Business: Tebow Plumbing Co.

When Craig Tebow gets a phone call and hears, "It can't wait until tomorrow," he's on the clock, no matter what time of the day or night it is. The emergencies usually happen during the colder months, because if a pipe is going to burst, of course, it's going to be when the wind is howling, it's 5 degrees outside, and the ground is frozen solid.

Otherwise, it's Monday through Friday from 8 a.m. to 5 p.m. for Tebow Plumbing Co. Craig's got Everett, his nine-month-old grandson, balanced on one arm as he waits on a customer in the shop that his parents, Howard and Cathy, opened in 1963. The building was once a showroom for a Ford dealership. Now, it's filled with things like faucet fixtures and stainless steel kitchen sinks and water softeners, and every kind of plumbing supply you could imagine. It stands a few doors down from the *Courtland Journal*, and the front door is purple.

"K-State," Craig's wife, Lisa, laughs.

Tebow Plumbing has five employees. Paul was with them for thirty-five years, Jerry has been with them for thirty years, and they've been banking with the Swedish-American for fifty years. Tebow's specializes in HVAC, plumbing, backhoe trenching, sewer work, and they can figure out why you've got a dead outlet in your living room because Craig's also a licensed electrician.

His office is tucked into the back of the shop, right behind the counter where Lisa is stationed. Next to the cash register is a filing cabinet that contains every job order that Tebow's ever completed dating back to 1963. This is also the area where all the good signs are hanging.

"Everybody brings joy to this office. Some when they enter. Some when they leave."

"Don't ask me to think. I was hired for my looks."

"Labor Rates: Regular—$24.50. If you laugh—$75.00."

Craig and Lisa were school sweethearts. Dated for five years. And have been married for thirty-five.

"The secret?" she laughs. "I think we complement each other. I'm high-strung with big goals."

"I like to watch TV on the couch," he says.

They have always worked together. And unlike some of the farmers' wives who feel like they're just along for the ride when it comes to decision making, Craig treats her like his equal.

Sometimes, he'll come home and say, "So, did you have a bad day?" This is usually after he gets wind that one of the farmers started chewing Lisa out over a bill or something that has nothing to do with her. Craig's usually the last one to know about it. And Lisa doesn't like the drama, doesn't want to tell him that someone was chewing her out, and kind of rolls her eyes when the person doing the chewing calls Craig to say that they *think* they owe his wife an apology, instead of just calling her and apologizing.

Lisa is petite and blonde and very friendly, has a tattoo on her left foot, and will stand there at the counter while you blow off steam about an invoice you think is too high or whatever else is bothering you until she's had enough. "Oh yeah, that happens," she says. "Even in a town that's so small, you can't avoid each other. Sometimes you can tolerate it, sometimes you can't. But I'm the oldest of six kids. You can't bully me. And most of our ugly customers have died, so . . ."

Craig handles most of the dirty work. "I do not like snakes, spiders, or creepy things," she says. Occasionally they'll go out on calls together. But most of the time, she handles the books, deals with the customers, orders things like rex crimps and auger wire and bulk hoses, and answers the phone.

"Tebow's. Good morning!"

When they're not at work, they're relaxing at home on the farm his mom grew up on or visiting their three kids and three grandkids. Whenever Craig and Lisa drive somewhere, she turns the radio off. "We're talkin'!" she'll say.

Much like Pinky's, C&W Farm Supply, and every other business in town, whether Tebow Plumbing is having a good year or a bad one is largely dependent on whether the market is good, and the weather is cooperating. "Our business really depends on the farmer," he says. "Bigger guys can do a job for nothin', but I can't afford to do that." They've seen the economy here go up and down and just deal with it because what else can you do? A farmer can't change the market or the weather and neither can a plumber.

What they can do is get away for a few days, but never more than three at a time. Lisa likes to go to Vegas. "Oh, I love it. The heat and the lights and the

excitement," she says. If they're not going to Vegas, they're using their season tickets to see what the Kansas State Wildcats can do in the Big 12.

They'll squeeze a trip in over a holiday weekend or when it's slow or when they just need a break. But they're never gone for more than three days. Three days max in thirty-five years.

"That's just our life," she says, "and it works."

The Women: Peggy Nelson

It's installing the sheetrock that Peggy Nelson hates. All that mud and dust.

"No, thanks," she says. "Demolition is *amazing*, though."

And wallpapering? Wallpapering, eh, she doesn't mind it. She's in the middle of removing it right now. Maybe eight layers in with two or three to go, strip upon strip upon strip that's just clinging together with far more glue than what seems reasonable.

"Those last layers are just kind of meshed into one," she says.

Her house was built in the thirties. And she's done a lot of renovating. Especially since she retired in December of 2016. The house has new windows now. New heating. New cooling. And soon, no more wallpaper. There's still a little bit of the knob and tube wiring, though. Which is okay.

Peggy also loves canning. Pickles and salsa and tomatoes and pizza and spaghetti sauce. She is a straight shooter, a meticulous organizer, and has no qualms about swinging a hammer. She is taking a break from the glue and the wallpaper, just finished having lunch at AnTeaQues and, in general, is still trying to figure out the whole retirement thing. "Some days it's good. Some days I'm bored as hell. I'm a people person. And being in that house . . . well, I guess that's why I'm a pain in everyone's ass, talking all the time."

She was the fourth of eleven kids and grew up in central Kansas. Russell. Small town, but a big, small town with its population of four thousand.

"I was a little farm girl. My father farmed. You wanted something done, you did it," she says. "And as I tell kids all the time; if you don't know, *ask*."

Her first husband was from Courtland. They married when she was just nineteen years old.

"If *you* marry young," she told her kids, "I'll kill you."

But he was her first serious boyfriend. Back then, it was just expected that you'd finish school and get married to your first serious boyfriend. So, they

did. It was 1971. Their marriage lasted five years. Long enough for them to have a couple of kids.

"I grew up that night I brought my daughter home from the hospital," she says. "I was bawling. I kept looking at her thinking, 'I'm responsible for this little person.'"

Eventually, she had three little people. Two daughters and a son, who at the age of seventeen came home from school and announced to his mother that he had joined the Marines.

"I could either fight it or go with it," she says. "I went with it. When they graduated, I saw them all in these little groups and thought, 'Oh my god, they're just babies.'" When his training was over and it was time for him to ship off to Iraq, she and a friend went down to Raleigh to pick up his truck and other stuff. For the next eight months, Peggy didn't watch the news. Just like Betty never does while her son is in Afghanistan.

Her son is home now. Got married and has a few kids. "He's a good father and a good husband," she says. "I decided he got the best part of my ex-husband."

Peggy's worked for most of her life. Usually two jobs at a time. Right before she got married in '71, she graduated from vo-tech with a degree in business and data processing. Afterward, she got a job at the telephone office in Belleville as a service rep. "This was when everything was on paper," she says. She loved it. "My favorite part was toll investigations. One incident, I'll never forget, ended up with the Secret Service in Texas, but it turned out not to be a problem."

She was able to be a stay-at-home mom for eleven years until her kids got a little older. To earn some extra money, she cleaned houses, cooked at the Republic County Hospital in Belleville, worked for the Swedish-American in Courtland, and then she and a friend operated the Pike Trail Café here on Main Street.

"I was in it for a year. Not for me," she says. "But I can make a really great pie."

After that, she worked as a teacher's aide at the school for about ten years. Went back to the bank for a few more. Then retired. "This hair," she says, pointing to auburn strands cut short. "I told my kids that when I'm seventy, I'm goin' silver. No more dying it. I'm a dino. I use a flip phone, a Trac Phone, just when I'm traveling alone. I'm not on Facebook. My kids want to bring me into the twenty-first century, but meh . . . "

Peggy is married to Don the EMT, whose son is married to Peggy's daughter. "Obviously, we're on our second marriages, and yeah, keepin' it in the family for real."

And in addition to renovating the house she's in now, she also renovated Don's old house on Courtland Avenue, right next door to the Mayor and across the street from Norm Hoard. In the basement are shelves and shelves filled with jars and jars of her canned goods. "That house did not have a single remodel since it was built in 1975. Including the carpet," she says.

So, Peggy took one look at that gold carpet and said, "That's gotta go."

And then she started looking around.

At the wall that separated the dining room and the living room.

That's gotta go.

At the popcorn ceiling.

That's gotta go.

At the small, useless cabinet hanging next to the kitchen sink.

That's gotta go.

At the soffit.

That's gotta go, she told Don, pounding away at it with a hammer. *Pound! Pound! Pound!*

The hammer felt good. So did the pounding. *Really* good. Especially with everything going on. Family stuff. Personal stuff. Loving retirement. Being bored with it. Life. Love. Just . . . way too much.

"You know what they say, though. If you're going through hell, just keep going. Well, that's where we're at."

The Nurse

Angie Hanel is rocking a baby in her arms. His name is Kollins. Three and a half months old. He is very quiet and very calm and just woke up from a nap and couldn't be happier.

"This is what I love," she says, patting him gently on the back. "I could do pregnancy and delivery and this part over and over again."

Angie is married to Brock, the veterinarian. She's an RN at the hospital in Belleville, the OB coordinator, and manages Bright Beginnings Birthing Center and Breastfeeding Support. "We birthed sixty babies at Belleville last year," she says. "I love it. If I could do it all day long, I would." She works two twelve-hour shifts a week, is usually on call for another twelve to twenty hours, but sometimes will be on call for thirty to forty hours a week depending on nurse availability. Last month, she had ninety-one hours on call, on top of being called in twice in the middle of the night. Which can get interesting when you have three kids to worry about and a husband whose job also puts him on call when there's a cow calving at 3 a.m.

"We have to plan and have a plan B," she says. "Daytime is usually not a problem. It's nights that are hard. While I'm at work, we have day care until 5:30 p.m. so either Nana Jan Carlson (Mrs. C) or my parents do day care pickups if Brock is busy. That's the one downfall of working twelve-hour shifts. I bring the boys to day care at 6 a.m. and they sleep until the other kids show up. It takes an army with three kids and two full-time jobs. We are so thankful for Nana Jan. She's not blood, but she's just as much family as my parents are."

Angie is very calm and relaxed and has a very soft, reassuring, lulling voice. The kind of voice you would really appreciate hearing when your epidural has worn off or something is bleeding profusely. Her toenails are painted a pretty, pastel pink and right now, she's not on call but is keeping an eye on Brock's veterinary office that sits behind their newly renovated ranch on Highway 36, just east of town. "My one must-have was my white farmhouse sink," she says.

Angie is keeping an eye on the office because Brock is inside the house, sick.

"My fourth child," she smiles.

Angie is thirty-one. She and Brock have been married for nine years and they have three kids: Maddy, Gage, and now Kollins, and she loves the fact that Mrs. C can babysit for her while she's at work, or when she and Brock want to get away to Vegas for a few days. When she posts things on Facebook, it's photos of their kids with hashtags like #blessedwiththebest and notes like "Mom, thank you for everything you do and have taught me. . . . And to our Nana Jan. Jan Carlson you are so good to us, thank you for helping keep my mind sane, helping me on a whim, and always being there for support and advice. You ladies are a great inspiration to be a better momma, wife, and person!" "I'm not quite sure if I'm done yet," she says, patting Kollins gently as she shifts him from one arm to the other. "I might be. But I haven't totally decided yet. We'll see."

Angie grew up thirty minutes north of town in Ruskin, Nebraska. "Smaller than Courtland," she says. When she was in high school, she got a job as a CNA. "In this small little nursing home. I had helped my dad out on the farm, but this was my first 'real job.' And I loved it. The way you can just bond with people on a different level." She also used to work in home health care, helping the elderly stay independent and in their own homes instead of a nursing facility. "My grandpa had to go to a nursing home . . . ," she says, tearing up. "I'm sorry. It's just . . . sorry," she says, taking a breath. "I just loved helping people stay in their own environment."

She went to college in Lincoln. "I'm a Huskers fan. Huskers for life. Brock hates that. He's K-State."

And don't get her wrong; it's fun to travel to a city like Vegas every now and again and enjoy the convenience and the shopping and all that glam. "But I like to come home. And that was fun when I was in my twenties, but once you have kids, you're so busy anyway. And you never know what's out there. It's safe here. People think that if you live rural, there's nothing to do. But there's always something to do if you want."

Angie doesn't really have time to get bored in Courtland. It's getting together with friends who tell you to come on over and bring a side dish because they're going to smoke some meat. "There are so many young couples here. People moving back and starting families."

It's taking Maddy to cheerleading practice and softball practice. It's playing sand volleyball every Monday in the summer. "I have a team. Luke Mahin has

a team. There are twelve teams of six players each and we have two courts. In a town this big. It's crazy."

It's buying and renovating the building next to AnTeaQues, the one with turquoise painted brick with two lush, green planters on the front stoop. "I was twenty-eight weeks pregnant, taking drop ceiling down. It was my little demolition project. And I didn't want to take away or hurt the other beauty salon in town, but the gals we have working for us are younger and so they can pull in a younger crowd. I tell people all the time, 'Make a day out of it! Go to the Depot and Soul Sister and Acquisitions and then get your hair and nails done. Girls' day out.'" She named it Salon 417. Hair. Nails. Tanning. Waxing. Facials. Mrs. C is a big fan of their pedicures.

Angie also bought the building next door to the salon and spent a few days high up on a ladder painting it black. "My goal is to put in a gym within the next year or so. But it's expensive." The closest gym is in Belleville, close to the hospital. "But when I get done after twelve hours, I'm tired. And on my days off, I really don't feel like driving twenty miles to go to the gym."

Angie loves living in a rural area. She does not worry about things like how long it's going to take the ambulance to get to her emergency. "I mean, I'm a nurse, but I don't think any of the other women really worry about it, either. Even a woman in labor. There are enough people in town that are trained medical professionals who will be able to help using whatever they have on hand until the ambulance gets there. Shannon and Linda at AnTea-Ques are both RNs. I'm an RN. We've got a few more RNs in town, too, and Don's got his EMT training. My gosh. He's so brilliant. He could figure out how to use duct tape as an effective tourniquet."

"How are you feeling?" she asks Brock as he comes into the office.

"Like shit," he says.

"What's your temperature?" she asks as she places Kollins in a walker.

"Normal," he says.

Angie loves being a mom. She loves caring for people when they need it the most, being calm, cool, and collected no matter what comes into the hospital: heart attacks, kidney failures, first breaths, last breaths. "When you're rural, you have to know everything that's walking in the door. It's what I love about working in the ER, the changes. It's always something different. And you can be scared shitless, but you never show it to your patient," she says.

"Oh, man, I think he needs a diaper change," Brock says, pointing down to Kollins. "Shit! It's running down his leg!"

"Oh, I'll get it," she says calmly, rolling her eyes.

"I can't even handle that," he says.

"You're ridiculous," she laughs, picking Kollins up. "You preg check a cow and have cow poop up to your shoulder almost every day. Turn the sink on for me, please."

"Yeah, I know . . . but that's totally different," he says, handing her some paper towels as he turns on the water.

Angie has no desire to live anywhere else. She wants Maddy, Gage, and Kollins to grow up here, but she also wants them to go out into the world and decide for themselves if they want to come back.

"It makes you appreciate it that much more," she says, placing Kollins in the sink. She takes off his onesie, then his diaper. She cleans him off and laughs when Brock starts to make gagging sounds.

"That is so foul," he says, turning his head.

"Life is good here," she says, not missing a beat. "I wouldn't want to change it for anything."

The Homeopathic

Everyone is always fascinated by the ear candling.

"Oh, everyone always wants to look inside an ear candle," laughs Lynette. "They want to see all the junk that gets pulled out of their ears."

Just like Angie, Shannon, and Linda, Lynette Engelbert is a nurse. She is sixty-five, retired, and is very peaceful and very mellow, just like Jake, her husband. Jake is the head of maintenance at the school and is usually in and out for a morning coffee at Pinky's before Steve and Larry even get there.

Lynette and Jake live in a nice, very tidy house just a few blocks from town. It's Sunday afternoon. Jake is in the living room reading a book. And Lynette is opening one door and then another to get to her shop. She named it Rural Remedies. "Helping you get back to basics, NATURALLY!"

"Sometimes you get a lot of looks, like, 'Seriously?' And I do believe that Western medicine has its place, but natural products and herbs have their place, too," she says.

Lynette offers a lot of homeopathic remedies.

"People love these, too," she says, lining a foot tub with a plastic liner before filling it with lukewarm water. "The water is ionically charged and pulls toxins out of your body through the feet. Just wait and see what the water looks like when it's done. It's scary."

Lynette's the one you call if you need gluten-free products or want to buy some organic ingredients to cook and bake with; things that you are not going to find at the Food Mart over in Belleville. Like almond flour, tapioca flour, flaxseed, hemp protein powder, crystallized ginger slices, raw pumpkin seeds, turbinado sugar, liquid stevia, MCT oil, and coconut oil.

"Is the water turning yellow?" she asks, looking at the tub. "Oh yeah. That's your urinary tract and kidneys being detoxified."

Lynette makes Kombucha and sells Kombucha making kits, and will give you recipes for Keto Rolls, and healthy versions of desserts like Pumpkin Flan and Lemon Blueberry Scones.

"Oh, those are the most popular for sure," she says.

She sells essential oils that are 100 percent pure and come in fragrances like lavender, orange, clove, eucalyptus, peppermint, jasmine, tea tree, citronella, tangerine, and rosemary, and also carries things like Endurance ("Our hydrating tea and fruit fusion that is the perfect alternative to sports drinks") and Summer Allergy Patches ("You place them on dry skin on the arm, shoulder or chest and they will provide up to twelve hours of relief from things like pollen, dust, mites, and even grass"). And on a very large, L-shaped counter that runs the entire length of the store are the herbal supplements. Bottles that are neatly categorized in alphabetical order and neatly stacked on top of one another.

"I'm a wholesaler, for NOW, Nature's Way, and Highlands," she says. "The water's turning brown? No, that's a good thing. It should look swampy. That is the colon being detoxified."

Lynette carries a remedy for everything that plagues you. There is cinnamon bark ("for blood sugar"), elderberry ("great for colds and flu"), olive leaf ("works wonders for upper respiratory infections"), and uva ursi ("helps fight infections like UTIs"). There is beet root ("for constipation"), bilberry fruit extract ("for the eyes"), hawthorn ("good for the heart"), and astragalus root ("It's an adaptogen. It'll do whatever you need it to do").

She sells copper mugs, too. "Great for arthritis. Fill it up with water, put it in the refrigerator overnight, and drink it in the morning."

She also carries CBD products. Oils, candy, and lotions from brands like American Shaman. The CBDs are her best sellers. "Oh, by far," she says. "CBD works for pain, anxiety, cramps, migraines. . . . It helps heal the body." It scares her, the way people are popping pills for every little ache and pain that comes their way. The way that doctors just scribble out prescriptions like it's candy. "It's so frightening."

When Jake had his shoulder surgery, the pharmacy had nothing to do with his recovery. Instead, Lynette gave him a cocktail of horsetail, magnesium, gotu kola, arnica, and CBD oil. "It healed him beautifully," says Lynette.

"How'd you do this?" the doctor wondered.

"Tell me your recipe for what you did," begged the physical therapist.

"I had no pain," says Jake.

She opened Rural Remedies in October of 2017. Traditional ads in the *Courtland Journal* and local magazines didn't do much to generate any business, so instead, she focused on social media. She posts regularly. "Be sure to see our Tick Spray recipe, products, and kits. We have supplies to keep you and your family safe this summer."

She runs contests, too. "Love one of our products? Leave a post on our review page to be entered in the next Drawing!'"

And she also gets the word out about special events and workshops. "Rural Remedies is hosting a winter wellness class. Learn to stay healthy through flu and cold season."

She thought about opening her shop on Main Street. Thought about opening it down in Concordia, too. "The landlord wanted $400 for rent and the overhead would have been another $400. He also wanted me to sign a two-year lease. It just didn't make sense. Besides, I like working here. I can just go in one door and out the other and I'm home."

Lynette has her Facebook page, business cards, and brochures, but Jake is by far her best means of advertising. "He's always talking to people about it," she says. "I make about $2,500 a month in sales." People message her through Facebook, text her at 6:30 a.m., just show up and knock on her door . . .

"I'm basically open 24/7, 365 days a year," she says.

She offers free pickup in Courtland, free delivery to Scandia, and ships all over the place. "Oh gosh, almost daily." California, Pennsylvania, anywhere.

"Yep," she says, peering into the water when the foot detox is over. The water is brown and swampy and something that looks like sediment has gathered at the bottom of the tub. "See those black flakes in the water? Those are heavy metals that were pulled out of your body, right through your feet. And this water actually doesn't look that bad. I've seen the water turn completely black with some people."

Lynette's got the same mindset that Shanna and Michelle have at Soul Sister and Shannon and Linda have at AnTeaQues. She doesn't price gouge. She doesn't mark her products up. Nowhere near to what the wholesalers tell her she could charge.

"Normally, it's a 100 percent markup. I don't go 50 percent. I don't even go 40 percent," she says. "And they will say to me, 'You could be making more money.' And yeah, that's true, but I want to be able to help people and that also means keeping it affordable."

The Morning Coffee: Monday

Carlson is moving his cattle this morning. Thirty cow/calf pairs that he needs to wrangle out of two separate pastures and into the one behind his house on old Highway 36. He wants them to feed on the Sudan grass he's planted so they can fatten up and catch a primo price when he sells them at the Mankato sale barn in a few weeks.

The total distance he'll be driving his thirty cow/calf pairs is one mile.

"Oh hell, that could take all day," Larry says. "Has he ever drove them before?"

"No!" Joerg says. "For thirty years they've been haulin' them outta there on the trailer. I have no idea why we're drivin' 'em out. He's been cube'n them, though. They love those alfalfa cubes. It's like candy."

"Yeah," Larry says. "One mile could end up being twenty miles, though."

"You remember that song? 'I wanna be a cowboy,'" Steve sings.

"Well, he has the cows trained on the alfalfa cubes but not the calves," Joerg says. "I just hope they don't all scatter."

"Damn firecrackers in July sent a hundred an' forty of my head scattering," Steve says. It ended up taking him ten days to catch all of them. Some wandered up to the Pawnee Indian Museum, three miles east and eight miles north of town. The phone calls he kept getting that day were funny even though they weren't. *Hey Brownie! Think we found some more!*

"Well, it just happens sometimes."

"They get a mind and just scatter."

"They are females. . . . What do you expect?"

While Carlson is out driving his cattle, Steve and Larry will probably try to cut some more beans now that the ground has dried out. Everyone heard about Larry and the combine rolling on him. It was the hot topic of conversation.

"I found a muddy spot," Larry says. "That was bad. Probably cost me five hundred to a thousand bucks. I wasn't payin' attention to my left side, which was stupid. Matt Jensen hooked it four times before he was finally able to pull it out. Yesterday was a good day, though. We got 'em cut. Might put my wife on it today."

Joan Brown is in her seventies and can run any piece of machinery that's on the farm. The Case IH Combine with the twenty-five-foot-wide wheat header. The thirteen-speed Chevy Bison dump truck. She was born and raised on a farm. When she was fourteen, her dad bought her a little John Deere 520. In twelve months, she put six hundred hours on it, mowing and planting. "She is more at home out in the fields than she is in that house. That's a fact," says Larry.

"There's a guy over there in Mankato that always hires high school girls to cut," Steve says. "He says they don't tear the fields up like the boys do, aren't as hard on the equipment, and don't go out every night getting all drunk. He hires girls every year."

"No one around here is smart enough to know everything that those combines can do these days," Larry says.

"The manual for one of those things is this thick," Steve says, holding his fingers three inches apart. "But yeah, there are women who run the combine."

"Women are doing everything these days. They can join the Boy Scouts now, you know."

"That ain't right. Imagine what would happen if a boy tried to join the Girl Scouts or anything else that was women only."

"We have women in our men's bowling leagues and whatnot. Goddamn, they can't compete!"

"There's something different about 'em."

"That's a good thing!"

"We like 'em the way they are."

"You know, Indians used to hunt and fish and chew on buffalo hide all day while the women did everything else. Boy, did we mess up."

"It's like the guns. We used to take 'em to school with us or leave 'em in the car, unlocked, and no one would bother 'em. Them days are over. And didja hear? That old boy who shot up that synagogue in Pittsburgh was a Jew-hater."

"Terrible."

"Is he a Trump supporter?"

"No, he hates Trump. Says he's a Jew coddler."

"Terrible."

"Well, what about the family situation these days? That plays a part."

"What really bothers me is that they've taken the Bible out of school."

"Some of 'em schools don't even say the Pledge of Allegiance anymore. One person gets offended over something and that's it."

"My dad failed his first year of school because he couldn't speak any English, only Swedish. Now, if you have one kid who speaks Spanish, they'll hire Spanish-speaking teachers to teach him."

"Well," Jim says, coming in and filling his mug. He raises it in the air before taking a sip. "To the governor."

They stop talking long enough only to check the radar on their phones.

"Should stay dry today."

Then the market.

"Beans are down two. Wheat's down four. Corn is down two."

Then somehow, Cupcake comes up.

"Lord," Joerg says, shaking his head.

Back in the seventies, Cupcake made a name for herself on the CB. When truckers were passing through on Highway 36, she'd let them know that her kitchen was open 24/7, just in case.

"And she wasn't baking," Joerg says. "She was . . . "

"Yeah, we get it!" Steve says.

If a trucker was interested in Cupcake's . . . cookies, she'd meet them in the Balch Cemetery, right there along Highway 36, just down the road from Courtland.

"God, she was ugly," Joerg says. "The Pride of Formoso!"

Joerg is still wondering what in the world happened to the possum that he shot at 5 a.m. with his .12 gauge.

"I threw it in the back of my truck and that was the last I saw of it," he says.

"Did you actually kill it?" the young farmer asks, grabbing the coffee pot to give everyone a refill.

"Yes, he's dead! He probably just bounced out of the truck because I left the tailgate open," Joerg insists as the young farmer overfills his mug, coffee splashing onto the table.

"Sorry," the young farmer says sheepishly.

"Goddamn! Every time!" Joerg says, making a grab for some napkins.

"Is it true, what everyone is saying?" Betty asks, leaning in between Larry and Steve.

"I wouldn't believe a single word that people say in this goddamn place," Steve says.

"Except what you and I say," Larry says. "That's gospel."

What everyone is saying is that the kid they heard about on the news, the one that was shot up in Hebron, about twenty minutes north of Courtland just over the Nebraska state line, was the same kid who used to cut alfalfa for the Browns.

"I heard he was at a bar on Saturday night and got into a fight with another guy. Then, that guy left and came back with a shotgun to settle whatever it was they were fightin' about," Betty says.

"Musta been pretty bad," Don says.

"Stupid," Larry says.

"What was his name?" Steve asks.

Betty isn't sure and Steve didn't even hear about it so now no one knows if what everyone is talking about is true.

"I was at the elevator last night," Slug says, changing the subject. "All corn. Not one of 'em semis was beans."

The elevator was open until about 8:00 last night with semi after semi after semi rolling in to dump their corn or whatever else the farmers finally managed to harvest.

"I weighed everything around eight, but by the time I got lined up and dumped, it was eight-thirty," Slug says.

"If trucks are lined up like that, give 'em a week and it'll cool off," Larry says. "Can you see the light at the end of the tunnel?"

"Yeah," Slug says. "Got about ninety acres left because the ground is still wet down there. It's all silt on the south side of town. I tried to grease the combine yesterday to get my beans, but I didn't cut very much because we thought we were broke down. But we weren't. It was just a sensor that wasn't plugged in."

"Which can be a heck of a job, cleaning the dirt out of those sensors," Larry says.

"Oh, I had my toothpick out," Slug replies.

There were combines and grain carts and semis running all day yesterday but still a lot left to harvest. Even after a five-day clip of 60- and 70-degree temperatures, everyone thinks it'll be mid-November by the time they're done pulling everything out of the ground. This means there's probably no way that most of them will be able to get their wheat *into* the ground by November 1, which is in two days. And if they don't get their wheat in by November 1, then they can kiss their crop insurance goodbye.

"Then you're just doin' it on your own," Larry says.

Some of the combines that were running during the day ended up running after the sun went down when it was pitch black all around, but for the bright spotlights glowing from farm machinery.

"We used to get lost at night in the wheat fields," Slug says.

"Or, you can't see the pivots," Don says.

"And that would be bad. Real bad," Larry says as Steve gets up and abruptly walks out. "We used to cut way into the night. Anymore? I don't have the same fascination."

"Do you want breakfast?" Betty asks.

"I'll take one egg sandwich," Kenny replies.

"I'll take whatever you want to give me," Joerg says.

"Two black eyes comin' up!" Larry laughs.

"Where were you last night?" Carlson asks. "You're having breakfast so I know you were out somewhere."

"I wasn't," Joerg says, mashing up his eggs with his fork. "I ran out of milk at home."

"Did you have to pour beer on your Wheaties?" Carlson coos, throwing a hot pepper onto his plate.

"Goddamn!" Joerg says, throwing it back into Carlson's mug of coffee.

"Shit," Carlson says, looking into his mug before Jim gives him a refill.

Tomorrow is Devil's Night. Back in the day, Devil's Night meant that you'd spend every hour after dark putting everything you could on Main Street. Tires. School buses. Farm machinery they could pull from C&W's outdoor lot. An outhouse or two . . .

"They stopped selling eggs because it got so bad," Slug says. "Back then, if you got caught you had to wash a cop car. Now it's a zero tolerance."

Which is probably a good thing. Take a farmer's combine for a joyride now, when everyone's behind on harvesting and can't even think about the wheat they aren't planting, and it'll probably be the last ride you ever take anywhere.

"You'll get shot!" Larry says.

"He's only half kidding," laughs Kenny.

The Drive Home

It's midmorning. A few hours after Steve, Larry, Slug, Kenny, Carlson, Jake, Don, Jim, Joerg, and the young farmer finished their cups of coffee. And there are four guys on four different four-wheelers who are in the driveway of Carlson's farm about a mile west of town. It's mild outside, but Joerg has something like, three layers of clothing on.

"It's 50 degrees," Mikey points out.

"Not when you're going forty-five miles an hour on one of these," Joerg replies, pointing to the Yamaha Grizzly 550 FL that he rode from his house just north of here.

He and Lance and Mikey are going to help with Carlson's cattle drive. The idea is that they'll take the rear while Carlson leads in his partially enclosed, mud-splattered all-terrain vehicle that looks like a souped-up golf cart with its big, wide windshield and fat little low-profile tires. It's got a heater and an air conditioner and three bags of alfalfa cubes in the bed that will keep the cattle moving forward instead of running off.

"It's a heck of a plan. I hope they don't get into a cornfield," Carlson says. "If they get in there, they could only be twenty feet away, but you won't be able to see them."

He also hopes they don't scatter into Kenny's bean field. "That's bad, too. They'll shake the beans loose from the pods and that's money on the ground. Hopefully, they just follow us down the road. *Hopefully*. If they scatter, I'm going to the pool hall," Carlson says.

The cow/calf pairs are something new. Carlson usually runs steers. "The market has been so screwy that I thought I'd try something different," he says. The cattle that he is getting ready to drive home include what he calls Last Calf Heifers; old girls that had babies in the spring and won't be having any more before they end up being served medium well on someone's dinner plate. The likelihood that they're going to scatter into Kenny's bean field or wherever else they feel inclined, despite being tempted with alfalfa cubes, is a good one. This is why Carlson has enlisted Joerg, Mikey, and Lance to help, each of whom is tearing down the road on their four-wheelers, heading toward the first herd that will be wrangled out of a pasture and into a catch pen. All three of them leave Carlson and his souped-up golf cart in the dust. Mikey stands up in his seat the entire way.

When Carlson finally meets them a mile or so down the dirt and gravel road, he gets out and grabs one of the bags of alfalfa cubes, pours them into a plastic bucket, and then begins scattering them onto the ground.

"Boss! Boss! Boss!" he calls out. "C'mon girls!"

"Well, you got one taker," Mikey points out as a black heifer cooperates and begins munching on the cubes. The rest of them just stand there, stare for a few minutes, get spooked by something, and take off running in the opposite direction. This is when Joerg, Lance, and Mikey all climb back onto their four-wheelers and one by one, ride through the gate and into the pasture, coming up behind the cows to urge them back toward the catch pen. They don't need much persuading and begin running toward Carlson, who is standing at the gate.

"Run these calves in here and lock 'em in," Carlson calls out. "We have twenty-five more to bring together."

He stands at the edge of the gate, watching as they all gather into the catch pen. Back in the day, it was nothing for a cowboy to run a hundred cows five or six miles from stockyard to stockyard. But right now, Carlson would be happy getting his thirty cow/calf pair just a mile down the road without incident. If they were used to being driven a mile down the road from one of his pastures to another, he wouldn't be so worried about it.

"They'd instinctively know where they were going. But I just bought these cows and they have never been driven between my pastures, so I've got a fifty-fifty shot of my plan actually working."

Once the first group is secured in the catch pen, everyone rides a few hundred feet further to a pasture on the south side of the road that is very green and very muddy and bumps and bucks and heaves the all-terrain vehicles as they roll over it, searching for Carlson's cows. After a short while, he spies them, standing on a bank on the other side of the creek. He gets out and starts shaking the bucket of alfalfa cubes.

"Boss! Boss! Boss!" he calls as they stare blankly for a minute or two before deciding to take off in the opposite direction, disappearing over the hillside. In a few seconds, they come running back as Lance and Joerg roll up slowly behind them and Mikey stays slightly to the south to discourage any from getting further out to pasture.

"C'mon girls!" Carlson urges, shaking the bucket. "Boss! Boss! Boss!"

Soon, one of them begins making her way toward Carlson and his bucket. Then another. And then all of them, who crowd around looking for an alfalfa cube to chew on.

"Boss! Boss! Boss! C'mon girls!" he says, using a plastic Budweiser pitcher to throw some more of the cubes onto the ground before hopping back into the driver's seat. "Let's go to town!"

As he slowly maneuvers through the mud and under the concrete road trestle to the north side of the road, all twenty-five of the cows and their calves follow. He lures them down the road to the first group that is waiting in the catch pen, puts them all together, and then lets them all out at once for the final drive home.

"Oh, look at that line," he says, glancing behind him as the road fills up with his animals. "I love it. This way, it's over and done with before you know it. Otherwise, it'd take four to five trailer loads to get them moved. Boss! Boss! Boss!"

Mikey, Joerg, and Lance are still bringing up the rear, riding at a slow pace, while the cattle speed up alongside Carlson's ATV, mooing and slobbering and kicking up the dirt and the gravel that's covering what was once the main thoroughfare across the northern part of Kansas. Usually, there's not much of any traffic coming from either direction, but everyone has been able to run their combines today, which means that there is one semi-truck after another that's been periodically tearing down the road, hauling corn and beans to the elevator, and then heading back to the fields to do it all over again.

"If they see us, they'll pull over and wait," Carlson says. "Hopefully. At least, that's what they're *supposed* to do."

Who does see them and pulls over is Kenny, whose farm and bean field is just west of Carlson's. "He's more concerned about his beans than his house!" Carlson laughs as Kenny maneuvers his little red pickup truck alongside his bean field like a rolling shield, driving parallel to the four-wheelers and thirty cow/calf pairs to ensure that none of them make a mess of his beans. And all is well, until they suddenly get distracted by Kenny's freshly planted wheat field on the other side of the road, tiny sprouts that look all green and delicious.

"Uh oh," Carlson says as they all make a beeline for it. It takes a minute, but eventually, they lose interest and start migrating back onto the road.

"That's good," he sighs, sounding relieved as he pulls up to the pasture that surrounds his house while Joerg, Lance, and Mikey bring up the rear. "Most farmers are pretty tolerant because everyone has had their cattle wander off into some else's field. But it's good they're moving again. C'mon girls! Boss! Boss! Boss!"

Overhead, the sky is blue and cloudless. A mild, fall day. There's a good breeze whipping around, one that will help wick the last remaining bit of

moisture out of the ground so that the harvest can continue, and the wheat can get planted. Combines are running. Plumes of dirt rising off the open prairie again. Semis heading to the elevators.

There is God and all his creation alongside the American farmer and all his. Planting. Harvesting. Feeding the world. With nothing, but the dirt.

"C'mon girls," Carlson says as his cattle follow him through the gate and into a lush, green pasture. "Welcome home."

Epilogue

Pinky's changed hands in 2019 and was taken over by a young couple from Colorado who fell in love with Courtland during their own road trip. They survived a few days with the morning coffee crew before deciding the lunch, dinner, and weekend brunch crowd was more their speed. The interior of the bar got a complete makeover for a more family-friendly, modern vibe. Gone are the Formica tables, Bunn coffee machine, Betty's hockey pucks, schedules for NASCAR and the Kansas City Royals, and hours that began before sunrise and didn't end even with a "Closed" sign hanging on the door. A few of the benches remain outside on the sidewalk, but are no longer occupied by any of the Liars. In 2022, they changed the name to Adri's Family Restaurant after realizing that they couldn't make Pinky's what they envisioned it could be while running it as it always had been.

They also whipped up a new menu with a focus on locally sourced ingredients, and it includes things like honey vanilla Greek yogurt topped with super seed granola mix, bacon jam bean dip, Caesar salad, pulled pork sandwich, salmon burger on a toasted brioche bun, cauliflower crust pizza, porcini ravioli, and skirt steak flatbread with roasted sweet corn. All of which can be washed down with any number of cocktails: an appletini, lavender martini, bottle of cabernet sauvignon or pinot grigio, hard cider, bottle of Budweiser, or can of Pabst Blue Ribbon. You can also find San Pellegrino sparkling fruit drinks instead of Mountain Dew in the to-go cooler. Some residents love the change. Others not so much. Betty retired, moved an hour away to be closer to her grandkids, and has not been back to Courtland since. She still misses the joint, the crew, all the talk that would make her blush . . . almost everything about it. "It was my whole life," she says. "But I'll be fine."

The morning coffee crew, finding themselves displaced, were taken in by Shannon over at AnTeaQues, who began opening at dawn so that they had somewhere to go. The usuals continue to meet six days a week, offering each of them plenty of opportunities to needle, harass, poke, and worry about each other. Shannon continues to impress them with how well she can dish it out at such an early hour. For Joerg's birthday, she baked him a cake topped with a naked Barbie doll.

Dan and Kathy Kuhn spent months renovating the Depot Market after taking it down to the studs, reopening to much celebration. They began growing apples again, too: Red Delicious, Jonathan, Cameo, EverCrisp, Fuji, Pixie Crunch, Golden Delicious. In addition to the homemade ice cream, they now whip up freshly made donuts on Fridays and Saturdays: blueberry donuts for summer, apple cider donuts for fall. Visitors can also snag a grab-n-go, Farm to Table flower arrangement created from blooms grown on-site or pick stems from the Depot's lush, colorful flowerbeds. Their weekly ads still appear in the *Courtland Journal*. "Lettuce grow you some fresh produce this summer!" In 2021, Dan retired as president of the Courtland Pride Club after serving for twenty-five years. Both he and Kathy remain active in the community.

The Swedish-American State Bank also got a facelift, thanks to a fresh coat of black paint on the exterior. Online accounts and online lending are coming soon. So is a website.

Norm Hoard celebrated his eighty-sixth birthday. He still comes to work every day.

Shanna Lindberg is now the sole owner of Soul Sister Ceramics. She added women's clothing and accessories to the boutique, continues to source for Made in Kansas products, and celebrated the shop's third anniversary in 2021.

Jennifer and Luke Mahin got married in a beautiful summer ceremony with Gus being present for part of the festivities until the sheer volume of strange people got on his nerves. Five minutes after the "I Do"s, guests started suggesting baby names. *Hint hint.* They have made Irrigation Ales their own and Luke's dad will be helping with the brewing, enjoying his retirement. They took a hammer to the old senior center on Main Street, upgrading and modernizing the space with a hand-painted mural of the Republican River Basin's irrigation system, new windows, siding, and a new sign, began selling Irrigation Ales merchandise, and had their grand opening in February 2022. Unfortunately, Gus turned out not to be brewery dog material. "If he liked people, he could be the welcoming committee brewery dog, but he can't even handle people walking by on the street with the door closed," says Jennifer. He remains judgmental as ever. In 2020, Jennifer earned her master of science degree in instructional technology from Fort Hays State University and is now a STEM/Tech Integration teacher at East Elementary in Republic County.

Jenny Russell has expanded JenRus Freelance to include the hiring of an architect on staff. Her sights are set on trying to fix the rural housing problem.

Christy Newman has continued her successful run as one of the top producers for Mary Kay Cosmetics, having earned her seventh diamond ring and eighth car in 2021. She has also been writing for the *Courtland Journal*, covering Little League.

The *Courtland Journal* continues its weekly run and is still assembled by hand and driven across the border into Nebraska for printing. It has been in continuous circulation for almost 120 years.

Dan Reynolds retired after forty-one years driving Truck 2 for the Irrigation District and can now be found behind the wheel of a semi during the fall harvest, helping a neighbor. Thus far, he has not yet smashed the alarm clock with a baseball bat. Mary has continued working at the Depot Market twice a week and loves it. "I get to see people I don't normally see and many travelers coming through!" she says. She and Dan are thoroughly enjoying retirement and go to almost every one of their grandkids' ball games.

Mark Garman still works at the wind farm and just purchased his first bit of land, with fingers crossed that it will be an additional stream of revenue when he retires. He finally admitted to possessing a talent for singing/songwriting that he categorizes as "below average" but is actually well above average. He has been dating his "new" girlfriend for over a year and a half. At the time of this update, he was in the grain cart at 10 p.m. on a Friday, helping his family with the harvest.

Quinten and Melissa Bergstrom's farming entity stabilized significantly. They now offer custom cattle background feeding with a six-hundred-head capacity, providing a solid base of revenue to sustain the sheep farm, which also has flourished thanks to marketing improvements, new contacts, and a loyal client base. They still love the freedom and challenges of rural entrepreneurship. "It's a very real sense of making a livelihood from the God-given talents that we are blessed with, along with the virtues we choose to abide by, sprinkled with the cold fact of risk that we can never completely tame nor be crippled by the fear of. If we can believe it, we can achieve it!" he says. They also welcomed their eighth grandchild into the family.

The Mayor officially passed the torch, finally convincing residents to vote for someone else. He continues to maintain a seat on the city council, chauffeur the dearly departed to their final destinations, jam with his band, and fine-tune his signal over his ham radio. He never did find his kite on the Bergstrom farm.

Al and Amanda Jo Reisenweber sold their home, packed up their kids, and hit the road to pursue their dream of playing live music. Their band, Deliberate Kin, went on tour, had to take a hiatus during the pandemic, and were back on stage in 2021. "Nothing like uprooting your whole life to chase a dream that may or may not pay the bills," he said. "We just got to the point where we knew we didn't want to grow old and regret not trying and we aren't getting any younger, so . . . no time like the present. I suppose you just have to accept that things might not be easy or fun. But really, what's the worst that can happen? It doesn't work like you want and you have to go find a different job somewhere? Go for it. If it doesn't work you'll live through it. If it does work you'll live a life you love. Ha . . . that got a bit motivational poster-ish. Truth no less."